POSSESSIONS

P9-EGC-154

MINN. TERR.

L. Superior

L. Huron

MICHIGAN 1837

L. Michigan

WISCONSIN 1848

Mississippi R.

IOWA 1846

St. Lawrence R.

MAINE 1820

VT. 1791

N.H.

L. Ontario

NEW YORK

MASS.

CONN.

R.I.

L. Erie

PENNSYLVANIA

NEW JERSEY

THIRTEEN

ILLINOIS 1818

INDIANA 1816

OHIO 1803

MARYLAND

DELAWARE

UNITED STATES IN 1783

ORIGINAL

MISSOURI 1821

Ohio R.

KENTUCKY 1792

VIRGINIA

STATES

NORTH CAROLINA

TENNESSEE 1796

Mississippi R.

ARKANSAS 1836

SOUTH CAROLINA

GEORGIA

MISSISSIPPI 1817

ALABAMA 1819

LOUISIANA 1812

WEST

Annexed, 1812

FLORIDA

Annexed, 1810

FLORIDA CESSION 1819

1845

ATLANTIC OCEAN

BAHAMA ISLANDS

GULF OF MEXICO

CUBA

Norman Clark Adams

Liberty
and
Union

Liberty and Union

DAVID HERBERT DONALD

Little, Brown and Company

BOSTON · TORONTO

For

Aïda,

Who Knows Why

Preface

This is a book about a people, a period, and a problem. It is a history of the American people during a period when their country was distracted by sectional strife, devastated by a civil war, and finally reunited only after decades of bitterness. The problem is one central to any democratic society: how to reconcile the principle of majority rule with the guarantee of minority rights.

In offering another study of the Civil War era, I suppose I ought to begin with an apology, for surely more books have been written on this subject than on any other topic in American history. Yet there have been surprisingly few attempts to treat as a whole an era conventionally divided into the antebellum years, the Civil War epoch, and the Reconstruction decades. That periodization has led some historians to lose sight of the central issues of the whole era. For instance, an author who writes only of the pre–Civil War years can plausibly develop the theme of a conflict between capitalism and a form of feudalism. If he carries his story through the following three decades, however, he is obliged to explain why the seemingly antithetical Union and Confederacy followed pretty much the same policies during the Civil War and why the victory of the Union brought about so few changes in the Southern plantation economy. A narrative that ends in 1861 can emphasize the conflict between North and South; but a continuation of the story requires discussion of the deep divisions within both the Union and the Confederacy and an examination of serious postwar rivalries between East and West. A study that treats the Civil War as the culmination of a struggle between freedom and slavery had best end with 1865, or perhaps 1867; otherwise its author faces the uncomfortable task of explaining why white Northerners so promptly abandoned the Negroes for whose rights they had presumably fought.

In studying the years from 1845 to about 1890 as a whole, I have become convinced that these important economic, social, and ideological conflicts can best be understood as special instances of a more general problem that nineteenth-century Americans confronted. Nearly all of them accepted Abraham Lincoln's pronouncement: "A majority . . . is the only true sovereign of a free people." At the same time they believed in the "sacred principle" Thomas Jefferson announced in his inaugural address: "that the minority possess their equal rights which equal law must protect, and to violate which would be oppression." In short, as Mr. Justice Frankfurter was later to observe, the central dilemma of a democratic society was to "reconcile the conflicting claims of liberty and authority."

Throughout the nineteenth century, these two principles were in unstable equilibrium. During the decades before the Civil War, minority rights were protected to the detriment of the national interest. In the war years central authority, in both the Union and the Confederacy, flourished at the expense of local and parochial interests. Postwar nationalism was checked by the reemergence of powerful minorities, so that only modest changes, not a social and economic revolution, were the outcome of Union victory. By the end of the century a new balance had been achieved. It assured what none of the compromises proposed before the Civil War had been able to guarantee. The federal government retained enough strength and continuity to carry out the will of the majority of the American people, and at the same time local and minority interests won enough latitude so that they, too, could survive.

In presenting this version of nineteenth-century American history, I write with several preconceptions, of which a reader should be aware. First, I am an unabashed American nationalist, proud of my country, and happy that it was able to maintain its unity. I cannot see that the successful separation of the Confederacy from the United States would have benefited either North or South or that it would have helped either the white or the black race. To the contrary, I am convinced that division of the United States would have had disastrous consequences in later decades when America (or, had the Confederates succeeded, two Americas) became a world power.

Second, as a nationalist, I am not much impressed by the importance of sectional, or ethnic, or racial, or religious differences in the United States. I know that it is presently fashionable among historians to stress such matters—possibly because they are more readily quantified than ideas, beliefs, and values. But I was born and raised in the South, was educated in the West, and have spent most of my adult years in the East; and I have discovered that Americans of all sections, races, and creeds are much alike. Taken as a whole, they are far more different from Europeans, Africans, or Asians than they are from each other. In holding this position, I am not subscribing to a saccharine "consensus" view that there have been no real conflicts in American history. We have quarreled among ourselves vigorously and at times viciously; but I insist that our quarrels have been family quarrels.

Third, as a conservative I have little faith in legislated solutions or constitutional mechanisms to solve a nation's problems. For this reason my hero in nineteenth-century American history is Daniel Webster, that flawed giant, admirable even in his imperfections, who had a conservative's understanding that society is held together by shared sentiments, institutions, and history. For Webster's great rival, John C. Calhoun, who was his superior in logic, I have respect but not admiration; for in the end Calhoun tried to invent governmental machinery—a process of nullification, a system of dual Presidents—to deal with what was necessarily a matter of feeling and emotion.

Finally, in writing a book that deals with majority rule and minority rights in nineteenth-century America, I am necessarily influenced by the fact that I am living in the twentieth century, where this same problem, though in different forms, is still very much with us. Today, to be sure, no disaffected group proposes to secede or, except perhaps for a few anarchists, to destroy the Union. But we do face choices that are much like those that confronted our ancestors: Do we put the interests of one group or state or section ahead of those of the nation as a whole? Do we adopt affirmative-action policies to give special advantages to our long neglected minorities even at the expense of the majority of our citizens? Do we promote the advancement of women in education, business, and government, even if equally qualified men are held back?

On all these questions—as on the similar questions that vexed nineteenth-century Americans—my attitudes are ambivalent. Perhaps they are shaped by the fact that I have some experience of what it is like to be a member both of the majority and of a minority. I grew up, a white Southerner, in Mississippi, a state where the dominant white majority gave not the least attention to the rights of the numerous black minority. But as an adult I have been part of the Southern minority in the United States that has, whether willingly or under duress, been obliged to accept drastic social changes decreed by the national majority. As a consequence of this dual experience, I have not much faith in those who claim they possess magic formulas that will protect minorities, and I have even less faith in those who assert that the will of the majority is in all cases to prevail. If the story of the troubled decades of the nineteenth century has any message for us today, it is that compromise is better than conflict, that pragmatic adjustments are more lasting than programmatic solutions, and that the power of an individual, a group, or even a generation to effect drastic changes in the course of history is minuscule.

DAVID HERBERT DONALD
Villa Serbelloni
Bellagio, Italy

Contents

MAPS

Liberty
and
Union

DANIEL WEBSTER

The most eloquent spokesman for the Union, Webster believed literally in the national motto, *E Pluribus Unum*. His commanding presence lent force to his oratory. When Webster died in 1852, Ralph Waldo Emerson, long a political foe, grieved: "Nature had not in our days, or not since Napoleon, cut out such a masterpiece." (*International Museum of Photography.*)

1

E Pluribus Unum

The United States was a historical impossibility. From Aristotle to Montesquieu, political theorists agreed that democracy was an unstable form of government, tending to disintegrate into anarchy, which in turn led to despotism. Only in small, compact, homogeneous areas, like the city states of Greece or the cantons of Switzerland, could democracy serve as a permanent form of government. For anyone unpersuaded by theory, the experience of the French Revolution demonstrated what was bound to happen when a large, diverse country fell under popular rule; democracy brought on the Reign of Terror, which produced the Thermidorean reaction and the dictatorship of Napoleon. But the United States in the 1840s broke all the rules of theory and experience. Half a century after its creation, this huge, dynamic, and infinitely varied republic continued to flourish. So astonishing was its success that European travelers visited America every year to view this social pyramid, perilously balanced on its apex, as it defied the laws of political gravity. Eagerly they sought to discover how Americans were able to reconcile democracy and order, equality and stability, the interests of the whole country with the rights of its constituent minorities.

❧ I ❧

By the 1840s, however, observers had good reason to wonder whether the United States could much longer keep up this balancing act, whether it would remain a single nation. With the annexation of Texas in 1845, the

3

country included 2 million square miles of land—an area twice the combined size of Great Britain, France, Spain, Portugal, Belgium, the Netherlands, all the German states, and Austria. After the division of the Oregon region with Great Britain in 1846 and the acquisition of California and the Southwestern territories at the end of the Mexican War, the area of the United States was larger than that of Russia in Europe—which everybody knew was so vast as to require despotic rule. The compiler of the 1850 United States census intended to be exulting, but he might unconsciously have been predicting, when he boasted that his country now was "of equal extent with the Roman empire, or that of Alexander."

Distances within this American empire were vast. New York was farther from New Orleans than London was from Constantinople, or Paris from St. Petersburg. If a traveler took the almost impassable land route from New York to Astoria, at the mouth of the Columbia River, he covered a

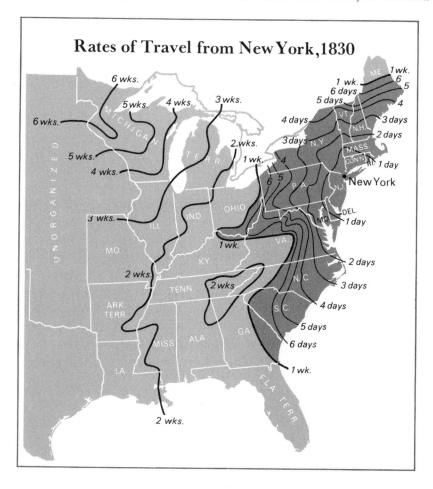

Rates of Travel from New York, 1830

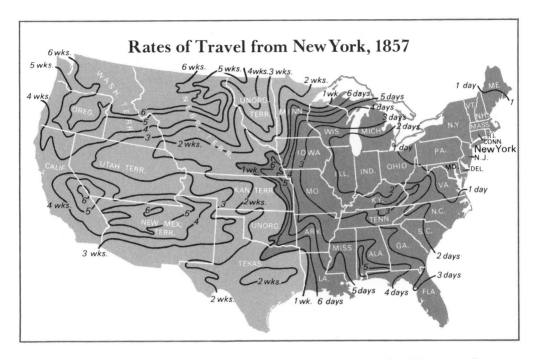

Rates of Travel from New York, 1857

distance nearly as great as that from Bremen to New York. If he went by water around Cape Horn to Oregon, his route was nearly as long as that from London to Canton, via the Cape of Good Hope. In such a huge, distended country, communications were slow and difficult. Before the railroads were built, it required at least two weeks for a newspaper printed in New York to reach Detroit or New Orleans, and an additional week to go on to St. Louis. As late as 1857, after the major intersectional rail lines had been completed, New Orleans was still a six-day trip from New York. It took four weeks for the news of the outbreak of the Civil War in 1861 to spread from the Eastern seaboard to San Francisco.

Heterogeneous was the only adjective that could describe the American people. At the time of the adoption of the Constitution, the authors of the *Federalist* papers had—with some exaggeration, to be sure—spoken of the inhabitants of the United States as "one united people—a people descended from the same ancestors, speaking the same language, professing the same religion, attached to the same principles of government, very similar in their manners and customs." But by 1850 the American population included representatives of almost every race and language in the world. Most of the 23 million inhabitants were of Western European origins, but they came from enormously varied ethnic backgrounds. Settlers of British origins still predominated, but after 1845 at least 150,000 immigrants,

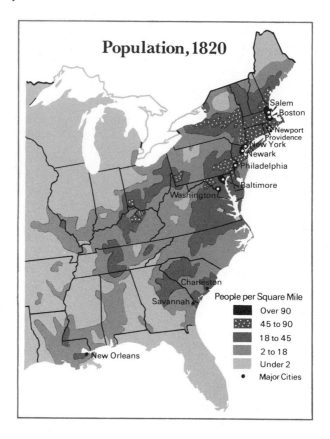

Population, 1820

People per Square Mile
- Over 90
- 45 to 90
- 18 to 45
- 2 to 18
- Under 2
- ● Major Cities

mostly from Ireland and the German principalities, came in every year. By 1850 43 percent of the foreign-born living in the United States had come from Ireland, and 26 percent from Germany. Quite apart from this majority composed of Western European stock was the minority of 3 million Afro-Americans, six out of seven of whom were slaves. In nearly every part of the United States all blacks were thought to belong to an inferior, or at least retarded, race, not eligible for full membership in civil society. Even more alien seemed the half million Native Americans (or Indians), whom most whites considered incapable of civilization and hence unassimilable.

These racial and ethnic groups were distributed unevenly throughout the United States. By 1850 most of the Native Americans lived west of the Mississippi. Here the great Western tribes, such as the Apache and the Sioux, had their hunting grounds, but here, too, the remnants of the Creeks, Choctaws, Cherokees, Chickasaws, and Seminoles, who had originally lived in the East, now had reservations. Blacks were heavily concen-

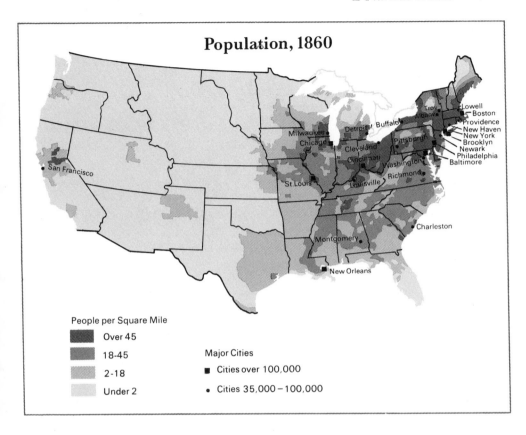

Population, 1860

People per Square Mile

- Over 45
- 18-45
- 2-18
- Under 2

Major Cities

- ■ Cities over 100,000
- • Cities 35,000–100,000

trated in the South, where they constituted over half the population of South Carolina, Mississippi, and Louisiana and made up more than 40 percent of the population of Florida, Georgia, and Alabama. In most states of the North and West, blacks were almost unknown; they formed less than 1 percent of the population of Maine, New Hampshire, Vermont, Massachusetts, Michigan, Illinois, Wisconsin, Iowa, and California. Recent European immigrants tended to settle in the North and the West. By 1850 one out of every eight inhabitants of Massachusetts had been born in Ireland. One out of every nine New Yorkers was of Irish birth, as was one out of every fourteen Pennsylvanians. But in North Carolina, Arkansas, and Florida the Irish comprised less than 1 percent of the population. Huge numbers of Germans resided in New York, Pennsylvania, Maryland, Ohio, and Wisconsin; but in all likelihood most residents of Maine, New Hampshire, Rhode Island, and North Carolina never laid eyes on anyone born in Germany.

The United States was as diverse economically as ethnically. To be sure,

NEW ENGLAND MILL SCENE (above); A COTTON GIN IN OPERATION (below)

The United States in 1850 was a country of small-scale enterprises. The looms used in early textile manufacturing in the North were not much more complex than the Southern cotton gins that separated seeds from lint. There were not many large manufacturing enterprises in the North; the average factory had fewer than eight employees. Similarly there were not many Southern plantations worked by hordes of slaves; in the entire slaveholding region, only 1733 persons owned more than 100 slaves. (*Above, American Antiquarian Society; below, Library of Congress.*)

a large majority of all Americans in 1850 still made their living from agriculture, and it is well to remember that as late as 1845 the hay crop in a relatively urban, industrial state like Connecticut was more valuable than the total output of its factories. But agriculture differed greatly from one section of the country to another. Except for corn, which was grown nearly everywhere, the major staples flourished in relatively limited areas. Louisiana alone produced 91 percent of the total United States sugar output; South Carolina and Georgia accounted for 92 percent of the rice; Kentucky and Tennessee grew 97 percent of the hemp, used in making rope. Four-fifths of all tobacco was grown in five states: Maryland, Virginia, North Carolina, Tennessee, and Kentucky. New York, Pennsylvania, Virginia, Ohio, Indiana, and Illinois produced 70 percent of the wheat. Though cultivation of cotton was widespread, four states in the Deep South—South Carolina, Georgia, Alabama, Mississippi—accounted for nearly three-fourths of the country's most valuable export.

Manufacturing was also geographically specialized. There were few factories in the staple-producing South. Textile manufacturing flourished in the Northeast. The mills in the New England states and New York represented three-fourths of all capital invested in cotton textile manufacturing; factories in the same states, plus Pennsylvania, attracted 85 percent of all capital invested in the manufacture of woolens. Iron production was concentrated in Pennsylvania, which alone in 1849 accounted for more than half of the country's pig iron.

Cities grew where there was immigration, industrial production, and commercial development. In consequence, in 1850 nearly two-thirds of the cities listed in the United States census were in New England and the Middle Atlantic states. New York, which did not yet include Brooklyn, led the way with over half a million inhabitants, followed, at a respectful distance, by Philadelphia and Boston. The only large Southern cities were on the periphery of that section: Baltimore, St. Louis, and New Orleans. By 1850 Massachusetts and Rhode Island had more urban than rural inhabitants, but even small cities were unknown in states like Iowa, Alabama, and Georgia.

⋊ II ⋉

Inevitably these immense differences in economic organization, social structure, and ethnic composition led to disagreements and quarrels over public policy, but fortunately during the first half century under the federal Constitution these controversies rarely reached the level of the national government. After the Federalists failed in their attempt to create a strong central administration, that government had minimal functions. It was in charge of foreign relations, but during the generation after the War of 1812 there were few diplomatic crises. It collected customs duties. It surveyed and sold the public lands in the West. And it distributed the mails. So insignificant was the work of the government in Washington that numerous congressmen resigned their offices or refused to stand for reelection, preferring instead to serve in the state legislatures, where the real issues before the country were being resolved.

It was in the state and local governments, during the first half of the nineteenth century, that fundamental decisions about the operation of democratic government were made. Again and again these governments had to deal with the perennial problem of any democracy: majority rule and minority rights. Was there any limit to the power of the majority, whose wishes, now that the suffrage was so widely extended as to include most white adult males, could easily be registered in the frequent elections? Or did minorities have rights that must be respected, regardless of the outcome of popular elections?

On the whole, local and state governments responded to the will of the majority of articulate voters, with little regard to the concerns of dissenting minorities. Indeed, the views of some minorities were not sought at all. When the Virginia legislature of 1831–1832 considered plans for ending slavery and colonizing free blacks abroad, nobody even thought of consulting the Virginia Negroes, slave or free. On other occasions minority voices were heard and then disregarded. The majority of the voters in Iowa, Arkansas, and Texas, believing that nothing else "ever devised by mortal man was so successful to swindle people" as the banks that issued paper money, overruled the wishes of commercial and financial interests and prohibited the establishment of any bank in those states. In 1833, a majority of Alabama whites, in an action followed by other Southern states, required any of the minority of slaveholders who wanted to free their slaves to send them out of the state. In New York City, despite the eloquent protests of Catholic Bishop John Hughes, the Protestant majority refused to share public revenues with the Catholic schools, attended mainly by the children of the immigrant minority.

On the national level the problem of majority rule and minority rights was more troublesome. States and regions that had special interests were not powerful enough to impose their will on the country as a whole. But majorities did not have a free hand either, since the Constitution left sovereignty divided between the nation and the states. Consequently local government had rights that no central authority could abridge (even when those same local governments were vigorously trampling on the rights of minorities within their own borders). Whenever, then, there arose in Washington a conflict between the desires of the majority of the American people and the objections of a minority—usually, in these years, a sectional minority—a crisis of popular government ensued. Three principal kinds of issues gave rise to these conflicts.

The least disruptive category of such issues related to economic questions. The controversy over the tariff during Jackson's presidency showed how, with careful management, it was possible to reconcile national and sectional interests. At this time Northeastern manufacturers, whose products were in competition with more cheaply produced European imports, mostly wanted high protective duties. Southerners, who needed cheap, imported textiles for slave clothing and who feared that any restriction on imports would result in a reduction of the United States export trade, chiefly consisting of their own tobacco and cotton, vigorously opposed protection. In 1828, partly as a result of political manipulation, partly as a consequence of mistaken calculation of economic interests, a coalition of congressmen from Northern and Western states succeeded in passing, over vigorous Southern opposition, the "Tariff of Abominations," which gave strong protection to New England textiles, Pennsylvania iron, and other commodities produced in the Northern and Western states.

To the Southern minority, adversely affected by this legislation, several courses were open. Southerners could accept the decision of Congress and try to live with it. They could try to reverse that decision in the next Congress. Or they could follow the advice of President Thomas Cooper of South Carolina College and begin to "calculate the value of the union." Southerners not directly affected by tariff legislation followed the first course. More of them adopted the second, anticipating that a fellow southerner, Andrew Jackson, would be elected President in 1828 and that John C. Calhoun, a South Carolinian, would again become Vice-President.

But many South Carolinians were not so optimistic and began exploring the third course open to them. Proud, imperious, and high-tempered, South Carolina leaders were always suspicious of any extension of the power of the national government. They feared that one day the federal government might fall under hostile control and interfere with the condition of the slaves, who outnumbered whites in South Carolina. Already feeling the competition from richer, fresher lands in the West, South Carolina was entering a prolonged period of economic depression, and its leaders blamed their misfortune on the tariff policies of the federal government. Many were ready to resist a law that they considered both ruinous and unconstitutional.

In this crisis the position of Calhoun, the most conspicuous political leader in South Carolina, was difficult and ambiguous. He was torn between a genuine devotion to the Union and a deep commitment to the rights of his state and section. He was also pulled in opposite directions by conflicting political considerations. Since there were no rival candidates, he was assured of reelection as Vice-President in 1828, and he expected to succeed Jackson four years later. He could not afford openly to support defiance of an act of Congress, however hurtful to his state. At the same time, Calhoun could not well flout the strong sentiment in South Carolina that the national majority was trampling upon its rights.

Calhoun resolved his dilemma by drafting the South Carolina *Exposition and Protest* (1828)—which was then published anonymously. In it he developed the theory of nullification, a theory that, on the one hand, estopped those who wanted to take South Carolina out of the Union and, on the other, offered a means for checking majority rule through safeguarding minority rights. As Calhoun expounded the doctrine, when the federal government exceeded the powers granted to it in the Constitution, a state could solemnly declare this action void and refuse to permit the unconstitutional piece of legislation to be enforced within its borders. Two resolutions of this standoff were too dreadful to be contemplated: the invocation of force by the federal government, and secession from the Union by the aggrieved minority. Instead, there would have to be a new national constitutional convention, which would decide whether to grant to the central government the authority it claimed—in this case, the right to enact tariff legislation that benefited one section at the expense of another. Presumably the voters in the majority sections, when they selected delegates to this convention, would soberly consider that injudicious action might precipitate a breakup of the Union; presumably the voters in the minority region would carefully weigh the importance of this one disputed power against all the rights and benefits that derived from belonging to the Union. Compromise would be almost inevitable. As a result of that compromise, majority and minority would achieve a better understanding of each other, and the ties of emotion, sentiment, and history that bound the Union together would be strengthened.

Things did not work out as Calhoun had planned. Jackson was elected and in 1829 he and Calhoun were inaugurated. But soon Jackson showed that it was not the South Carolinian but the New Yorker, Martin Van Buren, who was his favored adviser. In 1832 the Congress modified the 1828 tariff law, but not sufficiently to appease Southern interests. Aggrieved, the South Carolina legislature nullified the new law. President Jackson countered by calling on Congress to pass a Force Act, giving him authority to compel South Carolinians to obey the law. Resigning as Vice-President,

JOHN C. CALHOUN

Calhoun used his powerful logical mind to devise ways to reconcile the interests of minorities with the rights of the majority. "I never use the word Nation," he once explained. "We are not a nation, but a Union, a confederacy of equal and sovereign States." (Painting by Rembrandt Peale, *Collection of Carolina Art Association, Gibbes Art Gallery, Charleston, S.C.*)

Calhoun returned to Washington as senator from South Carolina, and he worked feverishly in cooperation with Henry Clay to prevent a showdown. After protracted debate, the Congress passed the Force Act in 1833, but it also passed a compromise tariff bill, which made some immediate concessions to Southern interests and offered a gradual reduction of duties over the next decade. Jackson signed both bills. Compelled to choose between federal military intervention and compromise, the South Carolina legislature grudgingly chose the latter, repealing its nullification ordinance but, in a useless, symbolic gesture, nullifying the Force Act.

Though Calhoun's scenario proved too slow and cumbersome to follow, the Nullification crisis of 1833 demonstrated that, on the national level, it was possible, if costly, to work out a compromise between a powerful majority and a deeply entrenched minority when economic issues were at stake. The compromise kept the peace and preserved the Union, but it left behind, on both sides, bitter memories. The action of South Carolina in nullifying the tariff gave that state a reputation for being precipitous, marked its spokesmen as "fire-eaters," and branded Calhoun, incorrectly, as a disunionist. In the Palmetto State the readiness of President Jackson to use force, if necessary, encouraged extremism, for it warned South Carolinians of their dangerous situation. As Robert Barnwell Rhett, the secessionist editor of the Charleston *Mercury,* admonished the South Carolina legislature: "A people, owning slaves, are mad, or worse than mad, who do not hold their destinies in their own hands. . . . Every stride of this [national] Government, over your rights, brings it nearer and nearer to your peculiar policy."

⋙ III ⋘

That "peculiar policy" posed a different sort of contest between majority rule and minority rights in the national government: a conflict over ideology. Such a controversy in nineteenth-century America was particularly hard to compromise, for justice, freedom, and equality were considered abstract rights, to be accepted or rejected, as a whole. "Principles," announced Alexander H. Stephens of Georgia, in rhetoric characteristic of the age, "are not only outposts, but the bulwarks of all constitutional liberty; and if these be yielded, or taken by superior force, the citadel will soon follow."

Fortunately for the continuance of the Union, most of the issues involving abstract principles never came before the United States government. Prohibiting the sale of alcoholic beverages, for instance, was a question that sharply divided members of local and state government, but it did not fall within the purview of the Congress. Similarly the nativist movement had relatively little impact in Washington, even though the antagonism between the native-born and the largely Catholic immigrant population was deep-seated and sharply divisive. Even when the nativist American (or "Know-Nothing") party elected numerous congressmen in the 1850s and ran Millard Fillmore as its presidential candidate in 1856, there was always a certain air of futility about the movement. Everybody knew that it was not the national but the state governments that had power over such matters as the regulation of Catholic convents—presumably the dens of shocking vice and depravity.

But some questions concerning Negro slavery did come before the national government, and they proved deeply troublesome. A large majority of the American people, at least up until 1845, wanted the federal government to take no action that interfered with the South's "peculiar institution," but a small, articulate minority sought to end a system of labor they considered both anachronistic and immoral. From the very beginning, the United States government supported the majority position on slavery. In the Constitution the Founding Fathers recognized the South's peculiar institution by basing direct taxation and representation in Congress on the number of white inhabitants plus three-fifths of "all other Persons." The Constitution also permitted a continuation of the Atlantic slave trade until 1808, and it required the free states to surrender runaway slaves "on Claim of the Party to whom [their] service of Labour may be due."

Though a good many American statesmen, from both the South and the North, expressed the hope that slavery would die out, they did little during the early years of the republic to check its expansion. In 1793 Congress passed the Fugitive Slave Act, which gave teeth to the constitutional provision for the rendition of runaways. President Thomas Jefferson's purchase of the Louisiana territory from France in 1803 opened the way for the creation of new slave states in the Southwest. Though the importation of slaves from Africa was prohibited in 1808, the Atlantic slave trade continued because the American navy would not cooperate with the British fleet in stopping and seizing slavers. The domestic slave trade operated within the full protection of United States law. Slave auctions were held in the District of Columbia, in sight of the national Capitol. Without federal protection, slavery would never have spread to the Mississippi Valley.

While a majority of Americans supported this consistent proslavery policy on the part of their national government, there was an articulate antislavery minority. Initially the antislavery movement was not exclusively sectional. In 1827 the abolitionist Benjamin Lundy said that there were 106 antislavery societies in the South, with 15,000 members, as compared to twenty-four such societies in the North, with 1500 members. Some of the most influential antislavery spokesmen, such as James G. Birney and Angelina and Sarah Grimké, came from the South. But by the 1830s, when the proslavery majority within the Southern states began to exercise its increasingly repressive power, most of these Southern opponents of slavery were silenced or driven out, and Northerners and Westerners assumed leadership in the movement.

With this shift in leadership came a shift in terminology. *Antislavery* was a broad term that described anybody critical of slavery, whether on moral, economic, or political grounds. It included those who had a vague

W Stands for **Woman.** In Slavery-life,
Full many are mothers, but no one is wife.
For decency's sake, form of wedding there is,
But the parties are claimed by the master as his;
And the children are sold, and the father is sold
To this or that trader, "to have and to hold;"
And the woman is whipped, for the motherly moan
And the cry of a heart that is left all alone.
O master all monstrous! is conscience amiss
In dooming the sham of a wedding like this!

"W STANDS FOR *Woman*."

This drawing appeared in an abolitionist primer designed to teach young Americans their letters and to inculcate a hatred for slavery. The stress in such illustrations on the abuse of black women was not designed primarily to titillate Northern readers, but to show that in a slave society the institution of the family—"the head, the heart, the fountain of society"—was corrupted. (*General Research and Humanities Division, The New York Public Library, Astor, Lenox and Tilden Foundations.*)

wish that the institution would die out, those who wanted to end it by colonizing blacks in Africa, and those who wanted to take practical steps to kill it. After 1830 the new leaders were not just antislavery men and women; they were abolitionists, pledged to the prompt, unconditional freeing of the slaves without compensation to their owners. Of these abolitionists, none was more articulate, more dedicated, and more unswerving in his opposition to slavery than William Lloyd Garrison, who began publishing *The Liberator* in Boston in 1831. None was more skillful as an organizer, lobbyist, and propagandist than Theodore Dwight Weld, whose *American Slavery As It Is* (1839), a graphic catalogue of the horrors of slavery as revealed in the news stories and advertisements from Southern newspapers, became the Bible of abolitionist organizers.

The influence of the abolitionist movement was disproportionate to its numbers. After ten years of agitation only one of every twenty Northern voters was an abolitionist, and the newly created antislavery Liberty party was conspicuously unsuccessful in the 1840 presidential election. But the abolitionist minority, with few members and few votes, could boast of real achievements. First, the abolitionists clarified the terms of debate over slavery. Stripping away the veil of vague antislavery sentiment, they showed that most advocates of colonization were, at heart, defenders of the peculiar institution. Second, they persuaded many Northerners who did not belong to their movement that the continued existence of slavery endangered the rights of free men. Abolitionists instituted a relentless campaign of sending petitions to Congress, urging it to act against slavery in the District of Columbia and in the few other areas where it clearly had constitutional power to do so. With the legislative hoppers flooded, both House and Senate in self-defense had to adopt "gag" rules, automatically tabling or refusing to receive all such petitions. Abolitionists then used this refusal to prove that the defenders of slavery were the opponents of free speech. Third, the abolititionists exhibited considerable political sagacity. Though their Liberty party never became a major political force, their presidential nominee, Birney, in 1844 received just enough votes to deprive the Whig candidate, Henry Clay, of the election and to ensure the choice of a Democrat, James K. Polk. Thereafter the abolitionist vote, though only a tiny minority of the total, was a factor to be considered in all national elections. In state elections, too, this organized minority, because it was strategically placed, was able to send to the Congress men belonging to one of the major parties but pledged to the abolitionists' goals: Joshua R. Giddings of Ohio; former President John Quincy Adams of Massachusetts; and John P. Hale of New Hampshire.

Unlike a dispute over the tariff, the contest between the abolitionist minority and the large popular majority that desired no interference with slavery could not be settled by compromise. Though Garrison did not speak for the whole antislavery phalanx in all his utterances, he voiced their immovable position in his initial announcement in *The Liberator:* "I will be as harsh as truth and as uncompromising as justice—I am in earnest—I will not equivocate—I will not excuse—I will not retreat a single inch—and I will be heard." Though Henry Clay was personally opposed to slavery and politically opposed to the Southern fire-eaters, he just as clearly spoke for a large majority of Americans in announcing an equally inflexible position: "The liberty of the descendants of Africa in the United States is incompatible with the safety and liberty of the European descendants."

ᕗ IV ᕤ

A third kind of problem that the United States government in the 1840s proved ill-equipped to deal with was political, involving the relationship between the members of the majority and the minority parties. In nineteenth-century America there was no such thing as proportional representation, and the party that received the highest vote in a state, even though it was a bare plurality, won all the state's votes in the electoral college for President. To a somewhat lesser extent, this same winner-take-all rule applied in the selection of congressmen (senators were still chosen by state legislatures), governors, and members of local legislative bodies. The consequence was a two-party system, since there were the strongest practical reasons against splintering the vote. Members of the largest party held a virtual monopoly of the patronage of the governments they controlled, whether local, state, or national.

Members of a minority party operated under a heavy disadvantage. They had almost nothing to say about appointments to federal jobs, even in their own states, and they were unrealistic if they aspired to the highest national offices. For instance, during the period of Jeffersonian hegemony, the principal politicians of New England, representatives of the shipping and commercial interests of that region, were mostly Federalists. Tainted with suggestions of monarchism and branded with failure since the ignominious defeat of John Adams in 1800, the Federalist party had lost most of its following except in the Northeast. Here the Federalists retained local power, but they knew that they had no influence on the course of events in Washington, no power even to affect the outcome of the next presidential election. It was the political frustration of these New Englanders as much as the economic suffering in their section during the War of 1812 that led many of them to join in the call for the Hartford Convention. It is significant that the official resolutions of that convention, expressing dissatisfaction with the war and with President Madison's administration, began with a complaint about an alleged "deliberate and extensive system" of politics, by which "the popular leaders in one section of the Union" were given "the control of public affairs in perpetual succession."

The election of Andrew Jackson in 1828 inaugurated a long period of Democratic hegemony during which defeat was the usual fate of the opposing national party—first, the National Republicans; after 1834, the Whigs. Though the Whigs had a broad, constructive program, powerful leaders, and a loyal following, the Democrats for a generation were the party of the normal popular majority. Again and again the Whigs learned that when they ran a recognized leader of their party, like Clay, for President, they always lost. Only when the Democrats made an egregious blunder or when the Whigs ran a bland, noncontroversial military hero—William Henry Harrison in 1840 and Zachary Taylor in 1848—could the Democrats be defeated.

Inevitably, Whig leaders, great and small, felt highly frustrated. Daniel Webster, for instance, yearned for the presidency as a child might long for a toy, and nothing could console him for his repeated failures. As late as 1852, during the final months of his life, he cherished the hope that the Whig party might, after all, nominate him. When old friends tried to console him by saying that this was an unworthy ambition for a man who had distinguished himself as representative, senator, minister to Great Britain, and secretary of state, who was unquestionably the greatest orator of his era and one of the best constitutional lawyers the country ever produced, the old man replied fretfully: "Perhaps it is as you say; perhaps I am just as well without that office. But, sir, it is a great office . . . the greatest office in the world; and I am but a man, sir, I want it, I want it."

Even more important was the effect that repeated defeats had on younger leaders of the Whig party. In Massachusetts, for example, so long as Webster continued his perennially unsuccessful presidential candidacy, there could be no movement up the national political ladder for able secondary Whig leaders like Edward Everett, the former president of Harvard College, Robert C. Winthrop, the judicious speaker of the House of Representatives, and Abbott Lawrence, the wealthy manufacturer. A group of still younger Massachusetts Whigs found their political prospects even more dismal. In other circumstances the commonwealth might have selected as governor, representative, or senator men like Charles Francis Adams, the son of one President and the grandson of another, or Charles Sumner, the eloquent favorite student of Supreme Court Justice Joseph Story, or Richard Henry Dana, Jr., the grandson of the first American diplomatic representative to Russia. But the path of these young Whigs to political advancement was blocked by older, more established state leaders, whose aspirations were, in turn, estopped by Webster's presence.

Political leaders who represented minority interests and who had little prospect of serving in the highest national offices often adopted a marked sectional stance. So long as Calhoun had hopes of being elected President, he muted his talk of sectionalism and tried to show that he had a broad national appeal. After about 1845, however, when it became clear even to Calhoun that he would never become President, he increasingly became a Southern, or even a South Carolina, spokesman. This transformation was not so much a matter of personal pique as it was of political necessity. If South Carolina politicians believed that Calhoun might soon sit in the

White House, where he would promote the policies they wanted and distribute the spoils of office to his political friends, he could keep the fire-eaters under control. When his hopes of high office dimmed, when he had no prospect of distributing loaves and fishes, his disciples became more openly advocates of sectionalism and even secession. In order to stay in public life, Calhoun had to have their support, and his own positions increasingly reflected theirs.

For politicians in the minority party who were on lower rungs of the political ladder, the incentives to become extreme advocates of local and parochial causes were great. Hope, however unrealistic, for the presidency might mute Webster's genuine aversion to slavery or Calhoun's narrow sectionalism, but secondary politicians in Massachusetts and South Carolina could cling to no such hope so long as Webster and Calhoun were in the field. They had nothing to offer their followers except a vigorous support for local interests. It is not surprising, then, that if Calhoun was a sectionalist, Robert Barnwell Rhett, who represented the next generation of South Carolina politicians, was a vocal advocate of disunion. Nor is it unexpected that Everett, Winthrop, and Lawrence were more outspoken critics of slavery than was Webster, while Adams, Sumner, and Dana were openly antislavery politicians.

Up until the mid-1840s these three types of conflict—economic, ideological, and political—involving the problem of majority rule and minority rights, emerged on the national scene at different times and over different issues. The true test of the permanence of the American republic would come if all three occurred simultaneously. If ever there emerged a powerful minority representing a great economic interest, voicing a distinctive ideology, and following a group of articulate, disaffected political leaders, the Union would be in danger.

⬧ V ⬧

Fortunately, the forces that united Americans were as powerful as those that divided them. Among themselves, especially in times of crisis, Americans tended to emphasize their divergent interests, their different social systems, their conflicting ideologies; but when they traveled abroad they were obliged to recognize that, for all their variety, American citizens were more like each other than they were like the people of any European state. Even in Great Britain, from which a majority of the American people had sprung, the traveler from the New World was made constantly aware that he was different. "An American seldom feels quite as if he were at home among the English people," the novelist Nathaniel Hawthorne concluded.

Of all the widely shared American beliefs, none was more pervasive, or more influential, than the doctrine of the free individual. So widespread was the faith that each man had the right, the power, and even the duty to act independently, "to sever himself from the mass of his fellows and to draw apart with his family and his friends . . . [leaving] society at large to itself," that the French traveler, Alexis de Tocqueville, was obliged in the 1830s to invent the term *individualism* to describe Americans' behavior.

To be sure, the doctrine of individualism, though almost universally acclaimed by Americans, was applied only within limited areas. Native Americans (Indians) were not considered part of the social organism, and nobody wanted to extend to them the protection society offered to other free individuals. Afro-Americans, and particularly those held in slavery, were also excluded. Most nineteenth-century Americans, including some abolitionists, were racists. Even Charles Sumner, the future antislavery senator from Massachusetts, viewed the slaves he saw on a trip to Washington in the 1830s as "nothing more than moving masses of flesh, unendowed with any thing of intelligence above the brutes." Women, too, fell into a special category, for most nineteenth-century American men were convinced that female intelligence and strength were inferior. Consequently women should express their individualism in the home, and men should serve as their spokesmen outside. Most Americans could neither understand nor approve the action of the little group of embattled feminists who met at Seneca Falls, New York, in 1848, under the leadership of Lucretia Mott and Elizabeth Cady Stanton and, borrowing the language of the Declaration of Independence, demanded an end to masculine tyranny.

But after all these important exceptions have been noted, the fact remains that Americans did share and cherish their right to behave like free individuals, unrestrained by social or intellectual distinction. This individualism stemmed from the history of the Americans—perhaps it would be more accurate to say that it derived from their lack of history. Except for the slaves, immigrants to the New World had made a deliberate and usually free choice to break with their past, to leave behind country, church, and king. Consequently the United States, unlike European states in the nineteenth century, had no feudal tradition, which conservatives could stoutly defend and liberals could attack. Indeed, America seemed a land without a past. The United States, as Henry James later lamented, was a country with "no sovereign, no court, no . . . aristocracy, no church, . . . no army, no diplomatic service, no country gentlemen, no palaces, no castles, nor manors, nor old country houses, nor parsonages, nor thatched cottages, nor ivied ruins; no cathedrals, nor abbeys, nor little Norman churches. . . ."

Without such landmarks, the United States seemed an open society, where each free individual could advance himself as far and as fast as his own exertions would carry him. The term *self-made man* was an Americanism introduced by Henry Clay, and it did seem to characterize the nineteenth-century American. Of course, not all successful Americans were self-made, for even in a land of plenty the winners in the race of life were often those to whom family wealth, education, or political influence gave a head start. But there was enough openness that a Massachusetts editor could reasonably argue that inherited wealth and position counted for little in the United States, since in the long run "men succeed or fail . . . not from accident or external surroundings" but from "possessing or wanting the elements of success in themselves." It followed, then, as the editor suggested, that every family should have as its motto: "Be somebody. Do something. Bear your own load."

Belief in political democracy was a logical extension of the idea of social individualism. By the 1830s the politics of deference, which had characterized the early decades of the republic, had virtually disappeared. Most states had, or were approaching, universal manhood suffrage for white males over the age of twenty-one. After the election of Andrew Jackson, aspiring political leaders had to be—or seem to be—men of the people, and the humbler their origins the better. Daniel Webster apologized for having been raised in a proper house—but offered as evidence of his lowly beginnings the fact that his brother had been born in a log cabin. In Illinois Abraham Lincoln, who had been born in a log cabin, was obliged to defend himself against charges of being an "aristocrat," since his wife belonged to a wealthy Kentucky slaveholding family. Future Governor Joseph E. Brown of Georgia won popular support by relating how, as a boy, he had been a day laborer on a farm; Representative Albert Gallatin Brown of Mississippi boasted that he had been a farm hand; Nathaniel P. Banks of Massachusetts, one day to become speaker of the House of Representatives, campaigned as the "bobbin-boy of Waltham."

But if Americans wanted their political leaders to be of lowly origins, they did not expect them to remain poor. Instead, the accumulation of property was regarded as evidence of virtue as well as of ability. Few Americans had much sympathy with the several communitarian experiments, from the Shaker settlements to the Fourierist colonies, where property was held in common. Instead, Americans wanted their own individual (or, at most, family) possessions. Perhaps the Americans' passion for the accumulation of private property derived from the fact that, in Europe, most of their ancestors had had very little in the way of worldly goods. Perhaps it was reinforced by the fact that in a country so diverse and mobile as the United

States, where there were no accepted criteria for locating a family on a social scale, wealth became a kind of universal pass, a badge of reputability as readily recognized as a European title of nobility. Whatever the cause, the American belief in the right to acquire private property, without restraint from government, was passionately and almost universally held. "In no other country in the world," as Tocqueville remarked, "is the love of property keener or more alert than in the United States, and nowhere does the majority display less inclination toward doctrines which in any way threaten the way property is owned."

To be sure, some influential groups in American society thought of themselves as exceptions to Tocqueville's generalization. For instance, New England manufacturers like the Lowell Associates, who built and ran the great textile mills at Lowell and Waltham, Massachusetts, boasted less of the financial rewards they were reaping than of the economic opportunities, the social stability, and the moral direction they were giving to labor in their region. Similarly, Southern planters often eschewed talk of profits in favor of romantic claims that they were re-creating a feudal society—rather like that portrayed in Sir Walter Scott's widely read novels—in which benevolent masters exercised kindly patriarchal guidance over their black "servants" or "families" (terms that these Southerners preferred to the blunter word, "slaves"). It is hardly surprising that these self-characterizations have misled some subsequent historians, particularly because, when judged by present-day standards, both manufacturers and planters ran poorly organized businesses and kept fairly primitive business records. But recent careful analyses by economic historians have shown that both groups tried to maximize profits and that both were equally successful, since in good years returns on capital invested in Southern tobacco, cotton, or sugar plantations, including slaves, were about equal to those on Northern investments in textile manufacturing or railroads. Whatever images Southern planters and Northern manufacturers had of themselves, they were in actuality capitalists, dedicated to the accumulation and preservation of private property.

Nearly all nineteenth-century Americans believed that one of the principal duties of their government—local, state, and federal—was to preserve and protect their ownership of private property. During the early decades of the century, when private capital was still scarce, they expected government to take an active role in promoting economic development. Government subsidies were sought, and granted, for the construction of roads, canals, and railroads. Such governmental intervention in the economy, as the chief justice of the Pennsylvania supreme court remarked as late as 1853, was considered simply a "public duty." "It is a grave error," the justice continued, "to suppose that the duty of a state stops with the establishment of those institutions which are necessary to the existence of government. . . . To aid, encourage, stimulate commerce, domestic and foreign, is a duty of the sovereign, as plain and as universally recognized as any other."

By mid-century, however, there was an increasing sentiment that government could best protect private property by refraining from further intervention in the economy. One reason was simply that there was now enough private capital to underwrite most profitable undertakings. But businessmen, whether Northern manufacturers or Southern planters, also came to see that the role of government in the economy was never a neutral one. If the Congress passed a tariff to protect American-made textiles, it adversely affected those who needed to import cheap European fabrics. If a state underwrote the bonds of one projected railroad, it thereby penalized the privately financed transportation corporations that sought to construct alternative routes. If a court permitted a landowner to dam a stream running through his property, the decision injured the property holders upstream, whose lands would be flooded, and perhaps the owner of an upstream mill, which lost power when the dammed-up water filled his mill race. Faced with such difficult choices, more and more Americans came to feel that these problems should be resolved by the impersonal working of economic forces, rather than by the sometimes capricious and unpredictable actions of government. In the future it would be best, the Philadelphia *Ledger* urged, to rely less on direct government intervention in the economy and more on "the keenness of self-interest," as manifested through the "enterprise of individuals or private companies."

It would be a mistake to interpret the Americans' concern with private property and its protection as mere acquisitiveness, or even materialism. Certainly many Americans were rapacious and retentive. But most who identified private profit with public interest, and private good with public welfare, believed that they were playing their designated parts in an elaborate historical drama. They were, in fact, helping to fulfill the American mission. This idea that America had a unique destiny dated back at least to the founding of the New England colonies, whose settlers had faith that they were not just populating another colony but were creating a city on a hill, which might serve as a beacon, a landmark, and a model for the rest of the world. The Founding Fathers of the American republic broadened and generalized this conception of the American mission. Thomas Jefferson saw America as "a standing monument and example" to the rest of the world still subject to the tyranny of despots. When, contrary to the theories of political philosophers, the American democracy not merely survived but flourished, the conviction grew that the United States was inhabited by a chosen people. As Andrew Jackson declared in his farewell message to Congress, Americans had been selected as "the guardians of freedom to preserve it for the benefit of the human race."

Naturally there was some disagreement as to how this providential mission should be carried out. For a very few, like young Samuel Gridley Howe, who was later to become famous as an educator of the deaf and blind, it meant actively supporting the cause of democratic liberty, for which America stood, wherever it was in danger. Fresh from college and full of youthful enthusiasm, Howe, like Lord Byron, saw the cause of liberty at stake in the Greek revolution against Turkey, and in 1824 he sailed from Boston ready to give "life and soul for Greece & liberty." Some saw the American mission

THE VERDICT OF THE PEOPLE

George Caleb Bingham's painting is a reminder that in nineteenth-century America elections involved more than issues and candidates. They were social occasions in an age when there were few public diversions—times for frolicking, drinking, wagering, and paying of election bets. But the architectural structure of Bingham's painting and the impressive solidity of the buildings make it clear that to the artist, as to his contemporaries, elections were also civic celebrations, which might bring out the weakness in people but showed the strength of the People. (*Collection of the Boatmen's National Bank of St. Louis.*)

as an imperative to extend the borders of the United States. In the 1840s there was much talk about America's "manifest destiny"—a phrase of the influential journalist John L. O'Sullivan—to "spread the blessings of Christian liberty" by extending "our free institutions as far and as wide as the American continent." Others, with an equally firm faith in the American mission, disagreed. To Calhoun, the notion of imposing liberty upon adjacent lands like Mexico was "a sad delusion." If the United States avoided war and acted with justice toward all other nations, he said, it might "succeed in combining greatness and liberty—the highest possible greatness with the largest measure of liberty—and do more to extend liberty by our example over this continent and the world generally, than would be done by a thousand victories."

Americans might disagree over the methods of carrying out their mission, but there was substantial unanimity behind the belief that, as Benjamin Franklin had predicted, the United States was destined to serve as "an asylum for those who love liberty." About this American mission there was, by midcentury, a sense of great urgency. Crushed out after the French Revolution, the idea of popular government had risen again in Europe in 1830 and in 1848, only to be cruelly suppressed. America alone seemed the destined home of freedom. Soon "the waters of despotism" would cover all the rest of the world, predicted an Alabama congressman, and, like Noah, "the votary of liberty" would be obliged to betake himself to an ark. When the flood of tyranny subsided, prayed the congressman, "let this government be the Ararat on which it shall rest." Webster put it more succinctly: "The last hopes of mankind . . . rest with us."

It is easy to smile condescendingly at the vanity of these nineteenth-century Americans, so confident of the future, so blind to the grave dangers ahead of their nation. But this remarkable shared belief in an American mission, with its constituent elements of individualism, democracy, social mobility, and private property, helped to avert those very dangers. So long as most Americans believed that the United States was "the last, best hope of earth," they would be less willing to see their country divided and more determined, in Abraham Lincoln's words, "that government of the people, by the people, for the people, shall not perish from the earth."

⚘ VI ⚘

Common values, a shared past, anticipation of a glorious future—these formed a reservoir of goodwill that Americans could draw on; but these sentiments were too generalized, too abstract, to be of much use in putting out the brush fires of economic, ideological, and political antagonism that flared up from time to time. For that purpose, Americans in the fifth decade of the nineteenth century needed fire extinguishers, and they were fortunate enough to have three that were closely related to each other and to the political process: a symbol, an institution, and a rhetoric.

The symbol was the Constitution of the United States. It is hard for a later generation to understand the reverence with which their nineteenth-century ancestors viewed that document. In a country that lacked a ruling family, a hereditary aristocracy, and an established church, the Constitution, next perhaps to the flag, was the symbol of American nationhood. Americans looked on it as a revelation of the ideal form of government and considered the Founding Fathers who had drafted it as a kind of American pantheon. Veneration for the Constitution was virtually universal. When William Lloyd Garrison and a group of abolitionists, believing that the Constitution authorized the continuance of slavery, denounced the charter as "a covenant with death, and an agreement with hell," and symbolically burned a copy of it, the act was condemned throughout the country, even by Northerners as opposed to slavery as Garrison himself.

Most Americans thought of the Constitution as a governmental yardstick. The "sages and patriots" who drew it up had made what Jackson called "sacred" arrangements in allocating power among the people, the states, and the federal government and in balancing the executive, legislative, and judiciary branches of the central government. Every action of a President, every law of Congress, every decision of a court could be measured against the Constitution. If any one of the branches of the federal government exceeded its powers, its action was invalid and hence not law. To be sure, nineteenth-century Americans found it difficult to use the Constitution as a measuring stick. It might seem that any debatable action of Congress could be checked against the carefully enumerated powers the Constitution gave that body; but the Constitution also included the ambiguous clause that allowed doing whatever was "necessary and proper" to carry out those enumerated powers. Was the creation of a national bank necessary and proper? Or the enactment of a protective tariff? Or the prohibition of the slave trade among states? On such questions eminent constitutional authorities differed, sometimes acrimoniously. But most Americans were not ready to believe that the law is what the courts say it is. Though often bewildered and confused, they clung to the Constitution as a symbol of their essential national unity.

The institution that did most to mediate conflict in the United States up until the 1850s had less lofty antecedents. Indeed, many of the Founding Fathers who drafted the Constitution solemnly warned against political parties. But by the 1830s a remarkable two-party system had grown up in the United States. If, as has been previously noted, the repeated defeats of

SYMBOLICAL PAINTING

Terence J. Kennedy's primitive painting recaptures the sense of American mission that prevailed in the 1840s and 1850s. Under the wings of his fierce eagle flourish fields and factories. American ships at sea are as secure as the cows and sheep that graze American pastures. All these diverse interests are sheltered by the American shield, with its motto, *E Pluribus Unum.* (*Reproduced through the courtesy of the New York State Historical Association, Cooperstown.*)

the Whigs (formerly the National Republicans) in presidential elections led to alienation among some leaders of that party, that frustration was alleviated by the recognition that, in the nation as a whole and indeed in every section, the two parties had almost equal strength. In New England, for example, Massachusetts voted against the Jacksonians in every presidential election from 1836 to 1852, but in all these contests New Hampshire consistently supported the Democratic candidates. The South was similarly divided. If the popular vote in all the slave states for Whig and Democratic presidential candidates from 1836 to 1852 is added, the two totals are separated by less than 0.2 percent.

So long as the two powerful national parties flourished, they served to buffer conflicting interests and ideologies. As party leaders from different sections and states worked with each other, they came to know each other better, to find shared interests and concerns, and to rethink the questions on which they differed. The structure of American political parties also helped to eliminate extremists and ideologues. Since a presidential nominee had to receive at least half of the votes of all delegates to the national convention of his party—and in the case of the Democrats he had to win two-thirds of the delegates' ballots—he could not be the spokesman of a local interest or of a minority region. Since, on the other hand, the successful presidential candidate had to win a majority in the electoral college, where smaller and less populous states were overrepresented, he could not be merely the voice of the popular majority. In consequence, from Martin Van Buren to James Buchanan, the roster of American Presidents is—with the exception of James K. Polk, whose vigor and tenacity surprised both his friends and his enemies—a list of amiable, elderly compromisers, noted chiefly for their resolute refusal to do anything notable. If to subsequent historians it has sometimes seemed that the national political conventions of this period selected their presidential candidates by arriving at the least common denominator, it should be remembered that that is a very important step in solving equations containing vulgar fractions.

Along with the symbol of the Constitution and the institution of the political party, the rhetoric of nationalism served as a powerful bond of American unity. This was the golden age of American oratory, when the spoken word carried out the functions of education, entertainment, and inspiration later performed by the radio, movies, and television. The American public seemed never able to hear enough oratory. Declamation was a required subject in schools, and long recitations of memorized patriotic addresses were features of every graduation exercise. Each year towns and cities celebrated the Fourth of July by inviting the most promising young lawyers and politicians to give commemorative orations. No man could hope for a public career who was unable to deliver an address lasting from two to four hours, an oration that would impress his audience by his snippets of quotations from the classics, that would move them with his swelling periods, and that in its surging peroration would bring his listeners cheering to their feet.

Public oratory in the antebellum period could, of course, be used to advance or challenge any cause—the Bank of the United States, the tariff, prohibition, abolition, or women's rights. But the most effective orators, the speakers remembered for their great set pieces that every schoolboy was expected to memorize and declaim with carefully rehearsed gestures, were those who minimized the divisive tendencies in American society and exalted the idea of the Union.

Some public figures of the era have, indeed, small claim to fame except as orators for national Union. In the long public career of Edward Everett, for instance, there is little that is memorable about his services as president of Harvard College, governor of Massachusetts, senator, and secretary of state. But he does deserve to be remembered—though not necessarily to be read—because of his orations upholding the importance of Union. Deeply troubled by the growing divisiveness within the United States and equally opposed to the abolitionists of his own section and the fire-eaters of the South, Everett sought to stimulate nationalism by reminding his hearers of the career of George Washington. Written with consummate care, painstakingly memorized and rehearsed, down to the last gesture, Everett's oration on Washington was delivered dozens of times to large, enthusiastic audiences in nearly every state of the Union. The proceeds from the sale of tickets of admission he donated to the organization of civic-minded ladies who had purchased and were restoring Washington's home at Mount Vernon; Everett raised nearly $70,000 for this purpose.

Just as he hoped that Mount Vernon would become a kind of shrine of American nationalism, so Everett sought in his great oration to persuade listeners, like Washington himself, to forget their local and selfish interests in favor of the national good. Comparing Washington to the Duke of Marlborough and Frederick the Great, to Cato and Demosthenes, to William Tell and King Alfred, Everett found the character of the American hero superior to them all. Consequently it behooved Americans of a later generation to give "practical deference" to Washington's superior wisdom. They should support Washington's policy of nationalism, lest the United States "follow the Old World example, and be broken up into a group of independent military powers, wasted by eternal border wars, feeding the ambition of petty sovereigns on the lifeblood of wasted principalities." If Americans continued to support the Union that Washington had so loyally served, then the name and memory of that greatest of Americans would be revered not only throughout the older, settled parts of America; it would "travel with the silver queen of heaven through sixty degrees of longitude, nor part company with her till she walks in her brightness the golden gate of California, and passes serenely on to hold midnight court with her Australian stars." It was all, of course, eloquent nonsense; but during the few hours he was on the platform Everett, with his fine, sculptured face, his manly presence, and his mellifluous voice, was able to persuade Americans that the interests of the one and the many were the same, that there were no conflicts between minority rights and majority rule.

Far more enduring than Everett's success, which owed much to personality and theatrical staging, was the ceremonial oratory of Daniel Webster. In addresses such as that commemorating the landing of the Pilgrims at Plymouth or the laying of the cornerstone of the Bunker Hill monument, Webster provided a rhetorical arsenal for nationalism. Unlike Everett's graceful fancies, Webster's rhetoric was as solid, as ponderous, and as enduring as the granite of his native New England.

Of Webster's oratorical defenses of national unity, none was more memorable than the speech he delivered in January 1830 during the course of a fierce sectional wrangle about the sale of the public lands. Apparently troubled that the rapid, unplanned settlement of the trans-Appalachian region was depressing the value of Eastern land and draining the population of New England, Senator Samuel A. Foot of Connecticut introduced a resolution calling for a reexamination of federal land policy. His proposal aroused the wrath of Missouri Senator Thomas Hart Benton, who saw in

WEBSTER REPLYING TO HAYNE

George P. A. Healy's painting, which was not completed until 1851, was not intended as a photographic representation of this high point in the history of American nationalism. Healy sought to give a symbolic presentation of the triumph of nationalism in the person of Daniel Webster—"the very man for the center of a large picture," Healy exclaimed—over the forces of sectionalism, as personified by Vice-President John C. Calhoun, half-hidden in the shadows on the left. (*Faneuil Hall, Boston.*)

Foot's resolution simply another illustration of how the Northeast, and New England in particular, selfishly sought to curb the development of the West. Senator Robert Y. Hayne of South Carolina, whose state was seething with talk of nullification and secession, sensed an opportunity to cement a South-West political alliance and adopted Benton's arguments. A continued liberal land policy, he argued, would help to check the already dangerous tendency toward "consolidation" of all power in the national government. He sought to encourage speedy settlement of Western states, which would be free to shape their own laws and institutions without fear of control by whatever majority temporarily dominated the government at Washington.

As the debate on Foot's resolution stretched over several days, Webster made not one but two replies to Hayne, the second of which was the more effective and memorable. In a brilliant stroke of rhetorical strategy, so skillfully executed that Hayne was left fairly gasping in an effort to keep in the fight, Webster changed the subject of controversy from supposed Northeastern discrimination against the West and seized upon some injudicious remarks Hayne had made about the alleged disloyalty of New England to the Union at the time of the Hartford Convention. Granting that in 1814 some New Englanders had assembled at Hartford to object to President Madison's policies, Webster contrasted their limited and strictly constitutional protest to the current nullification movement in South Carolina. In effect, Webster transformed what had started as a debate between East and West into one between North and South, and then he converted it into one over Union and Disunion.

Once on his own chosen ground, Webster proceeded confidently to demolish the supposed constitutional bases for nullification. The Carolinians were not respecting the Constitution, he claimed; instead, they were putting their own local and parochial interests ahead of those of the country as a whole. If they paused they would recognize that there were no really irreconcilable differences within the United States. Properly viewed, the interests of the majority and the minority were one. Indeed, it was to the Union that the sections, regions, and local interests owed their liberty; and it was from their liberty that the Union had gained its strength.

If the South Carolinians failed to pause, the result could only be disaster. Webster would not allow himself to speculate whether it would be possible to preserve local liberties without a national Union; he did not permit himself—as Thomas Cooper was urging Carolinians—to calculate the value of the Union. Instead, he grandly wrapped around himself the American flag for a peroration that would be declaimed from a thousand platforms during the next three decades:

When my eyes shall be turned to behold for the last time the sun in heaven, may I not see him shining on the broken and dishonored fragments of a once glorious Union; on States dissevered, discordant, belligerent; on a land rent with civil feuds, or drenched...in fraternal blood! Let their last feeble and lingering glance rather behold the gorgeous ensign of the republic, now known and honored throughout the earth, still full high advanced, its arms and trophies streaming in their original lustre, not a stripe erased or polluted, nor a single star obscured, bearing for its motto...blazing on all its ample folds, as they float over the sea and over the land, and in every wind under the whole heavens, that...sentiment, dear to every true American heart,—Liberty *and* Union, now and forever, one and unseparable!

STEPHEN A. DOUGLAS

Douglas appealed to self-interest in the hope of reconciling majority and minority interests. Carl Schurz described the Illinois senator as "a man of low stature, but broad-shouldered and big-chested. His head . . . was the very incarnation of forceful combativeness. . . . The whole figure was compact and strongly knit and muscular, as if made for constant fight." (*The National Archives.*)

2

Equilibrium

After 1845 these shared values, these reinforcing bonds of American nationality, were subjected to a series of severe tests. In part they were results of actions taken by the new President, James K. Polk, who assumed office in March 1845 with a clearly defined program, which he put into effect. But in larger measure the crises of the next decade were the work of no one man or administration but of great impersonal changes that required the government of the United States to take action. In a nation so tenuously united, any action was bound to be divisive.

The pressures on the United States government can be briefly summarized. After the repeal of the British Corn Laws, which served as a protective tariff, there was increased demand for the American grain abroad, and the shifting patterns of international trade gave rise to calls for revision of the United States tariff, little changed since the struggle over nullification. The rush of settlers, both from the East and from abroad, to the northern half of the Old Northwest, that area around the Great Lakes hitherto sparsely inhabited, led to demands for federal funding to improve canal, river, and lake transportation, so that the wheat and corn produced in the newly developed region could reach markets. The push of farmers and traders westward to the Pacific meant that the joint occupancy of the Oregon region (which included not only the present state of Oregon but also Washington, British Columbia, and Idaho) had to be terminated and a new, permanent

35

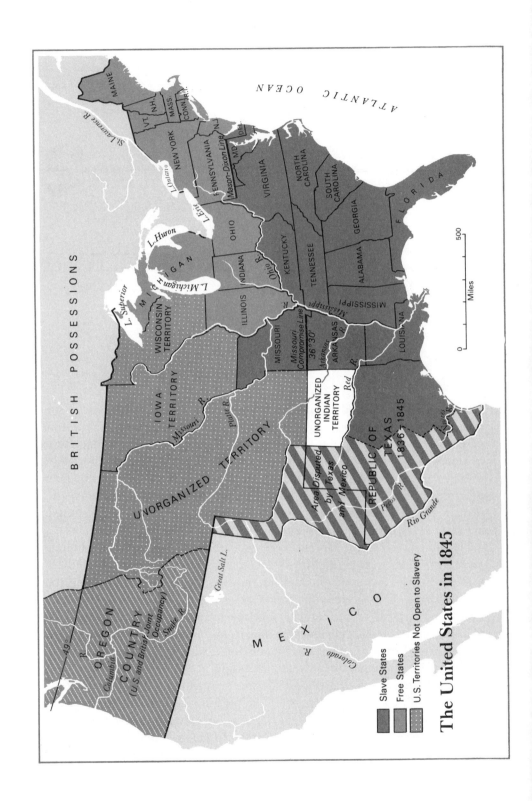

The United States in 1845

Slave States
Free States
U.S. Territories Not Open to Slavery

boundary with Great Britain negotiated. The annexation of the republic of Texas during the final days of President John Tyler's administration required Polk to make hard choices about the disputed boundary with Mexico. Long-standing and unsettled claims that American citizens had against the government of Mexico exacerbated relations with that proud and volatile country, and Americans' desire for the rich Mexican territory of California, with its magnificent harbor at San Francisco, further jeopardized peace.

⤸ I ⤹

On all of these issues the government of the United States was compelled to take a stand, and President Polk, backed by the Democratic majority in Congress, acted promptly. In every move, Polk sought to secure what he thought the majority of the American people wanted, and with every step

THE CAMP AT CORPUS CHRISTI LOOKING SOUTH

President James K. Polk's decision to order United States troops into the disputed territory between the Nueces and Rio Grande Rivers precipitated the Mexican War. This drawing shows Zachary Taylor's camp at Corpus Christi, at the mouth of the Nueces, just before the outbreak of hostilities. (*Courtesy of The New-York Historical Society, New York City.*)

he helped to create a powerful, angry minority opposed to his policies. Ordering General Zachary Taylor to lead American troops into disputed territory lying between the recently annexed Texas and an embittered Mexico, the President precipitated a war that was enormously popular in the South and West but was opposed in much of the East. Knowing he could fight only one war at a time, he compromised the dispute with Great Britain over the Oregon territory, and his agreement to extend the boundary of the 49° parallel to the Pacific pleased Southerners and Easterners but left Westerners feeling betrayed. Western anger grew when the President vetoed a federal appropriations bill for the improvement of rivers and harbors, though Southerners commended Polk for adhering to a strict construction of the Constitution. Lowering customs duties through the Walker tariff of 1846—legislation enacted only because the annexation of Texas gave the South a temporary majority in the Senate—alienated Easterners.

Of the minorities adversely affected by the actions of the Polk administration, those in the Northeast were the most vocal and vehement. They suspected that Polk was trying to put both the Democratic party and the federal government under Southern control. Democratic politicians in the East were offended by Polk's use of patronage, for he virtually excluded from federal offices the friends of Martin Van Buren, since they had opposed his nomination in 1844. Advocates of protection were troubled by the passage of the Walker tariff, not merely because it reduced duties but because it was an omen of what might happen if the slave states continued to have a majority in the Senate. That possibility had been increased by the congressional resolution for the annexation of Texas, which provided that as many as five states might be carved out of the former republic. It became even more threatening after the Treaty of Guadalupe Hidalgo ended the Mexican War and the United States acquired California and the sparsely inhabited New Mexico.* To these political resentments and economic fears of Easterners was added the powerful reinforcement of ideology: the growing Northern detestation of slavery and suspicion of a "slave-power conspiracy" to dominate the United States government. Thus by the late 1840s the three most dangerously divisive forces in American life—economic, ideological, and political—began to converge.

To protect their rights as a minority, a group of Northeastern Democrats devised a strategy for dividing the majority coalition of Southerners and

---

* This added territory, all of which technically had been under Mexican rule, included the prosperous Mormon colony in the Salt Lake Valley (now Utah), to which members of that faith fled after the murder of their leader, Joseph Smith, in Illinois.

Westerners who supported Polk. Their purpose was to exacerbate Western resentment against the Polk administration's opposition to internal improvements and its "surrender" in the Oregon controversy by showing that the President was simply a tool of the Southern proslavery interests. Anticipating that Polk would be obliged to request an additional appropriation in order to conclude peace negotiations with Mexico, several Northern Democratic representatives agreed to be ready in case any one of them could catch the speaker's eye during the debate. David Wilmot, a Pennsylvania Democrat of hitherto unquestioned loyalty to his party, was the first to secure recognition. On August 8, 1846, he introduced his celebrated "proviso" (or amendment) to the appropriations bill, prohibiting slavery and involuntary servitude in any territory acquired from Mexico. Though defeated, the Wilmot Proviso was repeatedly reintroduced by members of the Van Buren wing of the Democratic party whenever Congress considered any question concerning the cession of Mexican land, and each time it led to heated debates. By the time Polk left office in 1849, it was clear that, though he had accomplished more than any other President since Andrew Jackson, he had helped bring the country to the edge of the gravest crisis since the Nullification controversy.

Elected as a military hero, President Zachary Taylor immediately had to deal with the legacy of problems bequeathed him by the Polk administration. Each of them was serious enough to test the strength of Americans' loyalty to the Union; each of them aroused a determined majority interest and an entrenched minority opposition. Most of the difficulties were outgrowths of the Mexican War. There was urgent need to set up a government for recently acquired California, especially when the discovery of gold at Sutter's Mill in 1848 led to an influx of perhaps 100,000 new settlers during the next two years. Texas had a financial problem and a border problem, and the two were interrelated. During the years Texas had existed as an independent republic, it had issued bonds guaranteed by its customs revenues. Now that the United States collected the customs, Texas could not pay its debts unless the United States assumed payment of those bonds or unless Texas could sell the vast tract of land it claimed, which extended west to the Rio Grande River. But recognition of that Texas claim would almost wipe out the prosperous settlement around Santa Fe and make the needed organization of the New Mexico territory virtually impossible.

As each of these immediate problems aroused ill will among the sections, other old grievances came again to the fore. Northerners, including the majority who were not abolitionists but who simply disliked slavery, were embarrassed by the presence of the South's peculiar institution in the national capital, and they especially objected to the extensive slave markets and auc-

SAN FRANCISCO, 1847 (above); THE SAN FRANCISCO POST OFFICE DURING
THE GOLD RUSH (below)

The swift settlement of California following the discovery of gold at Sutter's mill
in 1848 helped to precipitate the sectional crisis. Before 1848 San Francisco was a
lazy trading town with about 800 people. By 1850 the population was nearly 35,000.
Gold seekers cherished the mail they received from back home in the East, but some-
times people had to wait in line for six hours before reaching the post office window.
(*Above, By permission of The Huntington Library, San Marino, California; below,
I. N. Phelps Stokes Collection, Prints Division, The New York Public Library,
Astor, Lenox and Tilden Foundations.*)

tions in Washington. Southerners, including the huge majority of planters who had never had a slave successfully escape, felt aggrieved that perhaps a thousand fugitives each year slipped into the free states, which had enacted personal liberty laws to prevent their owners from reclaiming them.

As the urgency of these problems became clear, several plans were advanced for a comprehensive solution. Polk, before leaving office, urged extending to the Pacific the Missouri Compromise line of 36° 30′, initially used to divide the free and the slave portions of the Louisiana Purchase; thus California would be divided into two territories, one of which would presumably become a slave state, the other a free state. Whig Senator John M. Clayton of Delaware favored referring the whole question of the status of slavery in the national territories to the Supreme Court for decision. Daniel Webster asked for the creation of a temporary government for the entire area ceded by Mexico, with strict enforcement of all Mexican laws— including the laws that prohibited slavery. Senator Stephen A. Douglas of Illinois sought to bypass the whole question of slavery in the territories by immediately admitting as a single state the entire territory acquired from Mexico. Incoming President Taylor, who had a better idea of the vast extent of the region, wanted a variant of this plan; he sent private emissaries to California and New Mexico, urging the inhabitants of both to draw up constitutions, which would exclude slavery, and to apply for prompt admission as states.

If adopted, any one of these proposals might have solved the most pressing problems facing the country and might thus have avoided the next fifteen years of sectional strife, but none was considered on its merits. During the years since Jackson's presidency, local interests in the United States, whether economic, ideological, or political—or often a combination of all three—had flourished almost without restraint from the inactive federal government. Everywhere the feeling had grown strong that any failure to protect these local interests against the power of the majority was a betrayal of principle. Northerners were increasingly unwilling to make any concession, real or imagined, to the South. Even so cautious and dedicated a Unionist as Edward Everett exclaimed angrily that "the only compromise that will satisfy the North . . . is, non-interference [with slavery] in the States, exclusion and abolition everywhere else." Southerners were equally adamant. Speaking for a large group of Southern congressmen, Calhoun insisted that slaveholders had a right to take their chattels into any part of the new national territory. If the North failed to honor their constitutional right, he announced, the South "would stand justified by all laws, human and divine, in repelling a blow so dangerous, without looking to consequences, and to resort to all means necessary for that purpose."

⋇ II ⋉

That the crisis of 1849–1850 was real cannot be questioned; that it was overdramatized is equally certain. Though Americans differed over significant and emotionally charged issues, they still shared most basic values and beliefs. Indeed, in some ways, the ties of unity were now stronger than ever. It was hard for any American not to take pride in the resounding military victories over the Mexicans, or not to believe that the acquisition of vast, rich lands was part of his country's manifest destiny.

It was appropriate that, when Congress assembled in December 1849, the architect of compromise should be the leading spokesman of American nationalism, Henry Clay. Over seventy years old, the Kentucky statesman emerged from retirement to seek, as he had done in the Missouri Compromise of 1819–1821 and in the Nullification controversy of 1833, a reconciliation of majority and minority interests. No item in the package of proposals that Clay presented to the Senate on January 29, 1850, was novel; it was the balance achieved by his plan that gave it strength. Clay urged that California should be admitted as a free state; that the remainder of the land acquired from Mexico should be organized as the territory of New Mexico, without any provision for the introduction or prohibition of slavery; that Texas would yield its claim to lands east of the Rio Grande and, in return, the United States government would assume the Texas public debt; that the slave trade—but not slavery—should be abolished in the District of Columbia; that a more effective fugitive slave act should be passed; and that Congress should declare that it had no power to interfere with the interstate slave trade.

If the specifics in Clay's compromise plan were not novel, neither were the arguments he used to support them. Holding aloft a fragment of Washington's coffin, he reminded his hearers that Americans had a proud history and that they acted from a shared belief in liberty. His compromise, Clay insisted, preserved that liberty to the fullest extent. It did not require any minority, whether Northern or Southern, abolitionist or proslavery, to make a concession of principle; it simply asked for tactical adjustments to reconcile minority and majority wills. The alternative to compromise was unthinkable, for intransigence could only lead to disunion, and disunion inevitably would result in civil war, "furious, bloody, implacable, exterminating."

Clay invoked, in support of his compromise plan, all three of the traditional ties of Union. Most skillful himself as a political organizer and manager, he sought to rally the national Whig party behind his proposal. Deliberately he did not consult with Taylor, the Whig President, before introducing his compromise, partly, no doubt, because the Whigs had selected that military hero in preference to himself as candidate in 1848. More important was Clay's feeling that Taylor had fallen under the influence of Senator William H. Seward of New York, who had told an Ohio audience during the 1848 campaign that "slavery . . . can and must be abolished, and you and I can and must do it." Clay wanted to read such anti-Southern spokesmen out of the Whig party, just as he wanted to exclude from it extreme Southern sectionalists like Robert Toombs of Georgia, who vowed, "in the presence of the living God," that he would vote *"for disunion"* rather than see California a free state. It was Clay's hope to restore the Whig party as a national organization, buffering local and sectional interests.

Clay also looked to the Constitution for support of his compromise. That document, he reminded the Senate, had been drawn up by the Founding Fathers "for posterity, undefined, unlimited, permanent, and perpetual." It did not contemplate or permit disunion; nor did it allow a majority to run roughshod over the rights of a minority. But for all Clay's unequalled charm and his silvery voice, he was never at his best in close constitutional controversy, and it remained for his sometime collaborator and frequent antagonist in the Senate, John C. Calhoun, to spell out the constitutional issues more clearly.

Calhoun was not in favor of Clay's compromise proposal; he considered it a mere palliative, because it failed to provide permanent machinery for protecting minority rights under majority rule. Too feeble to deliver his own speech, which a Virginia senator read for him, Calhoun looked back with longing to the early days of the republic, when the central authority at Washington had left undisturbed the local interests. Now, he claimed, minorities in the United States were imperilled by a consolidated government "as absolute as that of the Autocrat in Russia, and as despotic in its tendency as any absolute government that ever existed." Since the United States government in 1850 was one of the most decentralized and ineffectual in the world, Calhoun's address clearly overshot the mark, and the very extremism of his statement caused Southerners to pause before following their accustomed leader. But inadvertently, by reminding his listeners and his far more numerous readers that the Constitution guaranteed a federal system, with elaborate distinction between the powers assigned to the federal government and those reserved to the states and the people, Calhoun lent support to Clay's plan. A compromise in accord with that Constitution could not be bad.

To the third of the giants in the Senate, Clay turned for the eloquence needed to convert the compromise from a haggle over particulars into a broad act of statesmanship. In the crisis of the Union, Webster agreed to forget his previous disagreements with Clay and their long rivalry for the

Whig nomination and to give his full support to the compromise. On March 7, dressed in his blue dress coat with brass buttons, the uniform he always wore when delivering his greatest orations, Webster rose in the Senate to make the supreme effort of his long public life. "Mr. President," he began in his deep, almost cavernous voice, "I wish to speak today, not as a Massachusetts man, nor as a Northern man, but as an American. . . . I speak for the preservation of the Union. 'Hear me for my cause.'" Disregarding warnings that abolitionist sentiment was powerful in his state, Webster endorsed the compromise proposals even though they made concessions to slavery. He justified their constitutionality and argued that they treated North and South equitably. He concluded with an invocation of the spirit of Union and once again drew a picture of the horrors that would inevitably follow secession and civil war.

Constitutionalism, party loyalty, nationalistic rhetoric—all three of the forces that helped to bind the United States together were skillfully deployed in support of Clay's compromise measure, which opponents derisively termed the "Omnibus Bill," because it included so many diverse proposals. Yet this time the familiar appeals did not work. Clay's omnibus was derailed in the Senate. Behind its defeat lay President Taylor's obdurate insistence on his own solution of the territorial question, an insistence that kept Clay from uniting the Whig party behind the compromise. Taylor's unexpected death on July 9 and the accession of Millard Fillmore removed an enemy of the compromise from the White House and replaced him with a friend; but the change had its price, for the new President named Webster as his secretary of state and thus removed a mainstay of compromise from the Senate. Calhoun's death on March 31 also injured the cause of compromise. Though Calhoun had not supported Clay's plan, he opposed it in sadness rather than in anger. The younger Southerners who succeeded Calhoun now voiced in the national Congress the extreme views that they had rehearsed in the state legislatures. On July 31, through the work of a coalition of antislavery senators and proslavery senators, Clay's proposal went down in defeat. Old, tired, and discouraged, Clay fled the summer heats of Washington for the sea air at Newport.

⋈ III ⋊

But the idea of an adjustment was not dead. In Clay's absence Douglas took the lead of the compromise forces in Congress. Young, brash, and unpolished, Douglas was representative of a new breed of American politician, indifferent to ideology and unconcerned with morality, but intent upon getting on with the business of governing the country. Easterners thought

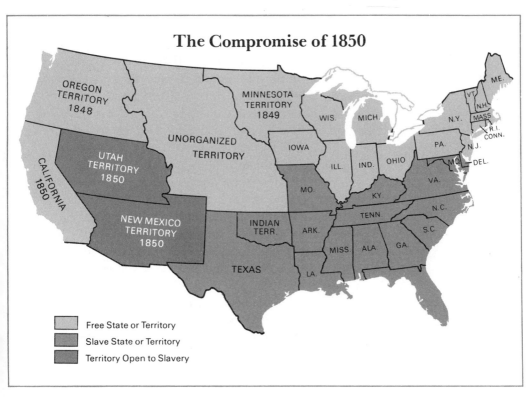

The Compromise of 1850

OREGON
TERRITORY
1848

MINNESOTA
TERRITORY
1849

WIS. MICH.

ME.

VT N.H.

N.Y. MASS

R.I.
CONN.

UNORGANIZED
TERRITORY

IOWA

PA.

N.J.

CALIFORNIA
1850

UTAH
TERRITORY
1850

ILL. IND. OHIO

MD. DEL.

VA.

MO.

KY.

N.C.

NEW MEXICO
TERRITORY
1850

INDIAN
TERR. ARK.

TENN

S.C.

TEXAS

MISS ALA GA.

LA.

Free State or Territory

Slave State or Territory

Territory Open to Slavery

the "Little Giant" of Illinois a vulgar upstart, who could do with a bath and a clean shirt, but Douglas showed that, whatever his deficiencies in etiquette, he was a master of parliamentary tactics. By September, despite the opposition of Northerners like Seward and the hostility of Southerners like Jefferson Davis, he succeeded in pushing the legislation known as the Compromise of 1850 through both Houses of Congress, and President Fillmore promptly signed it.

Taken altogether, these measures differed little from the provisions of Clay's Omnibus Bill. California was admitted as a free state. The remaining land acquired from Mexico was organized as the New Mexico and Utah territories, which would ultimately "be received into the Union, with or without slavery, as their constitution may prescribe." Texas was recognized as including a somewhat more generous area than Clay's plan had allotted to it, and the United States agreed to pay the bonds issued by Texas during its independence. The slave trade was prohibited in the District of Columbia, and a more stringent fugitive slave act was passed.

It is reasonable, then, to ask why Congress passed these measures in September 1850, when it rejected almost identical legislation the preceding

July. In part the change in the White House accounted for the different outcome. Fillmore was as enthusiastic a supporter of compromise as Taylor had been an opponent, and by fall the new Chief Executive was using all the power and patronage at his disposal to influence wavering congressmen. In part the change reflected the passing of time. As the summer wore on, reflective citizens in all sections learned more about the danger to the Union and stepped back from the brink of disaster. It became evident that extremists did not voice the public will. The failure of the Nashville Convention, which met in June, encouraged Unionists throughout the South. That body, called by the governor of Mississippi at Calhoun's suggestion, was attended by representatives of only nine of the slave states, and some of these had dubious credentials. Though the convention, after a good deal of debate, adopted an inflammatory address written by Robert Barnwell Rhett and pledged to hold a further session if the crisis was not resolved to the South's liking, most of its members came out in favor of the compromise plan.

But Douglas's role in the enactment of the Compromise of 1850 must not be minimized. While Clay had tried to promote his program through the traditional appeals to national unity, Douglas unabashedly went about harnessing to his legislation the most disruptive and centrifugal forces in American public life. He appealed to politicians' self-interest. Hesitant congressmen, along with their most influential constituents, were given an opportunity to invest in depreciated Texas bonds. If the compromise was passed, the bonds would be redeemed at par value. The records of these transactions are incomplete, and the number of highly placed public figures involved may never be known, but there are some instructive instances that can be documented. For instance, former governor James Hamilton of South Carolina, once an ardent nullifier, owned $110,000 in depreciated Texas paper, which promised to double in value when the compromise measures were passed. He traveled throughout the South, attempting to influence congressmen directly and, even more effectively, persuading their leading constituents to convince them to support the compromise. Bitterly the Virginia secessionist, Nathaniel Beverly Tucker, professor at the College of William and Mary, complained that bribery through Texas bonds was the real "key to the *Compromise*. It did not offer a *quid pro quo* to the South, but only to those who were in a position to betray the South."

To congressmen who would have scorned the thought of speculation in Texas bonds, Douglas was able to offer less blatant incentives. Always interested in the construction of railroads, Douglas was behind a proposal for a huge federal land grant to promote the building of the Illinois Central Railroad, which would ultimately link Chicago and New Orleans. Introduced at about the same time as the compromise proposals, the Illinois Central bill became intricately interconnected with the sectional compromise. By mid-summer it became clear that the one proposal could not be enacted without the other. As a result, congressmen who were personally interested in the new railroad or whose constituents stood to benefit from its construction, shifted from opposition to Clay's compromise in July to support of Douglas's bills in September. During these intervening months it appears likely that Douglas wooed a group of Whig congressmen from the Middle Atlantic states, who had mostly voted against Clay's Omnibus proposal in July. He may have offered them special opportunities for investing in the new railroad, and he agreed to naming Robert Schuyler, a New York Whig, as president of the railroad. Significantly, most Whigs from New York and Pennsylvania voted for the compromise legislation in September.

Douglas also used parliamentary tactics different from those of Clay. By binding the diverse bills into one legislative package, Clay had hoped to attract for the support of the whole proposal the supporters of each individual measure. The result, if it had been enacted into law, would have been a kind of solemn national judgment, settling once and for all the sectional issues before the country. Douglas tried exactly the opposite tack. He divided the Omnibus proposals into separate parts and pushed each one to a vote. Knowing that he could count on the votes of a considerable group of congressmen for all the compromise proposals, he sought to recruit just enough additional sectional or partisan support to give each one a majority. Thus the bill admitting California as a free state passed the House of Representatives with the unanimous backing of Northern congressmen, plus 27 additional Southern votes. On the other hand, all the Southern congressmen voted for the new fugitive slave bill, and they were joined by just enough Northerners to give it a majority. On this last measure many Northern congressmen, unwilling to vote for a bill strongly opposed by their constituents or to end the possibility of compromise by voting it down, skulked the vote. After the bill had passed, Representative Thaddeus Stevens of Pennsylvania sardonically proposed sending a page into the Capitol lobbies to notify his Northern brethren "that the fugitive slave bill has been disposed of, and that they may now come back into the Hall."

By postponing a civil war for a decade, ten years during which the free states grew much more rapidly in numbers and in economic strength than the slave states, the Compromise of 1850 had a decisive effect upon all subsequent American history, but it is well not to glorify it. Intended, as President Fillmore announced, to be "a final settlement" of all outstanding sectional issues, the Compromise of 1850 was a masterpiece of ambiguity and irony. The compromise measures were designed by men of one generation and adopted by those of another. They were devised in order to restore the nation to its wholeness, its organic unity; but they were enacted as piecemeal, fragmentary solutions to ad hoc problems. They were meant to appeal to the nation's conscience; they succeeded because they appealed to the legislators' self-interest. The compromise "solved" the pressing problem of slavery in the territories by not settling it at all. The legislation creating the New Mexico and Utah territories, Clay himself admitted, was "non-active upon the subject of slavery." "The bill admits that if slavery is there [under the Constitution], there it remains," the Kentucky Senator continued, in an explanation that explained nothing. "The bill admits that if slavery is not there, there it is not." In one sense, therefore, the Compromise of 1850 was not a compromise at all. This legislation represented no real reconciliation of minority rights with majority rule. Instead, the compromise was only a series of laws passed by transient majorities, whose members reserved for themselves the right of repudiating their actions.

⇘ IV ⇙

The most immediate consequence of the Compromise of 1850 was the demoralization of the Whig party. During the debates on the compromise measures, divisions within that party had gaped wide. Northern Whigs, on the whole, were more hostile to slavery than were Northern Democrats; yet it was Northern Whig leaders like Webster and Fillmore who enthusiastically supported the concessions the compromise made to the South. Long at odds with Fillmore's supporters, Seward's wing of the New York Whig party turned angrily against the President and began concerting plans to prevent him from securing the party's presidential nomination in 1856. With even greater bitterness, antislavery Whigs in New England repudiated Webster, denouncing him as a traitor, as another Benedict Arnold, as a "lion turned spaniel in his fawnings on the masters whose hands he was licking for the sake of the dirty puddings they might have to toss to him." Fillmore and Webster, in turn, used the patronage at their disposal to proscribe from public office those Northern Whigs who failed to support the compromise.

In the South the plight of the Whigs was even more desperate. Traditionally Southern Whigs had been more nationalistic, more moderate on questions relating to slavery, than Southern Democrats; yet it was not their party but Douglas's Democracy that succeeded in enacting a compromise that seemed both to sustain Southern rights and to preserve the Union. Southern Whigs felt that they had little choice but to rally behind the compromise, especially when groups of extreme states'-rights Democrats attacked it for yielding too much to the North. In Georgia, Whigs like Alexander H. Stephens and Robert Toombs found themselves political allies of such former enemies as Howell Cobb, a pro-compromise Democrat. The nonpartisan Georgia coalition favoring the compromise carried the fall elections in 1850, and their success dampened further secessionist efforts elsewhere in the South. But the platform adopted by the Georgia coalition— one widely imitated in other parts of the South—revealed how feeble was the Whig influence in an alliance dominated by Democrats. To be sure, the Georgia platform accepted the compromise measures. But it also announced that if Congress enacted any further restrictions upon slavery, Georgia would resist "even (as a last resort) to the disruption of every tie that binds her to the Union"; and it warned that "upon a faithful execution of the *Fugitive Slave Law* . . . depends the preservation of our much beloved Union."

Almost immediately it became apparent that the new Fugitive Slave Act could not, and would not, be widely enforced. Few pieces of legislation could have been designed more directly to affront public opinion throughout the North. To many inhabitants of the free states, the Wilmot Proviso, concerning the hypothetical extension of slavery to distant territory, was an abstraction. Not so the brutal reclamation of innocent black fugitives who peaceably lived in their midst. The new act permitted a slaveowner—and, even worse, his hired slave-catching agent—to seize a claimed fugitive simply by filing an affidavit of ownership with a United States commissioner. The fugitive received no jury trial in the free state where he was seized, and there was no assurance that he would receive a trial in the slave state to which he was returned. It was little wonder that Ralph Waldo Emerson called the act "a filthy law" and that Theodore Parker, the abolitionist preacher, termed it "a hateful statute of kidnappers." Nor was it surprising that when Southern owners tried to reclaim their runaways in the North, they met, at best, with sullen acquiescence and frequently, as in Boston, Syracuse, and Milwaukee, with outright mob resistance.

Even while Southerners and Northerners were engaged in testing the new Fugitive Slave Act, there appeared a work of fiction that did more than any piece of legislation to inflame sectional hostilities. Issued initially in serial form, *Uncle Tom's Cabin* sold 300,000 copies in 1852, when it was published as a book. For all its length, sentimentality, and sermonizing, Harriet Beecher Stowe's novel was a work of genius. Northern readers hitherto indifferent to slavery wept over Mrs. Stowe's account of the sufferings of the saintly Uncle Tom and were thrilled by her narrative of Eliza's escape to freedom. The story was all the more effective because it portrayed the evils of slavery not as the result of the wickedness of Southern

ELIZA'S ESCAPE TO FREEDOM

One of the most thrilling chapters in *Uncle Tom's Cabin* recounted the escape of the slave Eliza with her infant son from Kentucky across the frozen Ohio River to freedom. In this lithograph, Eliza is portrayed as nearly white, in order to avoid arousing Northern racist fears of blacks. (*Courtesy of The New-York Historical Society, New York City.*)

masters—the one truly malevolent slaveowner in the novel, Simon Legree, was born in the North—but as the necessary consequence of the Southern social system.

In just the measure that Northerners found *Uncle Tom's Cabin* convincing, so Southerners found it offensive. One Southern lady tried to read the novel but found that she could not, for it was "too sickening." "Flesh and blood revolt," she said, at such details as a "man sending his little son to beat a human being tied to a tree." Southerners noted that, though Simon Legree was a Northerner, his name was pronounced very much like that of one of the most distinguished and honorable families in South Carolina, the Legaré family. Southern critics claimed that Mrs. Stowe showed their society only in its excesses and that she never portrayed the typical

Southern planter, hard-working, businesslike, and carefully attentive to the needs of his slaves.

But what Southerners resented as much as the novel itself—and probably few of them actually read it—was the enthusiastic Northern reception of the book. In the negotiations and debates that led to the Compromise of 1850, Southerners had been seeking—perhaps not altogether consciously —a recognition of their right to have their own way of life (a right which white Southerners did not, of course, extend to the blacks in their midst) and an end to the incessant Northern moral condemnation of their section and its society. The Northern response to *Uncle Tom's Cabin* showed how futile was that hope.

ABRAHAM LINCOLN IN 1858

It is hard to remember that Lincoln in the 1850s was not the gentle, bearded figure so familiar through his wartime portraits. This ambrotype shows the rising politician, who was already known as one of the ablest lawyers in Illinois. He "was a great big—angular—strong man—limbs large and bony," wrote his law partner, William H. Herndon; "his mind was tough—solid—knotty—gnarly, more or less like his body." (*University Libraries, The University of Nebraska-Lincoln.*)

3

Testing

It was neither the reclamation of fugitive slaves nor the reception of an antislavery novel that led to the breakdown of the Compromise of 1850. It was, instead, the further agitation of the question of slavery in the national territories. This had been a central issue in the crisis of 1849–1850, until the compromise brought about what President Fillmore praised as a settlement "in its character final and irrevocable." Finality and irrevocability lasted just long enough to see that amiable mediocrity, Franklin Pierce, installed in the White House in 1853, when the territorial question erupted again. The Kansas-Nebraska Act of 1854, the rise of the Republican party, the Dred Scott decision of 1857, the Lincoln-Douglas debates of 1858, the split between the Northern and Southern wings of the Democratic party, the election of Abraham Lincoln in 1860, and the secession of the Southern states—all directly stemmed from the renewed dispute over the status of slavery in the territories.

❧ I ❧

In order to understand why this issue was, and remained, such a central one, it is necessary to recognize that, to a considerable extent, it was a surrogate. Under the Constitution there was nothing that the federal government could do about matters that most deeply troubled Southerners. Washington could not keep their section from falling behind the free states in

53

wealth and in numbers. The South lost control of the House of Representatives in the 1840s; with the admission of Wisconsin (1848) and California as free states, it no longer had a majority in the Senate; and, after the death of Zachary Taylor, no Southern man could realistically aspire to become President. But the Constitution gave the federal government no authority over these matters. The one field of legislation affecting the section balance in which the government clearly had power to act was the regulation of the national territories. Similarly Northerners, many of whom were deeply troubled by the moral, economic, and political consequences of slavery, recognized that the Constitution gave the federal government no power over the peculiar institution within the states where it existed. The national territory constituted one of the few areas where the federal government unquestionably did have authority to act adversely toward slavery.

But even this perspective on the territorial question is too narrow. When Northern spokesmen vowed to resist at all costs the further extension of slavery into the national territories, they were not merely expressing their general aversion to slavery; they were voicing a condemnation of the whole Southern way of life as being fundamentally un-American. Increasingly, many Northerners viewed the South, which they considered monolithic, as a barrier to the achievement of the American ideal of democratic equality. While the rest of the United States was making great economic progress, the South exhibited the symptoms of "premature and consumptive decline." In contrast to the thrift, industry, and prosperity of the free states stood the "worn out soil, dilapidated fences and tenements, and air of general desolation" of the South. Northerners were sturdy, equal, free men; Southern whites belonged either to a so-called aristocracy or they were "poor, shiftless, lazy, uninstructed, cowed non-slaveholders."

In this Northern view, slavery was responsible for the backwardness of the South. Condemnation of the peculiar institution did not derive primarily from the abolitionists' moral abhorrence of slavery. Indeed, David Wilmot explained that he and his fellow free-soilers had "no squeamish sensitiveness upon the subject of slavery, no morbid sympathy for the slave." Northern hostility toward the South and slavery stemmed, instead, from a sense that a distinctive culture was rising in that region, one that rejected the basic and hitherto shared American values of individualism and democracy.

Simultaneously, Southerners were developing a set of stereotypes concerning the North. They found it hard to distinguish between abolitionists and free-soilers and viewed all Northerners, with the exception of a few political allies, as enemies of the South, bent upon the total destruction of its society. In Southern minds it was the free, not the slave, states that were losing sight of the basic, cherished American values. The growth of Northern manufacturing and commerce, the rise in the North of cities as large and as pestilent as those of Europe, and the influx of vast numbers of Irish and German immigrants changed the character of Americans in the free states. "The high-toned New England spirit has degenerated into a clannish feeling of profound Yankeeism," lamented a Tennessee historian. "The masses of the North are venal, corrupt, covetous, mean, and selfish." The "Yankee-Union," agreed another Southerner, had become "vile, rotten, infidelic, puritanic, and negro-worshipping." Considering themselves as a permanent, self-conscious minority in the United States, Southerners felt they were daily threatened by an alien and fundamentally hostile Northern majority.

It is, on the whole, beside the point that neither of these opposing stereotypes bore much relationship to reality. Political democracy was about as

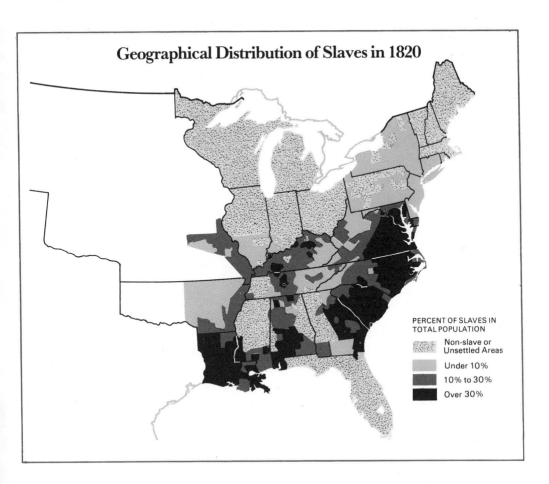

Geographical Distribution of Slaves in 1820

PERCENT OF SLAVES IN
TOTAL POPULATION

Non-slave or
Unsettled Areas

Under 10%

10% to 30%

Over 30%

prevalent in one section as in another. Most Southern whites were sober, hard-working yeoman farmers who had little or nothing to do with slavery; they were, in most respects, comparable to the small farmers of the North and West. There were very few large slaveholders in the South, just as there were very few wealthy Northern manufacturers; and the great Southern planters were, like their Northern counterparts, hard-driving, tight-fisted, and usually prosperous businessmen. But, as so often is the case, facts have less to do with determining the course of history than men's perceptions of them.

Even so, the existence of these obverse stereotypes of North and South did not necessarily lead to conflict except for the fact that, ironically, both value systems shared one fundamental belief: that slave society had to expand or perish. The origin of this idea is obscure. Perhaps it stemmed from the American experience that as the fertility of Eastern lands was depleted the center of agricultural production moved steadily West. The accuracy of this belief is debatable. Some historians argue that Southern lands were becoming exhausted, that the best tracts were being engrossed by large planters, and that small farmers had no choice but to emigrate to new territories where, perhaps, they might become great slaveowners. If there were no further slave territories into which they could move, they would be obliged to remain at home, where they would form a discontented element ultimately subversive of the slave-plantation system. Moreover, these historians add, the slave population in the United States was rapidly increasing; by 1890, it was predicted, the South would have ten million slaves. Since these could not all be profitably employed, their value would drastically drop unless they could be taken to new territory.

Other historians question this internal dynamic of slavery expansion. They point to the modern quantitative studies showing that the Southern economy during the 1850s was in very good condition, not merely in the recently opened lands of the lower Mississippi Valley but also in the older seaboard slave states. The rate of economic growth in the South, taken as a whole, was greater during the 1850s than the national average, and that section suffered far less than did the North from the panic of 1857. The per capita income of Southern white farmers (which is, of course, very different from the per capita income of all whites and blacks in the region) was not significantly lower than it was in the North. On the whole, they conclude, slavery was a very profitable institution where it already existed, and there was no special reason why—apart from the generally expansive temper of all Americans—for economic reasons it had to be extended into additional territory. But, once again, in history fact is often less important than belief.

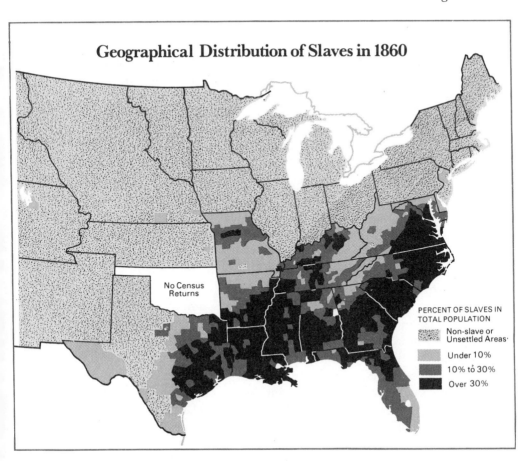

Geographical Distribution of Slaves in 1860

No Census
Returns

PERCENT OF SLAVES IN
TOTAL POPULATION

Non-slave or
Unsettled Areas·

Under 10%

10% tò 30%

Over 30%

Certain it is that virtually every Southern spokesman believed that slavery must expand or die. The same arguments for expansion appeared so frequently in the political rhetoric of the period that they became standard fare. Jefferson Davis perhaps best expressed two of the major doctrines. "We of the South," he explained, "are an agricultural people, and we require an extended territory. Slave labor is a wasteful labor, and it therefore requires a still more extended territory than would the same pursuits if they could be prosecuted by the more economical labor of white men." Restriction of slave territory, Davis noted in a secondary argument, would "crowd upon our soil an overgrown black population, until there will not be room in the country for the whites and blacks to subsist in, and in this way [it would] destroy the institution [of slavery] and reduce the whites to the degraded position of the African race."

Acting on such imperatives, Southern leaders had constantly to seek new areas into which slavery might be extended. Southerners were behind the numerous filibustering expeditions in the Caribbean during the 1850s. Southerners took the lead in attemping to annex Cuba, still owned by Spain. Meeting in Ostend, Belgium, in October 1854, Pierre Soulé of Louisiana, the American minister to Spain, John Y. Mason of Virginia, the American minister to France, and the pro-Southern American minister to Great Britain, James Buchanan, issued a manifesto calling for American purchase of Cuba. They announced that, if the Spanish government foolishly resisted the sale, "then, by every law, human and divine, we shall be justified in wresting it from Spain if we possess the power." Promptly repudiated by Secretary of State William L. Marcy and denounced throughout the North, the Ostend Manifesto fell into the wastebasket of history, and along with it went serious Southern hopes to acquire further foreign lands. But this rebuff made Southern leaders the more insistent that slavery must be given a chance in all the territory already part of the United States, since the peculiar institution must expand or die.

Northern free-soilers accepted this premise of slavery expansion but drew from it a conclusion exactly opposite from the Southerners'. If the extension of slavery could be prevented, they concluded, the whole slave system must collapse. Charles Sumner, the Massachusetts antislavery spokesman who succeeded in 1851 to Webster's place in the Senate, was confident that if slavery was restricted to the states where it presently existed it would soon die, "as a poisoned rat dies of rage in its hole." Then, Sumner predicted, the slaveholding oligarchy that now ruled the South would sink into impotence, and nonslaveholding whites would come to realize that just as a "blade of grass would not grow where the horse of Attila had trod," so could no "true prosperity spring up in the foot-prints of the slave." They would ultimately force "open the gates of Emancipation in the Slave States." Containment, in short, really meant abolition.

II

These rival sectional stereotypes, with their shared conclusion about the importance of the expansion of slavery, are what made the political controversies of the 1850s such intense struggles over what appears to be a very narrow issue. In every instance the pattern was the same: a powerful and growing majority based in the North opposed an entrenched and increasingly unified minority in the South. The consequence of the successive clashes was to weaken, one after another, the traditional bonds of Union.

After the enactment of the Compromise of 1850, the first great territorial question to come before Congress concerned Kansas—a vast area including not merely the present states of Kansas and Nebraska but most of the rest of the Louisiana Purchase west of Iowa. There were pressing reasons for creating a territorial government for this area. Settlers were already pushing into Kansas from Missouri and Iowa, but they could secure no valid titles to their farms until the federal government extinguished the Indian claims and made a land survey. Territorial organization was also necessary before a transcontinental railroad could be built through the region. Ever since the acquisition of California, the need for direct rail connection with the Pacific coast had been obvious. Some preferred a Southern route, and in order to facilitate its construction the Pierce administration in 1853 purchased an additional tract of land, known as the Gadsden Purchase, from Mexico. Others looked for a railroad connecting Lake Superior with the Oregon country. Stephen A. Douglas, the chairman of the powerful Senate Committee on Territories, was not opposed to either of these plans, but he also wanted a middle route, connecting San Francisco with St. Louis and Chicago. But before Congress could authorize such a road, it had to provide a government for the territory through which it would run.

By the 1850s any proposal to organize a new territory immediately raised the question of the status of slavery in that territory. In the case of Kansas, the answer at first seemed simple and obvious: the Missouri Compromise had excluded slavery from this region. But by this time Southerners, convinced that slavery must expand or die and unable to acquire further foreign soil, were unwilling to abide by that restriction. Perhaps few Southern congressmen, who were better informed than most of their constituents, ever thought Kansas would become a slave state, but they knew that if they accepted a prohibition on slavery they would be assailed at home. In Mississippi, John A. Quitman thundered that the expansion of slavery was a question of conscience, on which no compromise was ever possible. "Can we halve a moral duty?" he rhetorically inquired. The South Carolina fire-eater, Robert Barnwell Rhett, declared that Southern rights had to be maintained even if not a single Southern planter ever set foot in the territory. "But the right is important," Rhett insisted, "because it applies to future acquisitions of territory; and by refusing to acknowledge the obligations of the Missouri compromise, you force open the whole question of power." With such war drums beating in the background, Southern votes in 1853 defeated a proposal to organize Kansas as a free territory.

Douglas cared little about slavery one way or the other, but he cared a great deal about the organization of Western territories and the construction of a transcontinental railroad. In 1854, hoping to create a territorial government in Kansas, he sponsored a bill that discreetly failed to mention either slavery or the Missouri Compromise. When Southern senators, whose votes were needed to pass the bill, pointed out that his measure would, because of its silence, leave the Missouri Compromise restriction against slavery in effect, the "Little Giant" discovered that, through "clerical error," an essential section of his bill had been omitted, one that gave the inhabitants of the Kansas territory the power to deal with slavery. Southern congressmen claimed that not even this resort to popular sovereignty was enough, and Douglas further amended his proposal to declare explicitly that the Missouri Compromise was "inoperative" and "void." At the same time he agreed to divide the huge region into two territories, Kansas and Nebraska.

Charged by critics with caving in to proslavery interests, Douglas was, in actuality, attempting to repeat in 1854 the coup he had brought off in the Compromise of 1850. He was willing to add to his bill almost any amendments concerning slavery because he thought them irrelevant and inconsequential. Since, as he believed, "the laws of climate, and of production, and of physical geography have excluded slavery from that country," the wording of the legislation was a "matter of no practical importance." Douglas would, therefore, give the South the language it wanted and the North the

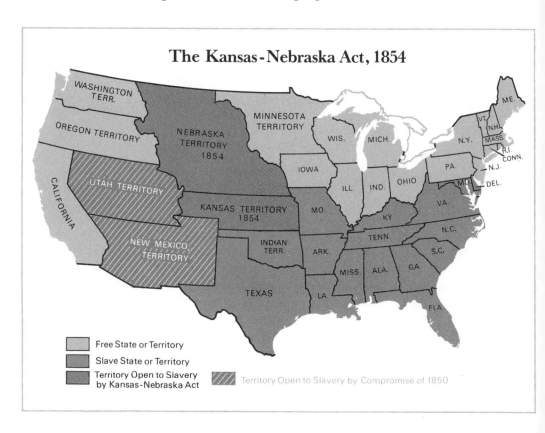

The Kansas-Nebraska Act, 1854

substance. To make this compromise palatable, Douglas sought to sweeten it for all parties—just as he had done in 1850—by sponsoring not one but at least three transcontinental railroad projects, which would give speculators, builders, and politicians in all sections urgent practical reasons for backing his measure.

But the strategy that had succeeded in 1850 failed in 1854. To be sure, Southerners, after an initial period of indifference, came out in support of Douglas's bill and they bullied President Pierce into endorsing it. Following one of the bitterest debates ever to occur in Congress, during which Douglas demonstrated again his superb gifts as a parliamentary tactician, both the Senate and the House passed the bill, and it received the President's signature on May 30. But this time there was no hurrahing that Douglas had saved the Union, no vast public celebration of the new compromise. Instead, when Douglas returned to Illinois at the end of the hard-fought session, he found his way from Washington to Chicago lighted by bonfires where he was being burned in effigy.

Three things had gone wrong with Douglas's calculations. First, the congressional debates on the Kansas-Nebraska bill were so protracted and intricate, so demanding on his time, that he was unable to give sufficient attention to his railroad proposals, which were bottled up in committee, where they died. In 1854, therefore, he could not rally behind his new compromise the powerful influence of America's first big business, the railroad. Second, by permitting Southerners to maneuver him into outright repeal of the Missouri Compromise, Douglas, as many Northerners believed, came close to tampering with the Constitution. Of course, the Missouri Compromise was not part of the written Constitution, but it was an agreement that had almost constitutional status, having been observed loyally for more than three decades and having acquired, as Douglas himself declared in 1849, respect as "a sacred thing which no ruthless hand would ever be reckless enough to disturb." Third, the congressional maneuvering on the Kansas-Nebraska bill suggested to many Northerners that the great national political parties, which had hitherto served as agents of national unity and sectional conciliation, could instead be exploited to ensure minority rule rather than majority rights. Given a free choice, virtually all Northerners in Congress would have opposed the Kansas-Nebraska bill, but the Pierce administration, using every appeal, from party loyalty to political patronage, applied pressure so intense that a majority of the free-state Democrats voted for it.

To many, this unprecedented misuse of a national party to promote a sectional interest served as a signal that a general political realignment in the United States was long overdue. As early as 1848, early moves in this direction had been made when young Northern Whigs opposed to slavery, disaffected Democratic followers of Martin Van Buren, and former Liberty party men coalesced to form the Free-Soil party. The Compromise of 1850 had weakened traditional parties in the South. Now further realignment was facilitated by the fortuitous appearance on the national scene of an anti-foreign and anti-Catholic party. This was the so-called Know-Nothing (or American) party, whose members were supposed to respond to all outsiders' inquiries about their organization, "I know nothing."

Important in itself as an expression of ethnic and religious tensions in American society, the Know-Nothing movement between 1854 and 1856 served as a convenient concealed conduit through which members of the older parties could gradually and inconspicuously move over into the camp of former opponents. In the years after the passage of the Kansas-Nebraska Act, increasing numbers of Southern Whigs, whose state parties were already in disarray, slipped through the covered passage of nativism into the Democratic party. As a consequence, all but one of the slave states voted for James Buchanan, the successful Democratic candidate for President, in 1856. But what the Democratic party gained in the South it lost in the North. Of the 86 Northern Democrats in the House of Representatives, 42 voted, despite all the pressure Pierce could bring to bear, against the Kansas-Nebraska Act. Though many of these remained in the Democratic party, others defected. As a result of these shifts, the center of gravity in the Democratic party shifted sharply to the South after 1854. The party that had once served as a strong bond of national unity now became an equally powerful force for divisive sectionalism.

Meanwhile a major new party opposed to the Democracy was emerging in the North. Early in the debates on Douglas's Kansas bill, antislavery leaders in Congress, including Salmon P. Chase and Joshua R. Giddings of Ohio and Sumner of Massachusetts, issued a widely circulated "Appeal of the Independent Democrats in Congress to the People of the United States," which denounced Douglas's measure "as a gross violation of a sacred pledge; as a criminal betrayal of precious rights; as part and parcel of an atrocious plot to exclude from a vast unoccupied region immigrants from the Old World and free laborers from our own States, and convert it into a dreary region of despotism, inhabited by masters and slaves." Skillfully incorporating two basic free-soil beliefs—that free labor and slave labor could not coexist within the same territory and that slavery blighted the economy wherever it was introduced—the Appeal served as a rallying point, during the protracted debates, for a protest movement throughout the North, in which antislavery Whigs, former members of the Liberty party, and free-soil Democrats joined. Initially given the awkward designation of the "anti-Nebraska" party, the coalition soon accepted the name "Republican," a term originally suggested at mass meetings in Ripon, Wisconsin, and Jackson, Michigan, in mid-summer of 1854.

The results of the political realignment in the North were evident as early as the congressional elections of 1854–1855. The Democrats lost to the Know-Nothings and anti-Nebraskaites (and often both parties supported the same candidate) 66 of the free-state seats in Congress that they had won in 1852. The 1856 presidential election revealed even more decisively the shift in Northern voting patterns. Though Buchanan was elected, he carried only five of the free states and received fewer votes than the combined totals of the American party candidate, Fillmore, and the Republican nominee, the explorer and adventurer John C. Frémont. When voting returns are analyzed on a county-by-county basis, it becomes evident that in most of the free states the Republicans were neither simply former Whigs nor former Democrats masquerading under a new guise; the Republican party was a genuine fusion of free-soil elements from all the earlier parties. The new party was even more strongly sectional than the Democracy, for it had virtually no strength in any slave state. Thus in the North as in the South the party system, once a strong unifying bond for the nation, became a powerful divisive force.

⋊ III ⋉

Equally ominous was the weakening of the American faith in the Constitution that resulted, though less promptly, from the Kansas-Nebraska Act. Almost immediately it became apparent that Douglas's measure, designed to settle the problems of Kansas, aggravated them. Many of the difficulties in that territory were those of other frontier regions: disputes over land titles, controversies over lucrative governmental contracts for trading with the Indians and carrying the mails, rivalries over the location of county seats, and struggles for the multiplying number of public offices paying generous salaries and profitable fees. But in Kansas these questions took on added significance, because the vehement congressional debates had singled out this territory as the battleground of slavery and freedom. (Everybody conceded that Nebraska would become a free state. Significantly the usual frontier difficulties in that territory received little general attention and were readily settled.)

Since everybody agreed that slavery had to expand or die, and since Kansas was the only national territory into which it could conceivably expand, proslavery and antislavery forces girded up for Armageddon. Throughout the North, organizations such as the New England Emigrant Aid Company recruited quasi-military bands of settlers and sent them to Kansas to help make it a free state. In the South, Jefferson Buford of Alabama sold forty of his slaves to help finance a 350-man expedition designed to save Kansas for slavery. Buford's followers carried Bibles provided by citizens of Montgomery and raised aloft banners that read "The Supremacy of the White Race" and "Kansas, the Outpost." Most of these systematic efforts to colonize Kansas were not successful, and most immigrants to the territory drifted in independently, looking for land and fortune. The Southern contingent of settlers had a ready reserve force in the proslavery inhabitants of Missouri, who were prepared whenever called to pour over the border to cast ballots in territorial elections or to harass free-soilers.

Something close to a state of civil war in Kansas resulted from the frequent conflicts between the free-state settlers and the Southern immigrants reinforced by these Missouri "border ruffians." Both proslavery and free-soil groups held elections for constitutional conventions, and each faction boycotted the election sponsored by its rival. Rival conventions met and drew up constitutions, one guaranteeing slavery in Kansas, the other excluding it; and contending delegations sent to Washington sought congressional approval. A series of territorial governors sent by the federal government could do nothing to bring the opposing sides together.

The danger grew that the usual frontier lawlessness in Kansas might turn into organized blood-letting. On the night of May 24–25, 1856, John Brown, a dedicated, single-minded abolitionist who had emigrated to Kansas after an unsuccessful career in the East as a tanner, sheep raiser, and land speculator, opened hostilities. Without warning, he led a small party, consisting mostly of his own sons, in an attack on the cabins of two Southern families who lived on Pottawatomie Creek and murdered five men, leaving their gashed and mutilated bodies as a warning for other proslavery families to leave Kansas. In revenge, Southern immigrants organized and attacked Brown at Osawatomie, where Brown's son Frederick was killed. Only Brown's departure for the East prevented further slaughter.

At this unpropitious moment, the Supreme Court of the United States decided to risk its prestige and the enormous respect that Americans gave to its exposition of the revered Constitution, in an effort to resolve the snarled question of the status of slavery in the national territories. The events leading up to the Dred Scott decision of 1857 were enormously complex, and no purpose is served by reviewing here the legal intricacies of the case before the Court. At issue was the legal status of Dred Scott, a Missouri slave, who had been taken in the 1830s by his owner, an army surgeon, first to Rock Island, Illinois, a state where slavery was prohibited by the Northwest Ordinance and its own constitution, and subsequently to Fort Snelling in what is now Minnesota, part of the Louisiana Purchase from

MYTH AND REALITY IN THE KANSAS STRUGGLE

Military operations in Kansas were on a very small scale. As this contemporary drawing (*above*) of a fight between proslavery and free-soil forces at Hickory Point shows, most involved only a handful of men. But in a Republican cartoon (*below*); proslavery armies are shown terrorizing the whole countryside, while Liberty is raped by President Pierce, who is abetted by James Buchanan, Lewis Cass, and Stephen A. Douglas. (*Above, Anne S. K. Brown Military Collection, Brown University Library; below, Courtesy of The New-York Historical Society, New York City.*)

DRED SCOTT IN 1858

In discussions of the celebrated Supreme Court case, Dred Scott himself
tends to get lost. Originally called "Sam," he was sold in about 1833
to a new owner, who renamed him. Unhappy, Scott ran away but was
promptly recaptured. His first wife was sold. By his second wife,
Harriet, he had two sons, both of whom died, and two daughters.
(*Missouri Historical Society.*)

which slavery had been excluded by the Missouri Compromise. Scott returned with his owner to Missouri, but later he sued for his freedom on
the ground that he had been resident first of a free state and then of a free
territory. After complex and contradictory rulings in the lower courts, his
case came before the Supreme Court for the definitive determination of two
broad questions: (1) Was a Negro like Scott a citizen of the United States,
who was, therefore, entitled to initiate a suit in the federal courts? (2) Was
the congressional prohibition of slavery in federal territories, whether in the
Missouri Compromise or in subsequent legislation, constitutional?

Initially the justices of the high court planned to avoid these sweeping issues and to deliver a limited opinion, following numerous precedents, declaring that the status of Scott, who continued to be a resident of Missouri, was determined by Missouri state law. Such a decision would have left Scott a slave, but it would have avoided initiating broader controversy. Just why the justices changed their minds and ruled on larger questions has been a subject of debate among historians. Some blame the two antislavery justices for insisting upon giving opinions favorable to Scott; their course of action, it is alleged, forced the other justices to address the issue that they raised. Other scholars censure Georgia Justice James M. Wayne for insisting that the Court discuss all apects of the case; it was Wayne's challenge, these historians claim, that elicited the sweeping dissents of the two antislavery justices. Nearly all specialists agree that President-elect Buchanan played a role in shaping the Court's decision. Upon learning that the Court probably would address the broad questions involved in Dred Scott's case, Buchanan feared the public reaction if that decision was supported by a majority consisting only of Southern justices, and he put pressure on Justice Robert C. Grier, a fellow Pennsylvanian, to join with the majority.

This controversy over the personal responsibility for the Dred Scott decision often overlooks the more important point that the Court, and particularly the aged, high-minded Chief Justice, Roger B. Taney, believed that the American public wished it to settle, once and for all, the critically divisive question of slavery in the territories. In the years since the introduction of the Wilmot Proviso, there had been numerous proposals that the Supreme Court be asked to decide the whole territorial issue. As has been previously noted, before the Compromise of 1850 the influential Senator John M. Clayton of Delaware urged that all questions concerning slavery in the territory acquired from Mexico be referred to the Supreme Court, which, he said, was a dial that shone brightly in the gloomy hour. As finally adopted, the compromise itself included a provision for direct appeal of all cases involving slavery in the New Mexico and Utah territories to the Supreme Court. In 1854 when Douglas initiated his bill providing for popular sovereignty in Kansas, President Pierce preferred instead that the Supreme Court should be asked to settle the whole problem. In short, the Court had good reason to think that the American people wanted a sweeping decision in the Dred Scott case.

Consequently, in March 1857, the Court gave such a decision. To be more accurate, it issued nine separate opinions, for each justice made a separate statement. Since these did not all address the same problems, it was not altogether easy to determine just what the Court had decided, but the chief justice seemed to speak for the majority of his brethren on the two essential issues. First he ruled that Scott, as a Negro, was not a citizen of the United States. Neither the Declaration of Independence nor the Constitution, he alleged, was intended to include blacks. The Founding Fathers, claimed Taney with a cheerful disregard of much historical evidence, lived at a period when Negroes were "regarded as beings of an inferior order, and altogether unfit to associate with the white race, . . . and so far inferior that they had no rights which the white man was bound to respect." As a noncitizen, Scott had no right to bring suit in United States courts. Addressing the second major issue, the chief justice announced that when Congress made regulations for governing the territories, its power was restrained by the Fifth Amendment to the Constitution, which prohibits the taking of property without "due process of law." All citizens had an equal right to enter any of the national territories with their property, and slaves were a variety of property. It followed that any congressional enactment— and specifically the Missouri Compromise—that excluded slavery from any national territory was "not warranted by the Constitution" and was "therefore void."

With the advantage of hindsight, it is easy to argue that the Dred Scott decision was of no great practical consequence. Four months after the Court's ruling, Scott's owner manumitted him and his family. The Missouri Compromise, which the Court struck down, had already been repealed in the Kansas-Nebraska Act. The Dred Scott decision did not open vast new areas for the extension of slavery, simply because since 1854 slavery was already permitted in all the territories into which it might conceivably go.

If the practical results of the Dred Scott decision were negligible, its consequences for the American faith in constitutionalism, hitherto one of the strongest bonds of Union, were fateful. As was to be expected, Southerners generally welcomed the decision as a vindication of their rights, and a good many agreed with Jefferson Davis that it meant Congress must enact a slave code that gave positive protection to slavery in all the territories. Southern enthusiasm was tempered, however, by a recognition that most Northerners would not accept the Court's ruling as definitive.

In truth, there was virtually universal condemnation of the decision in the North. Douglas and his Northern Democratic following were hard hit, because the Court appeared to have announced that popular sovereignty was unconstitutional. If Congress could not exclude slavery from a territory, a handful of settlers clearly could not do so either. Attempting to respect the Court, to preserve his doctrine of popular sovereignty, and to keep the Democratic party intact, Douglas devised an elaborate straddle. He conceded the abstract right of the slaveowner to take his chattels into the national territory but pragmatically noted that it was "a barren and worthless right, unless sustained, protected and enforced by appropriate police regulations and local legislation. . . ." Republicans, who had no Southern constituency, did not suffer from the same constraints as Douglas and angrily denounced the Court's "false and wicked judgment," which, as the New York *Tribune* claimed, was "entitled to just as much moral weight as would be the judgment of a majority of those congregated in any Washington bar-room."

≥ IV ≤

At just the time that the great unifying belief in constitutionalism was being eroded, the third great bond of Union, nationalistic oratory, was losing its force. In the South the death of Calhoun removed the last great orator for Union. Though Calhoun was a proponent of nullification and an advocate of Southern sectionalism, he always spoke of the Union with veneration. Even in his final address, explaining why he thought it too late in 1850 for meaningful compromise, he lamented the breaking of national ties.

Calhoun's successors had no such regrets. The most notable of the Southern sectionalist orators was William L. Yancey of Alabama, who was as unswerving in his hatred for the North as he was in his devotion to slavery. With spell-binding rhetoric, Yancey alerted his Southern audiences to the dangers that would result from the success of Northern abolitionism. The South, he predicted, would see a repetition of scenes from the Santo Domingo slave rebellion of the 1790s, "where wives were violated upon the bodies of their slaughtered husbands, and the banner of the inhuman fiends was the dead body of an infant, impaled upon a spear, its golden locks dabbled in gore, and its little limbs stiffened by the last agony of suffering nature." Openly an advocate of secession, Yancey explained the purpose of his orations: "All my aims and objects are to cast before the people of the South as great a mass of wrongs committed on them, injuries and insults that have been done, as I possibly can. . . . All united may yet produce spirit enough to lead us forward, to call forth a Lexington, to fight a Bunker's Hill, to drive the [Northern] foe from the city of our rights."

Equally ominous was the disappearance of the oratory of national conciliation in the North. Charles Sumner was not merely Webster's successor in the Senate; he was the new voice of Massachusetts. Drawing upon his Harvard education, his broad reading, and his first-hand knowledge of European developments, Sumner deliberately set about preparing orations that would unite the North in opposition to the South. The very titles of his major addresses indicated his purpose: "Freedom National, Slavery Sectional," "The Barbarism of Slavery," and so on. Because of its consequences,

Sumner's most famous oration was "The Crime Against Kansas," delivered in the Senate on May 19–20, 1856, as a commentary on the continuing violence in the Kansas territory. Taking as axiomatic the argument that slavery must expand or die, Sumner claimed that the disturbances in Kansas following the passage of the Kansas-Nebraska Act were evidence of the desperate attempt of Southerners to rape that "virgin territory, compelling it to the hateful embrace of slavery."

In his carefully prepared speech, Sumner attacked Douglas and made offensive personal references to the elderly South Carolina senator, Andrew Pickens Butler, whom he characterized as the Don Quixote of slavery, having "chosen a mistress to whom he has made his vows, and who, though ugly to others, is always lovely to him, though polluted in the sight of the world, is chaste in his sight . . . the harlot, Slavery." Butler was absent from the Senate during Sumner's speech, but his cousin, Representative Preston S. Brooks of South Carolina, seethed over the insult to his family and state. On May 22, before the Senate was called to order, Brooks entered the Senate chamber, approached Sumner, who was seated at his desk writing, and proceeded to punish him by beating him on the head and shoulders with a stout cane. He left Sumner bleeding and insensible in the aisle. It was nearly three years before Sumner recovered from his wounds. During that period, the Massachusetts legislature reelected him to the Senate, where his vacant chair spoke as powerfully for sectionalism as ever Webster had done for Union.

During these years of Sumner's silence, there sounded in the West an even more eloquent voice of sectionalism. Abraham Lincoln of Illinois paused long before announcing his hostility toward the Southern way of life. He was born in Kentucky; his wife came from a prominent Kentucky slaveholding family; his earliest political allegiance was to the great Kentucky compriser, Henry Clay. Unlike Sumner and many other Eastern antislavery spokesmen, Lincoln understood that Southerners did not cling to slavery simply from love of power or profit but because they could not conceive of a biracial society in which Negroes—far more numerous than in any part of the North—would be free. Indeed, Lincoln shared many of these Southern doubts and fears. At least up until he became President, he did not believe in the social equality of the races, and he was not even certain that free Negroes should have the vote. As late as 1862 he told a group of Negro leaders that it was impossible for whites and blacks to coexist peacefully within the United States, and he urged them to support his plans for colonizing freedmen in the Caribbean.

But for all his understanding of the Southerners' problems, Lincoln never approved of slavery. One of his first public actions, as a member of the Illinois legislature in the 1830s, was to draft a resolution condemning slavery as "founded on both injustice and bad policy"; and as a one-term Whig member of the House of Representatives in the 1840s, he initiated a plan for gradual abolition in the District of Columbia. But, along with most other Northerners, Lincoln did not believe that moral denunciation of slavery and of slaveholders would help to solve the problem, and he hoped that, with time, the peculiar institution would be contained and finally die out.

The Kansas-Nebraska Act ended those hopes. From the newspapers and through letters from friends who had emigrated to Kansas, he learned how that land, once sacredly reserved for free labor, was now falling under the dominion of slaveholders. Deeply aroused, in 1854 Lincoln became a leader in organizing the anti-Nebraska forces in Illinois. He was a prominent but unsuccessful candidate for senator the next year, and by 1856 he had enough of a national reputation to receive strong support for the Republican vice-presidential nomination.

It was the Dred Scott decision that impelled Lincoln to become a full-fledged Northern sectionalist. He hated the Court's decision not only for what it said but for what it portended. Believing that slavery had to expand or die, Lincoln thought that he could detect a pattern of conspiracy in the political developments of the past decade. First had come the annexation of the slave state of Texas. Then the Compromise of 1850 permitted slavery to exist in the New Mexico and Utah territories. Next Douglas, with President Pierce's backing, moved to repeal the Missouri Compromise and to open Kansas to slavery. Three years later Chief Justice Taney, abetted by President Buchanan, announced that Congress had no power to exclude slavery from any territory. It was clear to Lincoln that Stephen, Franklin, Roger, and James—Douglas, Pierce, Taney, and Buchanan—had all along been engaged in constructing a house and that now only the ridgepole was missing. That, Lincoln predicted, would soon come in the form of "another Supreme Court decision, declaring that the Constitution of the United States does not permit a *state* to exclude slavery from its limits." Unless Republicans throughout the North mobilized quickly to repudiate the whole Democratic party with its proslavery conspirators, Lincoln feared, "we shall awake to the *reality* . . . that the *Supreme Court* has made *Illinois a slave* state."

These utterances reveal more about the state of Lincoln's mind and the receptivity of the Northern audiences that cheered his speeches than they do about historical reality. There was no proslavery conspiracy of the sort Lincoln described. At the very time Lincoln spoke, President Buchanan and Senator Douglas were engaged not in collaboration but in fierce controversy that split the Democratic party. Buchanan, like Jefferson Davis, believed that the Dred Scott decision required a federal slave code for the territories; Douglas insisted that, through police regulations, the residents of a territory could still exclude slavery if they wished. When the pro-Southern element in Kansas, after a rigged election from which free-soilers abstained, drafted the Lecompton constitution protecting slavery and asked to be admitted as a state, Buchanan supported their application, but Douglas denounced it as a fraudulent distortion of his popular sovereignty doctrine. So completely estranged were the two Democratic leaders that, in 1858, when Douglas ran for reelection to the Senate, Buchanan used all his influence and patronage to support a rival independent Democrat. Lincoln, as the Republican nominee, was the beneficiary of this feud among those he labeled "conspirators."

But Lincoln, his emotions aroused over the extension of slavery and his ambition stirred by the prospect of the senatorship, fully believed the charges he made and, in a series of nationally publicized debates with Douglas in the 1858 campaign, he eloquently voiced both the aspirations and the fears of the free-soilers. If, to the present-day reader, the Lincoln-Douglas debates seem to revolve repetitiously around the one limited issue of slavery in the territories, it must be remembered that virtually every political leader in the North and the South agreed that that point was of the utmost importance, since slavery had to grow or it would wither away. After a strenuous campaign, Douglas was reelected to the Senate, but Lincoln emerged as the real victor. Throughout the North, antislavery men now perceived the issues in terms of the stark contrasts Lincoln had presented in the opening address of his campaign:

> "A house divided against itself cannot stand."
> I believe this government cannot endure, permanently half *slave* and
>   half *free*.
> I do not expect the Union to be *dissolved*—I do not expect the house to
>   *fall*—but I *do* expect it will cease to be divided.
> It will become *all* one thing, or *all* the other.

⋊ V ⋉

With the issue thus baldly stated, the outcome was simply a matter of time. The great forces that had once helped cement American unity—the Constitution, the political parties, the public oratory—now served to divide the people. The United States, it now appeared, was not, and never really had been, a nation; it was merely a loose assemblage of diverse and conflicting groups, interests, and peoples. By the late 1850s these had polarized into two groups, a majority in the North, and a minority in the South. Neither majority nor minority was willing to yield on what both regarded as the vital issue of the expansion of slavery. And the war came.

Though essentially correct as a broad outline of events, that sketch suffers from the oversimplification that has, unavoidably, been present throughout the previous pages. In order to present a clear picture of developments during the 1840s and 1850s, it has been necessary to gloss over the fact that neither North nor South was monolithic. Significant numbers in both sections dissented from what have been described as the dominant values. In the South, of course, blacks, whether slave or free, did not subscribe to the ideology of the master class. Nor did white residents of the Appalachians and Ozarks. Many large Southern planters, who had everything to lose in a sectional conflict, and numerous Southern seaboard merchants with economic ties to the North deplored the trend of events and denounced Southern sectionalists as mad fire-eaters.

In the free states, too, large numbers of people did not subscribe to free-soil doctrines and actively loathed abolitionism. The large Southern-born population in the lower part of Illinois, Indiana, and Ohio had ties of blood and affection to their native region and abhorred the idea of conflict with the South. Most German immigrants, though hostile to slavery, loyally supported the Democratic party in its efforts to avert sectional conflict. The numerous Irish population in Northern cities, fearful of economic competition from low-paid free blacks, had no enthusiasm for ending slavery. Many prominent Eastern manufacturers and businessmen deplored sectional agitation not merely because it might adversely affect their own ties with the South but, especially after the sharp panic of 1857, because it might retard general economic recovery.

When a historian speaks of "the North" or "the South" during these prewar decades, therefore, he is using a convenient shorthand to refer to the articulate groups who gained control of the political machinery in those sections. As late as 1859 that control was secure in neither section. There was always a chance that the sizable dissenting elements in both sections —which, if active and united, might have formed a majority in the country as a whole—would gain power, and that the United States would once more practice the politics of compromise rather than the politics of confrontation.

In the South, that possibility was drastically reduced after October 1859. Still reeking from the blood of Southerners killed in Kansas, John Brown had come East with a plan to attack slavery in its heartland. Securing the backing of abolitionists like Gerrit Smith of New York and Theodore Parker, Samuel Gridley Howe, and Thomas Wentworth Higginson in Mas-

JOHN BROWN

By the time of the raid on Harpers Ferry, Brown had grown a beard for disguise, but this clean-shaven picture gives a better idea of his character. Bronson Alcott described him: "He is of imposing appearance, personally—tall, with square shoulders and standing; eyes of deep gray . . . ; his hair shooting backward from low down on his forehead, nose trenchant and Romanesque; set lips, his voice suppressed yet metallic . . . ; decided mouth; the countenance and frame charged with power throughout." (*The Boston Athenaeum.*)

sachusetts, Brown organized a miniature army on the Maryland side of the Potomac, and on October 16 he led his band of eighteen followers, including three of his sons and five blacks, into Virginia. His plans are obscure, but apparently he intended to seize the federal arsenal at Harpers Ferry, to distribute arms to the slaves, who, he assumed, would flock to his banner, and then, from the mountain fastnesses in western Virginia, to wage guerrilla warfare against the slaveholders. Though he succeeded in capturing the arsenal, there was no slave uprising, and within a few hours Brown and the surviving members of his little force were captured by United States marines commanded by Colonel Robert E. Lee. After trial, Brown was executed for treason against the state of Virginia.

Brown's raid sent a shock of terror through the South. In fear and anger, Southern whites turned against all strangers in their midst, suspecting every Yankee peddler and colporteur of being an abolitionist emissary. As unfounded rumors of slave insurrections spread, even the mildest Southern criticisms of slavery were silenced. The raid also increased Southern hostility toward the Republican party. Brown's course proved to Southerners the falsity of Republicans' claims that they wished only to prevent the expansion of slavery, not to interfere with it in the states where it already existed. After all, John Brown moved from his murders in Kansas to his incendiary attack in Virginia. Southerners felt that the whole North must inexorably follow the same bloody path.

In the months after Brown's raid, even those Southerners who had not hitherto shared the dominant fears in their section came to feel that no Northerner could ever again be trusted to head the government of the United States. Naturally they rejected even the possibility of acknowledging as President a Republican leader like Lincoln, with his talk of a "house divided," or Seward, with his prediction of an "irrepressible conflict." Now they turned with almost equal unanimity against Douglas, the strongest candidate the Democratic party could nominate in 1860. In Southern eyes, Douglas was a threat to their section, more dangerous, because covert, than any Republican. He was a leader who promised much but delivered little. His Kansas-Nebraska Act had seemed to open the way for the extension of slavery, but few slaveowners proved willing to risk their valuable property in that troubled territory. Douglas ostensibly endorsed the Supreme Court's decision in the Dred Scott case, but he practically nullified it through his doctrine that local police regulations could exclude slavery from the territories. And, in the test of strength over the admission of Kansas under its proslavery Lecompton constitution, Southerners felt that Douglas had betrayed the South and prevented the creation of a new slave state.

The desire to defeat Douglas animated the Southern delegations to the Democratic national convention that met in Charleston, South Carolina, in April 1860. A majority in that convention supported the Illinois senator, but he lacked the two-thirds support required by the rules of the Democratic party. An early test of strength came in a conflict over the platform. When a majority favored a plank embodying Douglas's "nonintervention" position, promising vaguely to abide by decisions of the Supreme Court as regards slavery in the territories, Southern delegates, who since 1854 had seen just how much faith could be put in that pledge, bolted the convention. Subsequently two separate Democratic conventions were held: one, dominated by Northerners, which nominated Douglas; the other, consisting primarily of Southerners, which named Vice-President John C. Breckinridge of Kentucky as its nominee.

Jubilant over this split, Republicans assembled in convention at Chicago. The division in the Democracy virtually assured a Republican victory. The party could consequently afford to pass over both the most conspicuous candidate, Seward, who had made too many enemies during his long political career, and the more conservative possibilities, such as the old-line Whig, Edward Bates of Missouri. Instead it nominated Lincoln. Though the platform was careful to explain that there would be no interference with slavery within any state, it firmly denied "the authority of Congress, or a territorial legislature, or of any individuals, to give legal existence to Slavery in any Territory of the United States." In both the North and the South, that was recognized as code language for the determination that, if successful, the Republicans would, in Lincoln's phrase, put slavery "in the course of ultimate extinction."

Alarmed by the polarization of sections, a group of conservatives, consisting mostly of former Whigs who had supported Fillmore on the American ticket in 1856, formed a new Constitutional Union party dedicated simply, if vaguely, to the reconciliation of the majority and minority sections. They chose as their candidates John Bell of Tennessee, one of the few Southern senators who had voted against the Kansas-Nebraska Act, and Edward Everett, the most famous living orator who still invoked the ideal of national unity.

The election demonstrated how completely sectionalized American politics had become. Only the Constitutional Union party and Douglas's wing of the Democracy made real attempts to wage a campaign in all sections, and these two parties came in last at the polls. Breckinridge's branch of the Democratic party was essentially a Southern organization, with substantial strength in some parts of the North. The Republican party was a Northern party, which received not a single popular vote in ten slave states. Though Lincoln received only a plurality of the popular vote, he won an overwhelming majority in the electoral college.

The news of Lincoln's election triggered steps toward the secession of the slave states, plans for which Southern extremists had long been plotting. This time they intended to avoid the mistakes they had made in the past. They would not allow delay until Lincoln was inaugurated and committed some act adverse to Southern interests; previous experience in 1833

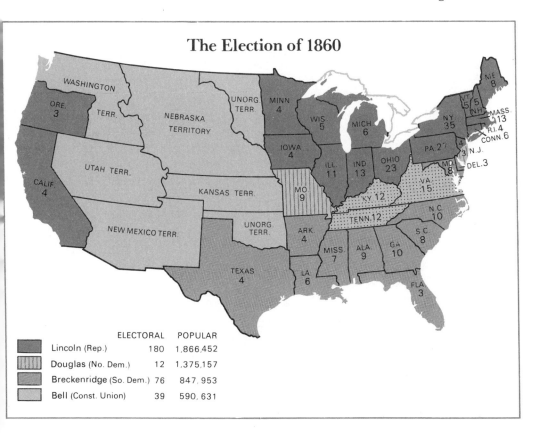

The Election of 1860

	ELECTORAL	POPULAR
Lincoln (Rep.)	180	1,866,452
Douglas (No. Dem.)	12	1,375,157
Breckenridge (So. Dem.)	76	847,953
Bell (Const. Union)	39	590,631

and 1850 had taught that the popular enthusiasm for secession might quickly fade and that Southern opinion could be divided over just what constituted a hostile act. Nor would they call a convention representing all the Southern states, as they had done in Nashville in 1850; that process would also require time, and the opposition, or even the hesitation, of one state might hold up the whole process. Instead, they pressed for separate conventions in each of the slave states to consider, in the words of the call for the South Carolina convention, "the danger incident to the position of the State in the Federal Union." The South Carolina convention met first and, with the impetuosity characteristic of that state, voted on December 20 to secede from the Union. Alabama, Mississippi, Florida, Georgia, and Louisiana followed before the end of January, and Texas seceded the next month. The victorious secessionists chose delegates to meet at Montgomery, Alabama, in February in order to draw up a constitution for the newly created Southern nation.

The Northern response to these swift Southern actions was confused and slow. After years of hearing blustering about secession, many Northerners could not believe that the South was in earnest. During the 1860 campaign, for instance, the exceptionally well informed German-American, Carl Schurz, who was campaigning for Lincoln's election, ridiculed talk of secession. "There had been two overt attempts [at secession] already," he said, "one, the secession of the Southern students from the medical school at Philadelphia, which he ridiculed abundantly; the second, upon the election of [Republican] Speaker Pennington [in 1859], when the South seceded from Congress, went out, took a drink, and then came back. The third attempt would be, he prophesied, when old Abe would be elected. They would then again secede and this time would take two drinks but would come back again."

Action by the federal government during the secession crisis was palsied by the fact that the President was the seventy-year-old Buchanan, who was torn between his long-standing pledge to maintain "the constitutional rights of the South in opposition to all the projects of the abolitionists and quasi-

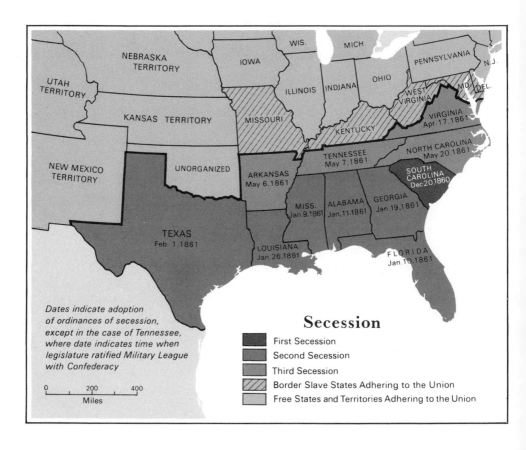

Dates indicate adoption of ordinances of secession, except in the case of Tennessee, where date indicates time when legislature ratified Military League with Confederacy

Secession

- First Secession
- Second Secession
- Third Secession
- Border Slave States Adhering to the Union
- Free States and Territories Adhering to the Union

abolitionists" and his oath to protect and defend the Constitution of the United States. Ineffectually Buchanan announced that the Southern states had no constitutional right to secede, but that the federal government had no constitutional power to keep them from so doing.

Congress, which assembled in December 1860, was little more effective. It still contained many members who recalled the better days of the republic, when compromises had been arranged between majorities and minorities. The leading proponent of compromise was John J. Crittenden of Kentucky, Henry Clay's successor in the Senate. His followers were mostly other congressmen from the border states, who knew how precariously the slave states of the Upper South were balanced between Union and secession and who recognized that, in the probable event of civil war following secession, their own homes and firesides would be devastated. The efforts of the congressmen to devise a compromise were supported by a peace conference, consisting of delegates appointed by the governors of the several states; former President John Tyler of Virginia emerged from retirement to lead this forlorn effort. Proposals for a package of compromises included an un-amendable amendment to the Constitution forbidding Congress ever to meddle with slavery in any of the states; perpetual protection of slavery in federal forts or installations located in the slave states; a more vigorous enforcement of the fugitive slave acts, with compensation to owners who were unable to reclaim their runaways; and, chiefly, a reinstitution of the Missouri Compromise line through the national territories, this time guaranteeing slavery on one side of the line and forbidding it on the other.

The fate of these proposals did not rest with the stalwart group of compromisers in Congress but with the Republicans and with the representatives and senators from those slave states that had not yet seceded. Though both of these groups were willing to accept parts of the compromise package, neither one could or would agree to what they considered its essential feature. For the Southerners, the drawing of a line through the national territory beyond which slavery should never go meant the ultimate death of the peculiar institution and, consequently, the unraveling of the whole fabric of Southern society. To the Republicans, on the other hand, a guarantee of slavery south of the Missouri Compromise line and the enactment of a federal slave code meant a base betrayal of their 1860 platform and an abandonment of the one principle that held the new party together. Beyond these considerations was the Republican belief that if the South, by bluffing about secession, could extract this concession it would use the same tactic to secure the annexation of further slave territory in the Caribbean.

If any Republican congressmen wavered on this point, they were drawn up sharp by letters from their President-elect. Observing the crisis as closely as he could from Springfield, Lincoln was willing to make concessions on all but the one essential point. "Let there be no compromise on the question of extending slavery," he enjoined his fellow Republicans in Congress. "If there be, all our labor is lost, and, ere long, must be done again. . . . Have none of it. Stand firm. The tug has to come, and better now than at any time hereafter."

⧜ VI ⧜

In chronicling the course of events between 1845 and 1861, the historian is forced to ask whether secession and the civil war that followed were inevitable. On this question there have been stridently differing opinions, but the disagreement often seems to result from a lack of semantic clarity. In one sense the Civil War obviously was not inevitable. Had Lincoln and his party agreed to the Crittenden Compromise, they might have forestalled, at least for a time, the secession of all the Southern states except South Carolina. Had Southern fire-eaters delayed action until the Lincoln administration adopted some policy hostile to slavery, secession might never have occurred. Had Douglas withdrawn his name from consideration by the Democratic convention in Charleston, quite probably that party could have chosen a nominee who would have been elected in 1860.* Had President Buchanan rejected the Lecompton constitution on the legitimate ground that it was not submitted for a general referendum, there would have been no split in the Democratic party in 1858. Had Chief Justice Taney held to his original view that the Supreme Court should issue a limited, technical ruling in the Dred Scott case, Northern fears about the extension of slavery would never have been so aroused. Had Douglas postponed the territorial organization of Kansas, the bargains of the compromise of 1850 might have held. And so, on and on, one can push the story of fateful, but not preordained, actions that led to war.

But emphasis on these actions of individuals and small groups minimizes the influence of larger issues and broader forces. The central problem that divided the United States during these troubled years was that of reconciling the power of majorities and the rights of minorities in a democratic government. Americans of the pre–Civil War era were unable to discover any formula for solving this dilemma. Certainly none of the mechanisms

---

* To be sure, had Douglas's and Breckinridge's votes in 1860 been delivered to a single candidate, Lincoln would still have won the presidency in the electoral college; but a strong, united Democratic party could probably have put on a more effective campaign than either of its two factions did.

proposed by Calhoun and others, such as a dual presidency with one Chief Executive from the North and the other from the South, would have worked.

Perhaps in theory the problem was unsolvable, but the reconciling of divergent and conflicting interests had previously proved possible for Americans so long as they considered themselves part of the same great people, sharing basic values and united by strong ties. But by the 1850s the reservoir of goodwill and compassion that Americans had hitherto shared was being drained. Slowly and usually reluctantly, more and more came to think of themselves as forming not one but two distinct peoples. For Ralph Waldo Emerson, the moment of realization came when he learned that his friend Sumner had been struck down in the Senate chamber. "I do not see how a barbarous community and a civilized community can constitute one state," the philosopher soberly reflected. "I think we must get rid of slavery, or we must get rid of freedom." For many Southerners, the moment of truth came when they learned of the election of Abraham Lincoln, a Black Republican. "These [Northern] people hate us, annoy us, and would have us assassinated by our slaves if they dared," one slaveowner wrote at that time. "They are a *different* people from us, whether better or worse and *there is no love* between us. Why then continue together?"

To the extent that this sense of difference—this feeling that Northerners and Southerners no longer spoke the same language, shared the same moral code, or obeyed the same law—prevailed, the secession of the South was inevitable; and war was an almost inevitable consequence of secession. But whether, in fact, these differences between North and South were so profound, as leaders in both sections by 1861 conceived them to be, would be revealed only in the four years of fighting that lay ahead.

GENERAL GEORGE BRINTON MCCLELLAN, U.S.A.

A serious student of warfare, McClellan was a disciple of Jomini. He personified the traditional kind of warfare both the Union and the Confederacy waged during 1861 and 1862. (*The National Archives.*)

4

Stalemate

During the first two years of the Civil War, as the Union and the Confederacy grappled with each other inconclusively, it seemed that two distinct and incompatible nations had emerged from the American soil. Certainly the aims announced by their leaders were totally inconsistent. President Abraham Lincoln announced that the United States "*will* constitutionally defend, and maintain itself"; the territorial integrity of the nation must remain inviolate. For the Confederate States, President Jefferson Davis proclaimed that his country's "career of independence" must be "inflexibly pursued." As the rival governments raised and equipped armies, attempted to finance a huge war, and sought diplomatic recognition and economic assistance abroad, the people of the two nations increasingly thought of each other as enemies: "Yankees" and "Rebels." It is easy to understand why Lord John Russell, the British foreign minister, concluded: "I do not see how the United States can be cobbled together again by any compromise. . . . I suppose the break-up of the Union is now inevitable."

A shrewder observer might have reached precisely the opposite conclusion. Perhaps the most striking thing about the war in America was the fact that both sides carried it on through virtually identical methods. The Union and the Confederate governments faced the same wartime problems and arrived at the same wartime solutions. Northerners and Southerners on the battlefields found each other, not two alien peoples, but mirror images. That identity made the conflict truly a brothers' war.

⊱ I ⊰

The government of the Confederate States of America was, in most respects, a duplicate of that of the United States, from which the Southern states had just withdrawn. Framed by delegates from six states of the Lower South (delegates from Texas, which seceded on February 1, 1861, arrived late), its Constitution largely followed the wording of the one drawn up in Philadelphia in 1787. To be sure, the new charter recognized the "sovereign and independent character" of the constituent states, but it also announced that they were forming "a permanent federal government," and it listed most of the same restrictions on state action included in the United States Constitution. Unlike that document, it used no euphemism about persons "held to Service or Labour" but recognized explicitly "the right of property in negro slaves." Otherwise, the two documents were substantially and intentionally identical. As secessionist Benjamin H. Hill of Georgia explained, "we hugged that [United States] Constitution to our bosom and carried it with us."

For President of the new republic, the Montgomery Convention* chose an inflexible defender of Southern rights, determined to protect his minority section, with its peculiar institution, from the national majority. But if the crowds that thronged Montgomery's streets on February 18, 1861, to watch the procession of military companies wearing red jackets, battle-green jackets, and gray jackets and flashing their shiny new bayonets hoped to hear a stirring inaugural from the South's new head of state, they were disappointed. Stepping forward on the portico of the Alabama state house, Jefferson Davis of Mississippi gave a long, legalistic review of the acts of Northern aggression that had led to the formation of the new state. While Davis pledged that he would, if necessary, "maintain, by the final arbitrament of the sword, the position which we have assumed among the nations of the earth," he spoke in a tone more melancholy than martial. He saw himself as the leader of a conservative movement. "We have labored to preserve the Government of our fathers in its spirit," he insisted.

---

* The Montgomery Convention drew up a provisional Constitution of the Confederacy, constituted itself the provisional legislature of the new republic, and named Jefferson Davis the provisional President. It also drew up a permanent Constitution, which was submitted to the states for ratification. After that, regular elections were held in the fall of 1861 both for members of the Confederate Congress and for President. Reelected without opposition, Davis was formally inaugurated as the first and only regular President of the Confederate States on February 22, 1862.

JEFFERSON DAVIS

Frail and often ill, the President of the Confederate States was also handicapped by his ideological rigidity, which prevented him from recognizing that modern warfare involves the whole society. Yet it would be hard to identify a Southerner who would have made a more effective leader of the Lost Cause. (*Library of Congress.*)

Just two weeks later, from the portico of the yet unfinished Capitol in Washington, another President took his inaugural oath. The capital was thronged, as Nathaniel Hawthorne wrote, with "office-seekers, wire-pullers, inventors, artists, poets, prosers (including editors, army correspondents, attaches of foreign journals, and long-winded talkers), clerks, diplomatists, mail contractors, [and] railway directors." On public buildings along the route of the inaugural procession, sharpshooters were strategically placed to prevent any pro-Southern interruption of the proceedings. Few in the crowd could hear Abraham Lincoln's words, but when they read his address in the newspapers, they might have been struck by its similarity in tone to Davis's. Vowing that the Union would be preserved, Lincoln gave a low-keyed version of the previous sectional quarrels, explained his personal views on slavery, and pledged that he contemplated "no invasion—no using of force" against the seceded states. In a warning softened by sadness, he reminded his listeners of the oath he had just taken to preserve, protect, and defend the government of the United States and entreated his Southern fellow citizens to pause before they assailed it. "In *your* hands, my dissatisfied fellow-countrymen," he concluded, "and not in *mine,* is the momentous issue of civil war."

In the weeks immediately following the two inaugurations, the central problem confronting both Davis and Lincoln was not so much whether either one should start a civil war but whether they could form viable governments. In Davis's Confederacy everything had to be started afresh. Even the most routine legal and governmental matters could not be taken for granted. For instance, it was not certain, until the Confederate Congress passed an act, whether the laws of the United States enacted before 1861 and the decisions of the United States courts were binding in the seceded states. The new nation had to choose a flag—over the opposition of some purists who claimed the Confederacy, representing the true American spirit, ought to retain the stars and stripes and let the Union look for a new banner. It had to provide for the printing of money and postage stamps—no small undertaking in a land where engravers were so few and incompetent that their unprepossessing likenesses of Jefferson Davis and other Confederate worthies caused suspicion of the loyalty of the artists.

In selecting his cabinet advisers, President Davis theoretically had a free hand, but in fact his range of choice was severely limited. No man of doubtful loyalty to the new government could be permitted a place in his cabinet; no Southern Unionist in the tradition of Henry Clay, John J. Crittenden, and John Bell was invited. On the other hand, because Davis wanted the world to see that the Confederacy was governed by sober, responsible men, he excluded from his council all the most conspicuous Southern fire-eaters. Then, too, he had to achieve some balance between former Whigs and former Democrats, and he felt obliged to secure a wide geographical spread by selecting one member of his original cabinet from each of the seven Confederate states, except Mississippi, which the President himself represented. As a result of these elaborate calculations, Davis's cabinet consisted of neither his personal friends nor—with the exception of Secretary of State Robert Toombs of Georgia, who served only briefly—the outstanding political leaders of the South.

Such a cabinet might have sufficed in a country where administrative procedures and routines were firmly rooted. Instead, in the Confederacy there was everywhere a lack of preparation and a lack of resources for running a government. Typical was the Confederate treasury department, which initially consisted of one unswept room in a Montgomery bank, "without furniture of any kind; empty . . . of desks, tables, chairs or other appliances for the conduct of business." For the first rickety furniture, the secretary of the treasury had to pay out of his own pocket. During the early weeks of the new nation, when an army captain came to the treasury department with President Davis's warrant for blankets for one hundred men, the sole clerk in the department pulled out his purse, which contained five or ten dollars, and offered it to him. "This, Captain, is all the money that I will certify as being in the Confederate Treasury at this moment," the

THE BALTIMORE RIOT OF APRIL 19, 1861

Rushing to the defense of the capital, Massachusetts troops were attacked while changing trains in Baltimore. Four Massachusetts infantrymen were killed and thirty-six others were wounded. The riot emphasized the importance for the Lincoln administration of keeping Maryland and the other border states in the Union. (*Prints Division, The New York Public Library, Astor, Lenox and Tilden Foundations.*)

clerk explained blithely. "I have been on a considerable frolic in Montgomery for the past two weeks and my finances are at this moment somewhat demoralized."

Disorganization and improvisation also characterized Lincoln's government in Washington. The Union had the advantage of owning the Capitol, the White House, and the permanent records of the United States government, and it had a recognized flag and a postal system. But in other respects it was thoroughly demoralized. Lincoln's government had no clear mandate from the people, for the President had received less than 40 percent of the popular vote in the 1860 election. It had an army of only 14,657 men, and every day military and naval officers announced that they were defecting to the South. Its treasury was empty, and it could not meet its payroll without borrowing at exorbitant rates of interest. Some of the most experienced clerks in the Washington offices were leaving to join the Confederacy, and others who remained were of suspect loyalty. Adding to the confusion was the fact that Lincoln's was the first Republican administration and, under the prevailing spoils system, party workers who had helped to elect the Republican candidate now flocked to Washington, expecting to oust and replace Democratic officeholders. The claimants for patronage ranged from elegant Brahmins, like the historian John Lothrop Motley, who sought a diplomatic appointment, to Lincoln's rough frontier acquaintances, but they all shared one characteristic: persistence. Accompanied by their representatives or senators and bearing huge rolls of recommending letters, the officeseekers besieged Lincoln in the White House. Wryly the President likened his plight to that of the inn-keeper whose clients demanded that he rent out rooms in one wing of his hotel even while he was trying to put out a fire in the other.

To make matters worse, not one member of the Lincoln administration had previously held a responsible position in the executive branch of the national government, and many, including the President himself, had no administrative experience of any sort. Like Davis, Lincoln made no attempt to form a coalition government; for his cabinet, he did not choose leaders of the Douglas Democracy or the Constitutional Union party. Nor, after a few timid and unsuccessful efforts, did he name Unionists from the South. Instead, all members of his cabinet were Republicans. That fact, however, scarcely gave his government unity, for several of Lincoln's cabinet appointees had themselves been candidates for the Republican nomination in 1860 and hence were rivals of Lincoln and of each other. The most conspicuous cabinet member was Secretary of State William H. Seward, wily and devious, extravagant in utterance but cautious in action, who felt he had a duty to save the country through compromise and conciliation despite its bumbling, inexperienced President. Seward's principal rival in the cabinet was Secretary of the Treasury Salmon P. Chase, pompous and self-righteous, who had an equally condescending view of Lincoln's talents and who lusted to become the next President of the United States. The other members, with most of whom Lincoln had only the slightest personal acquaintance before they took office, were appointed because they were supposed to have political influence or to represent key states.

⤜ II ⤛

Desperately needing time to get organized, these two shaky rival administrations immediately confronted a problem and a crisis, which were intimately interrelated. The problem concerned the future of the eight remaining slave states that had not yet seceded. Though linked to the Deep South by ties of blood and sentiment and fearful of abolitionist attacks on their peculiar institution of slavery, these states had refused to rush out of the Union. In January 1861, Virginia had elected a convention to consider secession, but it dillydallied and did nothing. In February, both North Carolinians and Tennesseans voted against holding secession conventions. When the Arkansas and Missouri conventions did meet in March, they voted not to secede. Up to April 1861, Kentucky, Maryland, and Delaware held no elections or conventions. But the loyalty of all these states to the Union was clearly conditional on the policy Lincoln's government adopted toward the Confederacy.

The crisis was the first test of that policy. It concerned the fate of the four United States installations in the seceded states that still remained under Federal control. Of these forts, two, Fort Taylor and Fort Jefferson off the Florida coast, posed no great problem; indeed, they remained in Federal hands throughout the war. More delicate was the fate of Fort Pickens in Pensacola Bay, where an uneasy truce held between the Union troops in the garrison and the Confederate force on the mainland. But the real trouble spot was Fort Sumter, in the harbor of Charleston, South Carolina. Its garrison, which consisted of about seventy Union soldiers and nine officers under the command of Major Robert Anderson, was no serious military threat to the Confederacy, but its presence at Charleston, the very center of secession, was an intolerable affront to Southern pride. For many Confederates, Sumter became a test of the resoluteness and effectiveness of their new government. They insisted that President Davis demonstrate his devotion to the Southern cause by forcing Anderson and his men out immediately. Conversely, many Northerners, who had despairingly watched during the final months of the Buchanan administration as fort after fort was turned over to the Confederates, also saw Sumter as a test of the strength and will of the Lincoln administration.

Despite these pressures, there were in both governments powerful voices that urged compromise or at least delay. All but two members of Lincoln's cabinet initially thought that Sumter should be evacuated, and Seward was so confident of a peaceful withdrawal that he pledged his word to the Confederate emissaries who had been sent to Washington in the hope of regularizing relations between the two countries. Davis's secretary of state was equally averse to hasty action. When the Confederate cabinet discussed attacking Anderson, Toombs solemnly warned: "The firing upon that fort will inaugurate a civil war greater than any the world has yet seen."

But Anderson's situation made some action necessary. After Charleston authorities prohibited further sale of food to the troops in the fort, his men faced starvation. The day after Lincoln was inaugurated, he learned that the garrison, unless supplied, could hold out no longer than April 15. Since Lincoln had just vowed that he would "hold, occupy, and possess" all places and property belonging to the government, he promptly directed his secretary of the navy to begin outfitting an expedition to provision Fort Sumter. At the same time, recognizing how dangerously explosive the Charleston situation was, he explored alternatives. One possibility was to reinforce Fort Pickens, in the relatively calm area of Florida; that would allow Lincoln to demonstrate his firmness of purpose, even if he was obliged to withdraw Anderson from the Charleston harbor. But the naval expedition sent to Florida miscarried, the Union commander at Fort Pickens misunderstood his orders, and the planned reinforcement could not be completed in time for Washington to know about it before Anderson's deadline for surrender. Another possibility was to consent to a peaceable withdrawal from Fort Sumter in return for assurances that the still vacillating border states would remain in the Union. "If you will guarantee to me the State of Virginia, I shall remove the troops," Lincoln confidentially promised a prominent Virginia Unionist. "A State for a fort is no bad business." But the Virginians delayed, a rainstorm kept a delegation of Unionists from reaching Washington, and they could give no firm promises. Seeing no other possible course of action, Lincoln let the expedition bearing food and supplies sail for Sumter.

President Davis understood that, in merely supplying Fort Sumter, Lincoln was not committing an act of aggression. Indeed, he predicted that "for political reasons the U.S. govt. will avoid making an attack so long as the hope of retaining the border states remains." But the Confederate President's hand was forced too. Hot-headed Governor Francis Pickens and other South Carolina extremists, impatient with Davis's caution, prepared to attack the fort. Rather than let Confederate policy be set by a state governor, Davis ordered General P. G. T. Beauregard, in command of the Confederate forces at Charleston, to demand the surrender of Fort Sumter. Anderson responded that he would soon be starved out, but he failed to promise to withdraw by a definite date. Beauregard's officers felt they had no alternative but to reduce the fort. At 4:30 A.M. on April 12 firing began. To the aged Virginia secessionist, Edmund Ruffin, who for a generation had crusaded for the creation of a separate Southern nation, was entrusted the honor of firing one of the first shots against the flag of the United States. Outside the harbor, the relief expedition Lincoln had sent watched impotently while Confederates bombarded the fort. After thirty-four hours, with ammunition nearly exhausted, Anderson was obliged to surrender.

Promptly Lincoln called for 75,000 volunteer soldiers to put down the "insurrection" in the South. On May 6 the Confederate Congress countered by formally declaring that a state of war existed. The American Civil War had begun.

Both at that time and later, there was controversy about the responsibility for precipitating the conflict. Critics claimed that Lincoln, by sending the expedition to provision Fort Sumter, deliberately tricked the Confederates into firing the first shot. Indeed, some months after the event Lincoln himself told a friend that his plan for sending supplies to Major Anderson had "succeeded." "They attacked Sumter," he explained; "it fell, and thus, did more service than it otherwise could." That statement clearly reveals Lincoln's wish that, if hostilities began, the Confederacy should bear the blame for initiating them, but it does little to prove that Lincoln wanted war. It is well to remember that, throughout the agonizing crisis, the Confederates took the initiative at Sumter. It was Charleston authorities who cut off Anderson's food supply; it was Confederate authorities who decided that, though the fort offered no military threat, Anderson must surrender; and it was the Southerners who fired the first shot. Writing privately to the Confederate commander at Fort Pickens, President Davis acknowledged that there would be a psychological advantage if the Southerners waited for the Federal government to make the initial attack; but, he added, "when we are ready to relieve our territory and jurisdiction of the presence of a foreign garrison that advantage is overbalanced by other considerations." These other considerations impelled Davis to take the initiative at Sumter.

If intent can be tested by consequences, it is evident that, initially at least, it was the Confederacy, not the Union, that benefited from the attack on Fort Sumter. The slave states still in the Union had now to make a choice of allegiances, and for a time it seemed that all would join the Confederacy. Virginia Governor John Letcher spurned Lincoln's call for troops as a bid "to inaugurate civil war," and on April 17 the state convention hastily passed a secession ordinance. Technically it was subject to popular ratification, but in actuality it immediately linked to the Confederacy the most populous and influential state of the Upper South, with its long tradition of leadership, its vast natural resources, and its large Tredegar Iron Works.

Other border slave states acted only a little less precipitously. On May 6 the Arkansas convention voted, with only five dissenters, to withdraw from the Union. When Lincoln's call for troops reached Governor Isham Harris of Tennessee, he replied haughtily, "In such an unholy crusade no gallant son of Tennessee will ever draw his sword," and began private negotiations with Confederate officials. On May 7 the Tennessee state legislature ratified the arrangements Harris had already made and voted to secede. On May 20 the North Carolina convention, under pressure from pro-Confederate newspapers to withdraw forever from "the vile, rotten, infidelic, puritanic, negro-worshipping, negro-stealing, negro-equality . . . Yankee-Union," unanimously adopted a secession ordinance.

Far to the west, the Confederacy scored another victory in the Indian Territory (later to become the state of Oklahoma). Confederate commissioner Albert Pike had little success with the Plains Indians there, but he won over most of the so-called civilized tribes, many of whom were slaveholders. The Confederacy agreed to pay all annuities previously provided by the United States government, and it allowed the Choctaws, Chickasaws, Creeks, Seminoles, and Cherokees to send delegates to the Confederate Congress. In return, these tribes promised to supply troops for the Confederate army. Most of them loyally supported the Southern effort throughout the war, and the Cherokee chief, Brigadier-General Stand Watie, did not formally surrender until a month after the war was over. A rival faction among the Cherokees, headed by Chief John Ross, and most of the Plains Indians favored the Union cause.

Elsewhere along the border, the Confederacy fared less well. Though a slave state with sentimental ties to the South, Delaware never really contemplated secession. To Lincoln's call for troops, the Delaware governor replied that his state had no standing militia, but he unenthusiastically recommended that citizens could form volunteer companies, which had the "option of offering their services to the general government for the defense of its capital."

Much more painful was the decision of Maryland, a state bitterly divided. In the southern counties and on the Eastern Shore, a tobacco-planting, slave holding region, sentiment was warm for secession. In the northern and western counties, yeomen farmers, often of German stock, were opposed to

A LOUISIANA CONFEDERATE

During the first years of the war, army uniforms were notably
individualistic. They ranged from improvised homespun clothing
to the impractical Zouave uniforms, consisting of kepis, short jackets,
and bloomer trousers. This stylish New Orleans soldier obviously had his
uniform tailor-made. Later uniforms of both North and South became
more standardized. (*The Valentine Museum, Richmond, Virginia.*)

slavery and loyal to the Union. Turbulent Baltimore, the scene of some of
the wildest riots of the antebellum era, was under the domination of pro-
Confederate mobs. For a few days in April, after one of these mobs attacked a Massachusetts regiment en route to Washington and effectively
cut communications between the Union capital and the rest of the country,
the secession of Maryland seemed a real possibility. But Lincoln, after deli-

cate negotiations with the timorous governor, arranged for further shipments of Union troops to bypass Baltimore until passions cooled. The
governor, in turn, helped to dampen secessionist sentiment by convening the
state legislature in stalwartly Unionist Frederick, rather than in secessionist
Annapolis. By the middle of May, Unionism was resurgent in Maryland,
and Federal General Benjamin F. Butler reopened the rail route through
Baltimore. With Butler's troops encamped on Federal Hill, ready, as the
general boasted, to lob mortar shells into the Maryland Club, the aristocratic hotbed of secessionist sentiment, the city remained quiescent. During
the next few months, the Lincoln administration did everything possible to
strengthen Unionist sentiment in Maryland. Suspected Confederate sympathizers, including nineteen members of the legislature and the mayor
of Baltimore, were unceremoniously arrested and jailed without trial. In
the 1861 fall elections, Maryland troops who wanted to go home to vote
received furloughs, while provost marshals kept from the polls any persons
believed to favor secession. As a result, Maryland elected an uncompromising Unionist as governor, and thereafter there was no further question of
secession.

In Missouri the Union cause was managed with much less skill. Here,
too, the populace was badly divided. The southwestern part of the state,
inhabited largely by migrants from the South, and the rich slaveholding
region along the Missouri River tended to favor secession. But the Unionist
element was strong, especially in St. Louis, where the influential German
community was hostile to slavery. Though Missouri's pro-Southern governor denounced Lincoln's call for troops as "illegal, unconstitutional, revolutionary, inhuman, diabolical," public opinion was so evenly split that
no steps toward secession probably would have occurred had it not been
for the hasty action of Unionist leaders. Encouraged by Francis P. Blair,
whose brother was Lincoln's postmaster-general, Union commander Nathaniel Lyon precipitated hostilities by overrunning an encampment of
pro-secessionist militia; he then made a spectacle of his prisoners by marching them through the streets of St. Louis. Confederate sympathizers rallied
to protect them, and for two days there was bloody street fighting in the
city. Lyon's precipitancy drove moderate Missourians, like Sterling Price,
into the Confederate camp, and open warfare followed. Union forces controlled the area around St. Louis; secessionists, commanded by Price, dominated most of the rest of the state. After General John C. Frémont
became commander of the department of the West, with his headquarters
in St. Louis, the territory under Union control was gradually extended;
however, Lyon, in a rash attempt to drive the secessionist forces from the
state, was defeated and killed at the battle of Wilson's Creek on August 10.

During the next three years, guerrilla warfare devastated the Missouri countryside, as neighbor fought neighbor. The bitterness was further aggravated when free-soil men from Kansas, remembering how Missouri border ruffians had once tried to extend slavery into their state, crossed the border to take revenge on secessionist sympathizers. In turn, Confederate gangs, the most notorious led by the horsethief and murderer, William C. Quantrill, preyed on Missouri Unionists.

Far more skillful was Lincoln's handling of Kentucky, which was his native state as well as that of Jefferson Davis. As in Missouri, the governor was an outright secessionist, but strong Unionist sentiment prevented the calling of a state convention. Out of this stalemate rose the anomalous situation of Kentucky's declaring herself neutral in any conflict between the United States and the Confederacy. Between May and September of 1861, both the Lincoln and the Davis government ostensibly acquiesced in this policy of neutrality; at the same time, each tried quietly to strengthen the hands of its partisans in Kentucky. Finally, suspecting that the Federal forces were about to seize a position in Kentucky, the Confederates moved first and took Columbus. Union troops then entered Paducah, and neutrality was dead. These months of indeterminate status gave Kentucky Unionists a chance to plan and organize, so that the state did not, like Tennessee, join the Confederacy nor, like Missouri, become a fierce battleground. In bringing about this outcome, Lincoln himself played a large role, for he gave Kentucky affairs close attention and took pains to assure prominent Kentuckians in private interviews that "he intended to make no attack, direct or indirect, upon the institution or property [meaning slavery] of any State."

Against the major Confederate victory in Virginia, the Union could count a lesser success in the western counties of that state, long disaffected from the planter oligarchy of the Tidewater region and little interested in slavery. When the Virginia convention voted for secession, a sizable minority of the delegates, mostly from these western counties, were opposed, and they went home vowing to keep their state in the Union. A series of exceedingly complex maneuvers followed, including the summoning of several more or less extralegal conventions and the creation of a new government for what was termed "reorganized" Virginia, which rivaled that at Richmond. This "reorganized" government then gave permission—as required by the United States Constitution—for the counties west of the mountains to form a new, and overwhelmingly Unionist, state of West Virginia. Not until 1863 were all these steps completed and the new state admitted to the Union. Thus, by that date, there were no fewer than three state governments on Virginia soil: the pro-Confederate government at

Richmond; the "reorganized" pro-Union government, which had only a small constituency and huddled under the protection of Federal guns at Alexandria; and the new Union government of West Virginia.

In summary, then, after the firing on Fort Sumter, the border slave states divided. Virginia, Arkansas, Tennessee, and North Carolina went with the Confederacy; Delaware, Maryland, Missouri, and Kentucky remained in the Union, where they were presently joined by West Virginia.

It is impossible to exaggerate the importance that these decisions, made early in the conflict, had on the conduct of the Civil War. For the Confederacy, the accession of states from the Upper South was essential. For all the brave talk at Montgomery, the Confederacy was not a viable nation so long as it consisted only of the seven states of the Deep South. So limited, the Confederate States could not dream of carrying on a war for independence. Its population was only one-sixth of that of the remaining states of the Union. In all the Gulf states of 1861 there was not a foundry to roll heavy iron plate or to cast cannon, not a large powder works, not, indeed, a single factory of major importance. But when Virginia, North Carolina, Arkansas, and Tennessee joined the Confederacy, they almost doubled its population. What is more, they brought to the new nation the natural resources, the foundries and factories, and the skilled artisans that made it possible to rival the Union. To recognize the economic and psychological strength added by these states of the Upper South—and also to escape the sweltering summer heats of Montgomery—the Confederacy in May 1861 removed its capital from Montgomery to Richmond.

But if the states of the Upper South brought the Confederacy strength, they also served to limit its freedom of action. So important were Richmond and Virginia that defense of this area became the absorbing passion of the Confederate government, which dictated its strategy in the campaigns east of the mountains and encouraged it to neglect the vital Western theaters of military operations.

For Lincoln's government, too, the border states were vital. If Maryland had seceded, Washington would have been surrounded by enemy territory, cut off from the Union states of the North and the West. The Baltimore & Ohio Railroad, the major rail connection between the East and the West, ran through Maryland and West Virginia. Confederate control of Kentucky would have imperiled river transportation along the Ohio, and the secession of Missouri would have endangered Mississippi River traffic and cut off communication with Kansas and the Pacific coast. While Lincoln grieved over the secession of the states that joined the Confederacy, he could take comfort in the fact that, by keeping four slave states in the Union, he was preventing the Southern armies from recruiting from a population that was three-fifths as large as that of the original Confederacy.

So important were the border states for the Union government that special pains had to be taken not to disturb their loyalty. In particular, Lincoln saw that there must be no premature action against slavery. European nations might fail to understand the nature of the American Civil War, and Northern abolitionists might denounce their President as "the slave-hound from Illinois," but Lincoln knew that to tamper with slavery would result in the loss of the border states, particularly Kentucky. "I think to lose Kentucky is nearly the same as to lose the whole game," he wrote to a friend. "Kentucky gone, we cannot hold Missouri, nor, as I think, Maryland. These all against us, and the job on our hands is too large for us. We would as well consent to separation at once, including the surrender of this capitol."

⋈ III ⋉

While Lincoln and Davis were moving in parallel fashion to win the support of the border states, ordinary folk, North and South, were rallying around their flags. Here, too, the pattern of response was remarkably similar in the Union and the Confederacy. On both sides, the firing on Fort Sumter triggered a rush to enlist. "War! and volunteers are the only topics of conversation or thought," an Oberlin College student reported when the news reached Ohio. "The lessons today have been a mere form. I cannot study. I cannot sleep, I cannot work, and I don't know as I can write." An Arkansas youth recorded identical emotions: "So impatient did I become for starting that I felt like a thousand pins were pricking me in every part of the body and [I] started off a week in advance of my brothers." For both North and South, Howell Cobb's observation held true: "The anxiety among our citizens is not as to who shall go to the wars, but *who shall stay at home*."

Ordinarily a volunteer offered to enlist in one of the regiments that was being raised in his community. Wealthy citizens and prominent politicians usually took the lead in recruiting these companies. The great South Carolina planter, Wade Hampton, for example, raised, organized, and equipped at his own expense the Hampton Legion of one thousand men. Inevitably these regiments displayed a wide variety of arms and accoutrements, ranging from rusty flintlocks to the latest sharpshooting rifles. Often their uniforms bore distinctive insignia; for instance, a Louisiana battalion recruited from the daredevil roustabouts of the New Orleans levees called themselves the Tigers, and their scarlet skullcaps bore mottoes like "Tiger on the Leap" and "Tiger in Search of a Black Republican." Perhaps the most colorful and impractical uniforms were those of the Zouave regiments, who dressed in imitation of the French troops in North Africa. These soldiers, wearing their red fezzes, scarlet, loose trousers, and blue sashes were magnificent in a military review, but when they had to wade across a stream, their baggy garments ballooned around them and they floated down the current like so many exotic waterlilies. When a regiment's ranks were filled, there was invariably a farewell ceremony, featuring hortatory addresses, lengthy prayers, and the presentation of the regimental flag, often hand-sewn by patriotic wives and sweethearts of the enlisted men. Then, loaded with hams, cakes, and sweetmeats provided by fond mothers and wives, the men went off to war.

Neither Union nor Confederate war departments knew what to do with this flood of volunteers. Leroy P. Walker, the first Confederate secretary of war, held office because Yancey, the leading Alabama secessionist, recommended him; he had no military training and no administrative experience. An amiable Southern gentleman of the old school, who was fond of prolonged conversation with visitors, of writing discursive three-page business letters, and of filing his correspondence by piling it in a chair after he had read it, Walker was wholly unable to cope with the situation. Complaining that he lacked equipment and arms, he refused the services of regiment after regiment. Perhaps 200,000 Confederate volunteers were thus rejected during the first year of the war.

The Northern war office was equally chaotic. Simon Cameron, the secretary of war, had been forced upon Lincoln as part of a political bargain. Known as "The Great Winnebago Chief" because of frauds he allegedly committed while an Indian agent, Cameron's main objective was to become

CONFEDERATE MONEY

Engravers and skilled printers were scarce in the South. Consequently the portraits of high officials that adorned Confederate currency often looked like caricatures.

the undisputed boss of Pennsylvania politics. There is no evidence that he used his cabinet position to line his own pockets, but he did employ his huge patronage to strengthen his faction of Pennsylvania Republicans. Lacking administrative talent, Cameron, like Walker, simply could not deal with the flood of volunteers, nor could he supervise the hundreds of contracts his office had to make for arms, ammunition, uniforms, horses, and dozens of other articles for the army. Inevitably there was haste, inefficiency, and corruption. For instance, in October 1861, General Frémont, desperately needing mounts for his cavalry in Missouri, contracted to purchase 411 horses. Subsequent investigation proved that 350 of the beasts supplied him were undersized, under- or overaged, ringboned, blind, spavined, and incurably unfit for service; five were dead. Unable to equip the Union volunteers as they rushed to defend the flag, Cameron thought it was his principal duty "to avoid receiving troops faster than [the government] can provide for them."

As the war wore on, the initial enthusiasm for volunteering inevitably abated, and many of the men rejected by Walker and Cameron in the early months of the conflict were never available again. Soon even those whose services had been accepted began to exhibit less enthusiasm for the war. Most had expected the army to be like the peace-time militia, to which all able-bodied white men belonged; the monthly militia rallies had been the occasion for fun and frolic, punctuated by a little uneven military drill, a considerable amount of political oratory, and a great deal of drinking. Now they discovered that war was not a lark. Belonging to the army meant discipline, spit-and-polish cleaning of equipment, and hours of close-order drill. A soldier's life was one of endless monotony, punctuated occasionally by danger from enemy bullets and more frequently by sickness resulting from inadequate food and clothing, lack of vaccination, filthy drinking water, and open latrines. By the end of 1861 many Union volunteers were beginning to count the weeks until their term of enlistment expired and they could go home. Confederate regiments, which had been enrolled for twelve months, were about ready to disband in the spring of 1862.

Of necessity, then, Lincoln and Davis moved, almost simultaneously, to strengthen their war departments in order to give more central direction to their armies. In January 1862, having persuaded Cameron to become American minister to Russia, Lincoln named a former Democrat, Edwin M. Stanton, to the war department. Brusque and imperious, Stanton was also hard-working, efficient, and incorruptible. Quickly he reorganized the war department, regularized procedures for letting war contracts, and investigated frauds. No longer were there private deals and special arrangements in the Union war office. Standing behind an old-fashioned writing desk, looking like an irritable schoolmaster before a willful class, Stanton heard all war department business in public. Patronage-seekers, even when accompanied by congressmen, he curtly dismissed; contractors had to state their prices in clear, loud voices; and even a petitioner bearing a letter of introduction from the President might be abruptly shown the door. Working incessantly, Stanton saw to it that the Union army became the best supplied military force the world had ever seen.

It took a bit longer for Davis to find a war secretary to his liking. When Walker, to everyone's relief, resigned in September 1861, Davis replaced him briefly with Judah P. Benjamin, who subsequently became Confederate secretary of state, and then with George Wythe Randolph, who did much to see that Robert E. Lee and Thomas J. "Stonewall" Jackson had the necessary arms and supplies for their 1862 campaigns. But when Randolph and Davis disagreed over strategy, the secretary had to go, and in November 1862 James A. Seddon succeeded Randolph. Sallow and cadaverous, looking, as one of his clerks remarked, like "an exhumed corpse after a month's interment," Seddon was nevertheless diligent and efficient. Moreover, he had the good sense to give solid support to subordinates of great ability. Perhaps the most competent of these was General Josiah Gorgas, head of the Confederate Ordnance Bureau. Thanks to Gorgas's exertions, the Confederacy, which in May 1861 had only about twenty cartridges for each musket or rifle, had by 1862 built powder plants capable of producing 20 million cartridges—enough to supply an army of 400,000 men for twelve months.

While both Presidents were strengthening their war departments, they also moved in 1862 to take a more active role in recruiting troops. Because the twelve-month period of enlistment of Confederate troops expired in the spring, Davis warned that the Southern army would be decimated just as Federal forces were approaching Richmond. Uncomfortably ignoring the principle of state sovereignty proclaimed in the Confederate Constitution, the Southern Congress on April 16, 1862, passed a national conscription act, declaring every able-bodied white male between the ages of 18 and 35 subject to military service. This first conscription law in American history was, however, less Draconian than it seemed; it allowed for numerous exemptions—ranging from druggists to Confederate government officials— and a subsequent law excused from military service planters or overseers supervising twenty or more slaves. The purpose of the Confederate conscription act was less to raise new troops than to encourage veterans to reenlist. If the men stayed in the army, the law provided, they could remain in their present regiments and elect new officers; if they left, it threatened, they could be drafted and assigned to any unit that needed them.

Lincoln's government moved toward conscription a little more slowly. After the bloody campaigns in the summer of 1862, volunteering all but stopped, and the army needed 300,000 new men. Union governors suggested to the President that a draft would stimulate volunteering, and on July 17 the Federal Congress passed a loosely worded measure, authorizing the President to set quotas of troops to be raised by each state and empowering him to use federal force to draft them if state officials failed to meet their quotas. Intentionally a bogeyman, which the governors used to encourage enlistments, this first Union conscription law brought in only a handful of draftees.

⅀ IV ⪡

If it became hard for both the Union and the Confederate governments to raise troops, it was even harder to supply and pay them. Though the United States in 1860 was potentially one of the great industrial nations of the world, it was still primarily an agricultural country, with five out of six of its inhabitants living on farms. The factories that would be called on to supply vast armies were mostly small in scale. Some 239 companies manufactured firearms in 1860; their average invested capital was less than $11,000. Textile mills, especially for the manufacture of woolens, were larger, but ready-made clothing was still sewn in small shops. The country produced an abundance of foodstuffs, but there was no effective wholesale marketing system for meat and grain. Maps showed that by 1860 the country was crisscrossed by 30,000 miles of railroads, but most of these were short spans, each under its own corporate management, often not connected to other lines at common terminals, and even having different rail gauges. The sending of a boxcar from, say, Baltimore to St. Louis was an undertaking that required diplomacy, improvisation, frequent transshipment, long delays, and a great deal of luck. Commercial transactions were impeded by the fact that the United States in 1860 had no national bank; indeed, it did not even have a national currency, for the bills issued by the numerous state banks, depreciating at various rates, formed the principal circulating medium.

Yet Union and Confederate leaders had somehow to mobilize this invertebrate economy so that it could support an enormous war effort. Both governments made a basic initial decision to rely primarily upon privately owned, rather than upon government-operated, factories to supply their armies. Behind this choice lay both a theoretical preference for free enterprise and a necessity; if individual businessmen and corporations had little experience in the large-scale production of goods, the civil servants in Washington and Richmond had even less. Where it seemed useful, both governments supplemented the output of private industry with that of government-owned plants. While purchasing firearms from Colt, Remington, and dozens of other manufacturers, the Lincoln administration continued to rely upon its armories, especially the one at Springfield, Massachusetts, for some of its best weapons. Because the South was even more largely rural and agricultural than the North, it had to be more active in establishing government-owned plants, the most successful of which was the huge powder factory built by George W. Rains at Augusta, Georgia. But for most of the arms, clothing, and other equipment needed for the armies, both governments contracted with private individuals and corporations. Because of the need for haste and the lack of experience, there was much laxity and some fraud in these arrangements. The extravagantly expensive contracts the Union war department approved in the early months of the war helped cost Secretary Cameron his job, and the Confederate system of approving contracts on a cost-plus basis, which guaranteed high profits to manufacturers, often led to waste and inefficiency.

It was easier to contract for supplies than it was to pay for them. Both Union and Confederacy began the war with empty treasuries. When Secretary of the Treasury Chase took up his duties in Washington, he was horrified to discover that between April and June 1861 the expenses of the Union government would exceed its income by $17 million. Inexperienced in financial matters, Chase, whose reputation had been built on his work as an antislavery lawyer and politician, desperately cast about for solutions. He managed to keep up a good façade, for visitors to his office thought this tall, broad-shouldered, and proudly erect statesman, with his regular features and "his forehead broad, high and clear," was the incarnation of "intelligence, strength, courage and dignity"; yet, inside, Chase was a jelly of confusion and uncertainty. So wavering was the advice he offered in cabinet that some of his colleagues thought he was pursuing some devious goal of his own, and Secretary of the Navy Gideon Welles concluded that he was "cowardly and aspiring, shirking and presumptuous, forward and evasive." But Chase's real problem was that he was an incompetent financier, who was placed in charge of unmanageable financial problems.

Even so, Chase's difficulties were nothing compared to those of his Confederate counterpart, Christopher G. Memminger, who had to make bricks without clay as well as without straw. Like Chase, Memminger had no experience in financial matters, and his neat, systematic mind was troubled by the free and easy ways of government finance during wartime. He did what he could to bring about order by requiring Confederate treasury employees to keep regular 9-to-5 hours, by outlawing traditional Southern sociability in the treasury offices—including drinking on the job—and by insisting that his visitors curb their customary garrulity and state their business. Such measures, however, did little to solve Confederate financial difficulties and only increased Southerners' suspicion of a man who had been born in Germany and raised in a South Carolina orphanage and was not, therefore, a proper gentleman.

However dissimilar personally, Chase and Memminger faced identical financial problems and finally opted for the same solutions. Neither secretary seriously thought of financing the war through levying taxes. For either the Union or the Confederacy to impose heavy taxation in 1861 might well have killed the citizens' ardor for war. Americans simply were not used to paying taxes to their national government; there had been no federal excise duties during the thirty-five years prior to the war. In 1860 the United States treasury had no internal revenue division, no assessors, no inspectors, and no agents. Since tariffs were a more familiar method of raising revenue, both secretaries hoped for large customs receipts. But when Republicans in the Union Congress passed the highly protective Morrill Tariff in 1861 and raised rates even higher in 1862, they effectively killed that source of revenue. Similarly, the Union blockade of the South reduced the amount and value of goods brought into Confederate ports and cut the Southern income from tariffs. In desperation the Union government resorted to a direct tax (levied on each state in proportion to population) of $20 million in August 1861; much of it was never collected. The same month the Confederates imposed a "War Tax" of 0.5 percent on taxable wealth. Davis's government, like Lincoln's, had to rely on the states to collect this tax, and most of them preferred issuing bonds or notes rather than levying duties upon their people.

In neither country was borrowing a realistic possibility for financing the war. Products of the Jacksonian era, with its suspicion of paper certificates of indebtedness, Americans of the 1860s were a people who preferred to hoard rather than to invest their surplus funds. The rival Union and Confederate governments were themselves affected by this same suspicion of paper and trust in specie. In the North, Secretary Chase insisted that the banks of New York, Philadelphia, and Boston subscribe to a $150 million federal bond issue, but he was unwilling to take anything but gold or silver in payment. The drain on the banks' reserves, coupled with uncertainty over the course of the war and the fear of embroilment with Great Britain over the *Trent* affair, forced Northern banks to suspend specie payment for their notes in December 1861. Nor was Chase more successful in his early attempts to sell Union bonds directly to small investors. The Confederacy followed much the same course in its borrowing. An initial loan of $15 million was quickly subscribed to, with the result that Southern banks, including the strong institutions of New Orleans, were obliged to give up all their specie to the new government; consequently they could no longer redeem their notes in gold or silver. Memminger's attempt to sell subsequent Confederate bonds directly to the Southern people ran into the difficulty that nobody had any specie. Urged by Vice-President Alexander H. Stephens and other Confederate orators, planters in the fall of 1861 subscribed tobacco, rice, cotton, and other commodities to purchase bonds. Since the Union blockade cut off the market for these products, the Confederate government realized little from the loan.

In consequence, by early 1862 both governments moved, slowly and ineluctably, to the issuing of paper money, backed only by the promise that it would some day be redeemed in specie. Both treasury secretaries came reluctantly to this policy. Memminger, a prominent hard-money advocate before the war, was obliged to resort to the printing presses in 1861. The Confederacy issued $100 million in paper money in August 1861 and the next year it printed millions of dollars more. So crude were these Confederate notes that counterfeits could be readily detected, since they were obviously superior in quality and design. Having denounced "an irredeemable paper currency, than which no more certainly fatal expedient for impoverishing the masses and discrediting the government of any country, can well be devised," Chase found it even more embarrassing than Memminger to resort to treasury notes, but by January 1862 he had no alternative. Declaring that an issue of paper money was now "indispensably necessary," he persuaded Congress to authorize the printing of $150 million in non-interest-bearing United States treasury notes (which were promptly dubbed "greenbacks," because of their color). Rarely does history provide such a tidy illustration of how huge impersonal forces overrule the preference and will of individual statesmen.

⇜ V ⇝

In diplomacy as in economic policy, the Union and the Confederacy moved along parallel paths during the first two years of the war. Neither Lincoln nor Davis had much knowledge of diplomacy or took an active role in the conduct of foreign policy. Both, however, had difficulties with their secretaries of state. Seward, Lincoln's principal adviser, would ultimately rank as one of the greatest American secretaries of state, but in the early stages of the Civil War he gave evidence of wild eccentricity, coupled with personal ambition. At the height of the Sumter crisis, he submitted to Lincoln a private memorandum complaining that the government as yet had no policy for dealing with secession, announcing his readiness to take over the President's function and shape a suitable policy, and suggesting that the proper course for the administration was to "change the question before the public from one upon slavery . . . for a question upon union or disunion" by precipitating a confrontation with foreign powers. If allowed, Seward would "seek explanations from Great Britain and Russia"—for what offenses he did not specify; he "would demand explanations from Spain and France, categorically, at once," presumably over their threatened intervention in the affairs of Santo Domingo and Mexico; and, if Spain and France did not respond forthwith, he would urge a declaration of war against these powers. Lincoln, to his enduring credit, quietly filed away this memorandum, refrained from dismissing a secretary who planned to bring on a world war, and allowed Seward time to return to his senses.

Despite Lincoln's reticence, word of Seward's bellicosity leaked out in conversation at Washington dinner tables, and diplomats at the capital soon had a pretty good idea of what was in the secretary's mind. From the diplomatic dispatches, European governments during the first two years of the war learned to view all of Seward's policies with skepticism, even after the secretary had returned to sobriety and moderation. Perhaps, however, the awareness of Seward's hair-trigger temper did something to make those governments more cautious in their relations with the United States and less willing to recognize the Confederacy.

Davis, too, had trouble with his state department. Toombs, the first Confederate secretary of state was as ambitious and overbearing as he was able. It was a relief when he decided that the road to glory lay on the battlefield rather than in the cabinet and resigned to take a commission in the Southern army. His successor, R. M. T. Hunter, was equally ambitious and—perhaps with an eye on the 1868 Confederate presidential election—he too promptly resigned, to become senator from Virginia. In March 1862 Davis finally found his man in Judah P. Benjamin, who had already been Confederate attorney-general and secretary of war. Serving until the end of the war, Benjamin cleverly reflected the changing moods of his chief, but he was not an innovator in foreign policy. In the words of a critical Northerner who visited Richmond during the war, Benjamin had a "keen, shrewd, ready intellect, but not the stamina to originate, or even to execute, any great good, or great wickedness."

Union and Confederate diplomatic appointments abroad were rather a mixed lot. If Lincoln lacked tact in appointing Carl Schurz—considered a

"Red Republican" for his participation in the German revolution of 1848—as minister to conservative, monarchical Spain, Davis showed a total failure to understand British antislavery sentiment by sending Yancey, the most notorious Southern fire-eater, as first Confederate commissioner to London. On the positive side, the Union minister to Great Britain, Charles Francis Adams, exhibited the patience and restraint required in his difficult assignment; and the pride, the chilly demeanor, and the punctiliousness of this son and grandson of American Presidents made him a match even for the aristocratic British foreign minister, Lord John Russell. Of the Confederate emissaries abroad, probably John Slidell of Louisiana proved ablest; wily, adroit, and unscrupulous, he was perfectly at home in the court of Napoleon III.

Much to the disappointment of Americans on both sides, the attitudes of European powers toward the Civil War were not shaped primarily by the actions of American ministers, secretaries of state, or even Presidents. Nor, during 1861 and 1862, were they shaped by appeals to economic self-interest. Firmly believing that cotton was king, that, as an Atlanta newspaper asserted, the need for cotton would "bring more wooing princes to the feet of the Confederate States than Penelope had," Southerners expected that pressure from British and French textile manufacturers would compel their governments to recognize the Confederacy and to break the blockade. But, as it happened, European manufacturers had an ample stockpile of cotton, purchased before the outbreak of hostilities, and were therefore not much affected when Southern cotton was cut off in 1861. By 1862 cotton mills in both Britain and France were suffering, but Union and Confederate orders for arms, ammunition, and other equipment counterbalanced these losses. There was great hardship and suffering among the workers in the cotton mills, especially in the Lancashire district of England, where unemployment was high, but their complaints were relatively ineffectual, since Britain still did not allow these men to vote.

Northerners were equally disappointed in their belief that European powers would see the American conflict as a war against slavery and would consequently condemn the Confederacy. Since Lincoln had announced that he would not interfere with slavery where it existed, since Seward in his dispatches called abolitionists and "the most extreme advocates of African slavery" equally dangerous to the Union cause, and since Union generals in the field were still returning runaway slaves to their Southern masters, it was unreasonable and unrealistic to expect European antislavery forces to rally behind the Union. Yet when Britons failed to see that the South represented "the cause of chaos against that of harmony, of anarchy against order, of slavery against freedom," even such conservative Northerners as the New York diarist, George Templeton Strong, denounced their "monstrous and incredible blindness."

What Northerners and Confederates alike did not understand was that the policy of European states toward the Civil War would be determined largely by considerations of national self-interest. Since the Crimean War, an uneasy balance of power had prevailed in Europe, and no nation was eager to upset it by unilateral intervention in the American conflict. But concerted action by the European powers was always difficult because of mutual suspicion, and in the 1860s it was virtually impossible because of the nature of the British government. The British prime minister, Lord Palmerston, who was nearly eighty years old, headed a shaky coalition government, which was certain to fall if it undertook any decisive action. With the British government immobilized, the Russians largely favorable to the Union cause, and the Prussians and the Austrians mostly indifferent to the conflict, the inclination of the ambitious Napoleon III to meddle in favor of the Confederacy was effectively curbed.

As a result, European nations announced their neutrality early in the war. Queen Victoria's proclamation of May 13, 1861, was typical in recognizing that a state of war existed between the United States and "the states styling themselves the Confederate States of America" and in declaring British neutrality in that war. Recognition as a belligerent—not as a nation —meant that the Southerners had a right to send out privateers without their being considered pirate ships and that the Union blockade of the South would have to be effective if other nations were to respect it. Initially these proclamations seemed to be a great Confederate success. They were, however, both necessary and warranted by international law and, despite Seward's ranting, were truly impartial.

In November 1861, the rash action of a Union naval officer threatened to upset this neutrality. Learning that Davis was replacing the temporary commissioners he had sent to France and Britain with permanent envoys, John Slidell and James M. Mason, Union Captain Charles Wilkes decided to capture these diplomats en route. Off the shore of Cuba on November 8, 1861, his warship stopped the British merchant ship, the *Trent,* Union officers boarded and searched the vessel, and Mason and Slidell were unceremoniously removed, to be transported to Boston for imprisonment. When news of Wilkes's action, in clear violation of international law, reached Europe, hostility toward the Union government flared up. "You may stand for this," Palmerston told his cabinet, "but damned if I will!" Russell drafted a stiff letter demanding the immediate release of the envoys. Through the intervention of Albert, the Prince Consort, the tone of the letter was softened, and through the cautious diplomacy of Lord Lyons, the

British minister in Washington, the threat of war was minimized, but it was still clear that the Lincoln government faced a major crisis if it held its prisoners. After conferring with cabinet members and senators, Lincoln decided on Christmas day to release the Southern envoys. He would fight only one war at a time.

Even with the firm intention of remaining neutral, European powers found their patience tested as the American war stretched on without apparent chance of ending. International relations were disturbed, commerce was disrupted, textile manufacturing was suffering, and neither North nor South seemed able to achieve its goal. Increasingly, support built up in both France and Britain for offering mediation to the combatants, and such an offer inevitably involved recognition of the Confederacy as an independent nation. In September 1862, Palmerston and Russell agreed to explore a mediation plan involving France and Russia as well as Great Britain. Carried away by the prospect, a younger member of the cabinet, William E. Gladstone, made a highly publicized speech at Newcastle, announcing that "Jefferson Davis and other leaders of the South have made an army; they are making, it appears, a navy; and they have made what is more than either,—they have made a nation." Perhaps the very vehemence of Gladstone's advocacy of the Confederate cause helped to kill ideas of intervention, for pro-Union members of the British cabinet, like the Duke of Argyll and George Cornewall Lewis, replied with strong arguments against mediation. Faced with dissension within his unstable coalition and given no encouragement by Russia, Palmerston by October 1862 changed his mind and concluded that the European states "must continue . . . to be lookers-on till the war shall have taken a more decided turn."

⊱ VI ⊰

But on the battlefields in 1861 and 1862 there were no decided turns. Engagement followed engagement, campaign followed campaign, but neither side could achieve a decisive victory. The stalemate was baffling to many arm-chair strategists, in both the South and the North, who had been sure that the war would be short and decisive, ending in an overwhelming victory for their own side.

Confederate war planners counted among their assets the fact that some of the best graduates of West Point led their armies and that President Davis himself had military training and experience. They believed that Southern men had more of a fighting spirit than Northerners, and they were probably correct in thinking that Southerners had more experience in handling firearms and were better horsemen. They knew that the Confederacy would generally act on the defensive and assumed that the offenive Union army would have to be at least three times as large as that of the South. Since Southern forces could operate on interior lines, they could move more quickly and easily than Union forces, which would have to travel longer distances. Recognizing the superiority of the Union navy, Southerners knew that the Confederacy had 3500 miles of coastline, with innumerable hidden harbors and waterways through which shipping could escape. When Confederate strategists added to all these assets the fact that Southern soldiers were fighting on their home ground, where they knew every road and byway, they saw no reason to doubt ultimate victory.

But an equally good case could be made for the inevitability of a Union victory. The population of the Union in 1860 was about 20.7 million; that of the Confederacy, only 9.1 million. Moreover, 3.6 million of the inhabitants of the South were blacks, mostly slaves, who, it was presumed, would not be used in the Confederate armies. Along with this superiority in manpower, the North had vastly more economic strength than the Confederacy. The total value of all manufactured products in all eleven Confederate states was less than one-fourth of that of New York alone. The iron furnaces, forges, and rolling mills in the United States were heavily concentrated in the North. The North in 1860 built fourteen out of every fifteen railroad locomotives manufactured in the United States. Northern superiority in transportation would more than compensate for Southern interior lines, for only 30 percent of the total rail mileage of the United States ran through the Confederacy. The Union navy, which experienced few defections to the South, was incomparably superior, and the blockade President Lincoln announced at the outbreak of hostilities would cut off, or at least drastically reduce, Southern imports from Europe. When Northern planners added to the advantages of their side the possession of the established government, the recognition by foreign powers, and the enormous enthusiasm of the people for maintaining the Union, they could not doubt that victory would be sure and swift.

In fact, these assets substantially cancelled each other during the first two years of the war and produced not victory but deadlock. As the armies engaged in complex maneuvers and in indecisive battles, they demonstrated not only that they were fairly evenly balanced but also that, even on the battlefield, Americans from the North were very much like Americans from the South.

It is hardly surprising that Union and Confederate commanders largely employed the same strategic plans, for most had been taught the art of war by the same teachers at West Point. In fifty-five of the sixty biggest battles of the war, the generals on both sides had been educated at West Point, and in the remaining five, a West Pointer led one of the opposing armies. At the military academy they had studied the theories of the French historian and strategist, Baron Henri Jomini. Some read Jomini's works in the original French or in translation; more, doubtless, absorbed his ideas from the abridgement and interpretation of his work, *Elementary Treatise on Advance-Guard, Outpost, and Detachment of Service of Troops* (1847), written by Dennis Hart Mahan, who for a generation taught at the academy and greatly influenced his students.

Although Jomini's military theories were a complex body of doctrine, subject to many differing interpretations, as understood by American commanders they stressed the importance of the conquest of territory and emphasized that the seizure of the enemy's capital "is, ordinarily, the objective point" of an invading army. Jomini envisaged a battle situation in which two armies were drawn up in opposing lines, one offensive, and the other defensive, and he even prepared a set of twelve diagrams showing the possible orders of battle. In all twelve, the determinant of victory was the concentration of force—the bringing to bear of a powerful, united force on the enemy's weakest point. Warfare was thus something like an elaborate game of chess, an art that only professional soldiers could fully master. Abhorring the intervention of politicians in military affairs and deploring great popular uprisings like those of the French Revolution, Jomini admitted to a prejudice "in favor of the good old times when the French and English guards courteously invited each other to fire first,—as at Fontenoy."

Most of the military operations during the first two years of the Civil War can best be understood as a kind of elaborate illustration of Jomini's theories, slightly modified to fit the American terrain. The first big battle of the war occurred on July 21, 1861, when Union General Irwin McDowell, under much pressure from Northern newspapers and much badgered by exuberant politicians in the Congress, reluctantly pushed his poorly organized army into Virginia. He expected to encounter the Confederates, under General Beauregard, near Centreville. In the ensuing battle of Bull Run (or Manassas), both armies tried to apply the same battle plan from Jomini's treatise; each attempted a main attack upon the enemy's left flank, to be followed by a secondary thrust at his center and right wings. If completely executed, the two plans would have had the amusing result of leaving each army in its opponent's original place. But the Confederates also followed another of Jomini's principles, that of concentration of force and, using the railroad, rushed General Joseph E. Johnston's

INFANTRY TACTICS: THEORY AND PRACTICE

The tactics taught at West Point stressed the charge, with soldiers closely aligned as in this sketch (*above*), by Alfred R. Waud, of the advance of the New York Excelsior Brigade in the battle of Fair Oaks. But improved rifles gave such an advantage to the defending force that officers and soldiers dropped the close-order drill, and engagements usually resembled this tangle of guns, troops, and wagons (*below*) that Henri Lovi sketched behind the Union lines at Shiloh. (*Above, Library of Congress; below, Prints Division, The New York Public Library, Astor, Lenox and Tilden Foundations.*)

troops from the Shenandoah Valley to join Beauregard's main force. The Union troops fought bravely and initially seemed to be carrying the day, but after Johnston's men were in position, the Union army was thrown back and then routed. Weary and disorganized, Federal troops limped back to the Potomac and to safety. The Confederates were almost equally demoralized by their victory and were unable to pursue. The South's easiest opportunity to follow Jomini's maxim and seize the enemy's capital had to be given up.

After this initial engagement, it was clear that both armies needed reorganization and training before either could attempt further campaigns. As a result, despite growing impatience for action, there was little significant military action during the rest of 1861, except for minor engagements in Kentucky and Missouri. During this period, General George Brinton McClellan, who was credited with some overrated minor successes in western Virginia, was summoned to Washington to bring order to the Union army. With enormous dash and enthusiasm, the young commander began to whip the Federal regiments into fighting shape. He insisted on careful drill and inspection; he demanded the best of food and equipment for his men; and he refused to move forward until his army was thoroughly prepared.

By early 1862 Union armies, not merely those in the East but in all the theaters of war, were ready to advance, and, taking advantage of their numerical superiority, Union commanders concentrated their forces upon a series of weak spots in the Confederate defenses, just as Jomini had directed. In January, General George H. Thomas defeated a Confederate force at Mill Springs, Kentucky, and made a break in the Southern defense line west of the mountains. The next month General Ulysses S. Grant made an even more important breach in that line. In collaboration with the Union gunboats on the Tennessee and Cumberland Rivers, he captured Fort Henry and Fort Donelson, requiring the Confederate army in the latter fort to accept his terms of unconditional surrender.

The Southerners now had to abandon Tennessee. Union armies under Grant and Don Carlos Buell pushed rapidly after them, so rapidly indeed that for the moment they forgot Jomini's maxim about concentration and allowed the Confederates a chance for victory. On April 6, while Buell's troops were still some distance from Grant, the Confederates, who had concentrated their forces in the West under Generals Beauregard and Albert Sidney Johnston, fell on Grant's unsuspecting army at Shiloh Meeting House and, during the first day's fighting, came near to pushing it into the river. But the death of General Johnston, the demoralization of the victorious Confederates, and the timely arrival of Buell's forces meant that on the second day the Federal forces, now fully concentrated, were able to

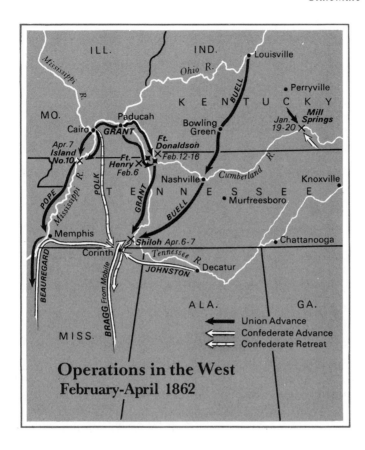

Operations in the West
February–April 1862

Union Advance
Confederate Advance
Confederate Retreat

sweep back the enemy and reclaim the field. Dissatisfied with Grant's generalship, General Henry Wager Halleck, who was the Union commander for the entire Western theater, took personal charge of the army after Shiloh. A disciple of Jomini, whose works he had translated, Halleck concentrated his force for a push on Corinth, Mississippi, in order to break the important rail connection that linked Memphis and the Western portion of the Confederacy with the East.

Meanwhile in March Union forces had decisively defeated the Confederates at Pea Ridge in northwestern Arkansas, and organized Southern armies had to be withdrawn from Missouri. Even farther west, Union forces captured Santa Fe and compelled Confederate General Henry H. Sibley to withdraw from New Mexico.

To the south, Flag Officer David Glasgow Farragut daringly pushed his fleet up the Mississippi, past Forts St. Philip and Jackson, and captured New Orleans, the largest city in the Confederacy. On April 29 General

Butler took command of the Federal forces in the city and prepared to give New Orleans secessionists the same treatment he had extended to those of Baltimore.

A simultaneous Union advance in the Eastern theater promised to be equally successful. After long delays, McClellan began his offensive against Richmond, not by going directly overland, but by transporting his troops to Fort Monroe, on the Peninsula between the York and James Rivers. Bitterly complaining because Lincoln violated the principle of concentration and held back 40,000 troops to defend Washington, McClellan nevertheless prepared to follow Jomini's maxims and seize the Confederate capital.

But at this point in the gigantic, synchronized Union offensive, designed to crush the Confederacy, everything began to go wrong. The difficulties stemmed partly from human inadequacies. Though good theoreticians and able administrators, Halleck and McClellan were indecisive fighters. Halleck took nearly two months to creep, snail-like, from Shiloh to Corinth, stopping to fortify his position each night so that there could be no repetition of Confederate surprise. By the time he reached his destination, the Southern army had moved south with all its provisions. Equally cautious was McClellan's advance on the Peninsula, where he allowed 16,000 Confederate soldiers under General John B. Magruder to hold up his magnificent army of 112,000 until the Confederates could bring reinforcements to Richmond. The trouble was partly that these Union campaigns attempted to coordinate movements of forces larger than anything seen before on the American continent, though few of the commanding officers had ever led anything larger than a regiment. But chiefly the Union failure was due to the fact that able Confederate generals had read the same books on strategy as the Union commanders and knew how to fight the same kinds of battles.

While McClellan slowly edged his way up the Peninsula, Confederate commander Joseph E. Johnston, who had rushed in with reinforcements, kept close watch until the Union general injudiciously allowed his forces to be divided by the flooded Chickahominy River. Applying Jomini's principle of concentration on the enemy's weakest spot, Johnston on May 31–June 1 fell upon the exposed Union wing in battles at Fair Oaks (or Seven Pines), which narrowly failed of being a Confederate triumph. When Johnston was wounded in this engagement, Davis chose Robert E. Lee to replace him.

Lee quickly revealed his military genius by showing that he knew when to follow Jomini's principles and when to flout them. Remembering from his days at West Point how slow McClellan was, Lee detached troops from

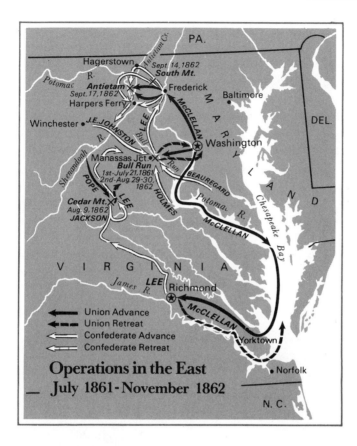

Operations in the East
July 1861 - November 1862

→ Union Advance
⇠- - Union Retreat
⇨ Confederate Advance
⇨ Confederate Retreat

the main army and sent them to reinforce "Stonewall" Jackson, who was operating in western Virginia. With these additional men, Jackson was able to make a daring raid down the Shenandoah Valley, defeating and demoralizing the Union forces. He so threatened Washington that Lincoln withheld reinforcements that he had promised for McClellan. When Jackson had accomplished this objective, Lee reverted to the principle of concentration and ordered Jackson promptly to rejoin the main army before Richmond. The combined Confederate force fell upon McClellan's exposed right flank at Mechanicsville. Since Jackson was not fighting at his best and his soldiers were exhausted, Lee failed to crush McClellan; but in a series of engagements known as the Seven Days (June 25–July 1) he forced the Union army to beat a slow, hard-fought retreat to the banks of the James River, where it lay under the protection of Federal gunboats. Lee had saved Richmond.

As the Union advances ground to a halt by mid-summer of 1862, the Confederates planned a grand offensive of their own. In the West, two

Southern armies, under General Braxton Bragg and Edmund Kirby-Smith, in August swept through eastern Tennessee; by September they were operating in Kentucky, where they were in a position to cut the supply line for Buell's army in Tennessee. The early phases of their offenses were brilliantly successful, but the campaign as a whole was fruitless because of a lack of coordination between the two Southern armies and because of Bragg's indecisiveness. After a bloody battle at Perryville (October 8), the Confederate forces withdrew toward Chattanooga, followed, at a very respectful distance, by the Union army.

The more daring part of the Confederate offensive was in the East. While McClellan's army was slowly being withdrawn from the Peninsula, Lee turned quickly on Union forces in central Virginia under the braggart General John Pope and, concentrating his entire strength upon this segment of the Federal army, scored a brilliant Confederate victory in the second battle of Bull Run (August 29–30). Free then to push into the

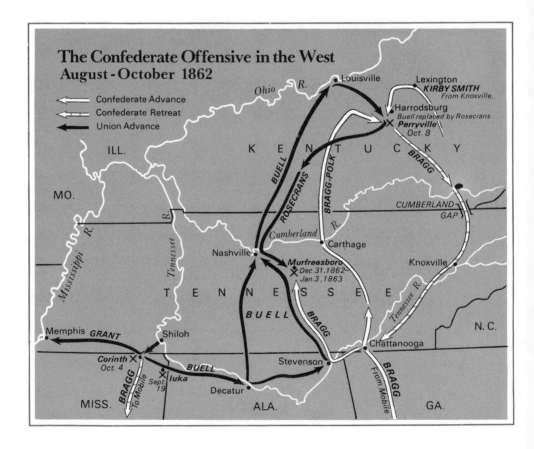

CAVALRY OFFICER

The cavalry considered itself the elite of the army, and both Union and Confederate horsemen clung to the tradition of devil-may-care individualism long after infantrymen accepted the need for regimentation. Winslow Homer's drawing of this dashing Union cavalry officer suggests his spirit of independence. (*Courtesy of Cooper-Hewitt Museum, The Smithsonian Institution's National Museum of Design.*)

North, Lee crossed the Potomac into Maryland, where he hoped to supply his ragged army and to rally the inhabitants of that state to the Confederate cause.

Lee's invasion of Maryland led to the battle of Antietam (September 17), an indecisive engagement whose very inconclusiveness spoke

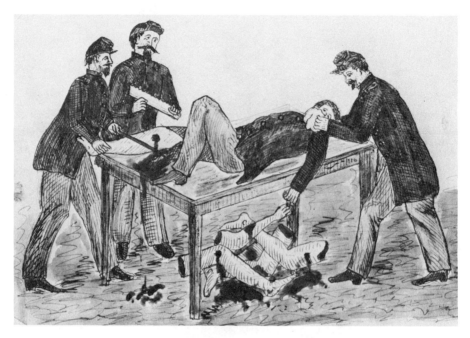

UNION DOCTORS AT WORK

After major battles, haste and crudeness characterized the medical attention received by the wounded. Private Alfred Bellard sketched this outdoor operating table with three Union doctors, one of whom holds a patient down while another administers ether and a third prepares to use a saw. (*Courtesy of Alec Thomas Archives.*)

volumes about the impossibility of ever ending the war so long as it was fought by the conventional rules. Union General McClellan, again in command, moved slowly to catch up with Lee's army, because he wished to concentrate all his forces for an attack. Lee in turn waited in a defensive position behind Antietam Creek at Sharpsburg, Maryland, because he too needed to concentrate his troops, a portion of whom had been sent on a successful expedition to capture Harpers Ferry. When McClellan was finally ready to take the offensive, he precisely followed one of Jomini's battle plans, and Lee defended his position by the same rules. The result was the bloodiest day of the Civil War. In areas of the battlefield, like the cornfield, the Dunker church, the Bloody Lane, and Burnside's bridge, men fell as in windrows. By the end of the day there were more than 25,000 casualties, with at least 5000 dead. The next day an eye-witness noted "the most appalling sights upon the battle-field . . . the ground strewn with the bodies of the dead and the dying . . . the cries and the groans of the wounded . . . the piles of dead men, in attitudes which show the writhing agony in which they died—faces distorted . . . begrimed and covered with clotted blood, arms and legs torn from the body or the body itself torn asunder."

Quietly Lee slipped back into Virginia, and McClellan did not pursue him. The Confederate offensive was over, and with it ended an era. If Jomini's strategy could only lead to stalemate, it was time for both Union and Confederacy to experiment with modern, organized warfare.

CHARLES SUMNER

Charles Sumner embodied the spirit of radical experimentation with which the war was conducted during its final years. The senator from Massachusetts was, a friend said, "the statesman *doctrinaire*," willing to do anything and everything necessary to promote human rights. (*Harvard University Archives.*)

5

Experimentation

"I have been anxious and careful," President Lincoln announced in his December 1861 message to Congress, that the present war "shall not degenerate into a violent and remorseless revolutionary struggle." Both he and President Davis assumed at the outset that the conflict would be a brief and limited one, waged in a conventional fashion by armies in the field and having little impact on the economic, social, and intellectual life of their sections. The events of 1861–1862 proved these expectations utterly wrong. It slowly became clear that to carry on the war Americans, in both North and South, had to break with tradition and to engage in broad experimentation. They had to try new forms of government action, new modes of social thought and economic cooperation, and new patterns of thought.

Because the Union was ultimately victorious, it would be easy to conclude that Northerners were more willing to experiment, better able to mobilize all their resources, for what has been called the first modern war. But such a judgment makes the historian the camp follower of the victorious army. The record shows, instead, that both the Confederacy and the Union attempted innovations that for the time were daringly original. It also shows that both combatants during the final years of the war resorted to much the same kinds of experimentation. Thus even while devising novel means for destroying each other, Northerners and Southerners showed themselves to be fundamentally similar, fundamentally part of the same great people.

≥ I ≤

The bloody and indecisive campaigns of 1861 and 1862 made innovators out of both Union and Confederate soldiers. Experience under fire convinced them not to follow Jomini's tactics. The French writer had conceived of a tactical situation where infantrymen, drawn up in close, parallel lines, blazed away at each other with muskets capable of being loaded perhaps twice a minute and having an effective range of 100 yards. But Civil War soldiers were equipped with rifles, which not only were more quickly loaded but had an effective range of about 800 yards. In Jomini's day the offensive force had the great advantage; rushing forward, with bayonets fixed, charging troops could break the defenders' line before they had time to reload. In the Civil War, on the other hand, the advancing force was exposed to accurate fire during the last half-mile of its approach. In consequence, nine out of ten infantry assaults failed, and the Civil War soldier had little use for his bayonet—except, perhaps, as a spit on which to cook meat.

Soldiers on both sides rapidly learned how to make defensive positions even stronger. At the beginning of the war, most military men were scornful of breastworks and entrenchments, arguing that they simply pinned down a defending force and made it more vulnerable to a charge. When Lee, upon assuming command of the Army of Northern Virginia in 1862, ordered his men to construct earthworks facing McClellan's advancing troops, Confederate soldiers bitterly complained and called their new general the "King of Spades." But when they saw how entrenchments saved lives, they changed their tune, and Lee became to the Confederate common soldier "Marse Robert," the general who looked after his men's welfare. What Confederate generals started, Union commanders imitated. Even William Tecumseh Sherman, who feared that fortifications would make his men cowardly, changed his mind after the Confederates swept through his unprotected camp at Shiloh. By the end of 1862 both armies dug in wherever they halted. Using spades and canteens, forks and sticks, soldiers pushed up improvised earthworks and strengthened them with fence rails and fallen logs.

Experience also quietly killed off Jomini's view that warfare was restricted to professionals. In the early days of the conflict, commanders believed warfare should not injure civilians. When McClellan's army pushed up the Peninsula, the general posted guards to keep his soldiers from raiding Confederate farmers' cornfields. Similarly Halleck permitted slaveowners to search his camp in order to reclaim their runaway slaves. By the end of 1862 such practices vanished. Soldiers joyfully foraged

ROBERT E. LEE

The commander of the Army of Northern Virginia was as willing to experiment and to break the rules in military affairs as Charles Sumner was in political and constitutional matters. This photograph, taken in 1862, is probably the first to show Lee with a beard. (*Andre Studio, Lexington, Virginia.*)

through civilians' watermelon patches, cornfields, and chicken roosts, while their officers ostentatiously turned their backs. If the civilians complained, the officers could truthfully reply that they had *seen* no foraging. Northern generals exhibited a growing reluctance to permit the recapture of fugitive slaves who had fled to the Union lines. As early as May 1861, General Butler at Fortress Monroe, Virginia, refused to return three such fugitives on the ground that they were contraband of war. *Contrabands* became a code name for escaped slaves, and in 1862 the Federal Congress showed what it thought of Jomini's notion of limited warfare by prohibiting any Federal military officer from returning runaways.

The deadlock of 1861–1862 also brought about a transformation of the command systems of both Union and Confederate armies. Because the Union lost so many battles during the first two years of the conflict, Lincoln was forced to experiment first. His initial venture came in mid-1862. Since he distrusted McClellan's capacity to keep an eye on the general progress of the war while also leading a campaign to capture Richmond, he brought in Halleck from the West to serve as his military adviser and gave him the grand title of general-in-chief. The position was an untenable one, for it placed Halleck in conflict with the other generals, especially McClellan, often put him at odds with Secretary of War Stanton, and exposed him to what he called the "political Hell" of pressure from congressmen. In addition, Halleck's slowness, his indecisiveness, and his rigid adherence to Jomini's principles made him hostile to all innovation, and Lincoln soon concluded that he was of little more use than a clerk.

Seeing no alternative, Lincoln, after McClellan's withdrawal from the Peninsula and Pope's defeat at Second Bull Run, again tried to direct military operations himself, and his efforts proved the desperate need for a unified system of command. For the rest of 1862 and most of 1863, Northern generals managed their own armies and planned their own campaigns, with Lincoln, Stanton, and Halleck providing only loose supervision and frequent injunctions to win speedy victories.

In the Eastern theater Lincoln replaced McClellan, after his failure to follow up his partial success at Antietam, with that bumbling incompetent, Ambrose E. Burnside, whose one redeeming feature was that he knew he was bumbling and incompetent. Burnside led the Army of the Potomac into the battle of Fredericksburg on December 13, 1862, one of the most disastrous, and surely the least necessary, Federal defeats of the war. Replacing Burnside with "Fighting Joe" Hooker, a boastful egotist fond of the bottle, brought no better luck to the Union cause. After directing an initially successful advance on Chancellorsville (May 1–4, 1863), Hooker lost his nerve, or ran out of liquor, and pulled back to a defensive position in the hope, as his fatuous order read, "that a suspension in the attack . . . will embolden the enemy to attack us." That is precisely what Lee did. Permitting "Stonewall" Jackson to slip through obscure byways to reach the unfortified right flank of Hooker's army, Lee caught the Union force in a vise. After Jackson's surprise attack crumpled Hooker's right wing, with "hundreds of cavalry horses, left riderless . . . dashing about frantically in all directions . . . battery wagons, ambulances, horses, men, cannon, caissons, all jumbled . . . together in an apparently inextricable

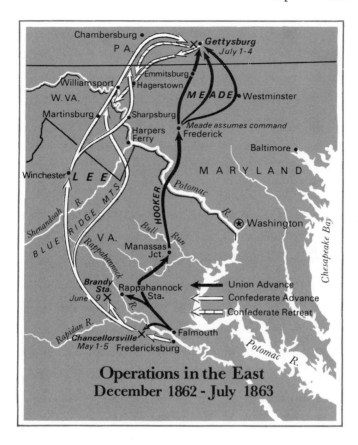

Chambersburg •

P A.

Gettysburg
July 1-4

Emmitsburg•
Williamsport
Hagerstown

W. VA.

M E A D E • Westminster

Martinsburg •   Sharpsburg •

Harpers
Ferry

Meade assumes command
Frederick

Baltimore •

Winchester • *L E E*

M A R Y L A N D

Potomac

R.

HOOKER

Washington

Shenandoah R.

BLUE RIDGE MTS.

V A.

Rappahannock

Manassas
Jct.

Bull

Run

Chesapeake Bay

*Brandy
Sta.*
June 9 X

Rappahannock
Sta.

Union Advance

Confederate Advance

Confederate Retreat

Rapidan R.

Chancellorsville X
May 1-5   Fredericksburg

Falmouth

*Potomac
R.*

Operations in the East
December 1862 - July 1863

mass," Hooker ordered retreat. Chancellorsville was still another Confederate victory—but one gained at a great price, for Jackson, accidentally fired upon by his own men, was mortally wounded.

Still trying to direct military operations himself, Lincoln watched anxiously as Lee in mid-summer of 1863 began his second invasion of the North, this time pushing into Pennsylvania. When Hooker appeared unable or unwilling to pursue the Confederates, Lincoln replaced him with the shy, scholarly George Gordon Meade, who assumed command of the army only three days before the climactic battle of Gettysburg (July 1–3, 1863). Rushing all available forces to that Pennsylvania town, Meade succeeded on the first day in establishing a battle line along Cemetery Ridge, just south of Gettysburg, where he awaited attack from the Confederate army, drawn up on the roughly parallel Seminary Ridge, a mile or so to the west. On the second day of the battle, both sides suffered heavy losses when the Confederates attacked a salient in the Union line, extending through a peach orchard and through rocky terrain that soldiers christened the Devil's Den, and then unsuccessfully tried to capture Little Round Top, a hill on the Union left flank, which would have allowed their artillery to sweep Cemetery Ridge. The decisive day of the battle was July 3, when a Confederate charge, led by General George E. Pickett, reached the very crest of Cemetery Ridge before it was finally turned back. At last the Army of the Potomac had won a victory—but Meade failed to pursue, and Lee's army recrossed the Potomac to safety. "We had them within our grasp," Lincoln lamented. "We had only to stretch forth our hands and they were ours. And nothing I could say or do could make the Army move."

When Lincoln tried personally to plan strategy for the trans-Appalachian theater of war, he was no more successful. After the battle of Perryville, it was clear that Buell must be replaced, and Lincoln chose W. S. Rosecrans, suspected of having military ability and known to have political connections. If Buell had been slow and cautious, Rosecrans proved to be slow and careless. Lincoln urged him to push on to Chattanooga, the rail hub of the Confederacy, but en route Rosecrans encountered Bragg's army in the bloody and indecisive battle of Murfreesboro (December 30, 1862–January 2, 1863). Though Rosecrans claimed victory, his army was so badly mauled that he could not advance for another six months. Finally, in June 1863 he maneuvered the Confederates out of Chattanooga, but in pursuing Bragg's army he received a smashing defeat at Chickamauga (September 19–20). Only the rocklike determination of General George H. Thomas prevented the reverse from becoming a rout, and Rosecrans's army limped back into Chattanooga. Disoriented by defeat, Rosecrans, as Lincoln said, behaved "like a duck hit on the head," and allowed Bragg to invest the city.

Farther west, Lincoln's personal direction of the Union armies proved equally inept. Here the main objective was Vicksburg, the last major city on the Mississippi River still in Confederate hands; when it fell, the eastern part of the Confederacy would be severed from the trans-Mississippi region. At first Lincoln thought Grant, who commanded Union forces in this area after Halleck's departure, ought to push overland from his base in northern Mississippi, but when Confederate General Earl Van Dorn's brilliant raid destroyed the Union base of supplies at Holly Springs, that approach had to be abandoned. Next Grant tried a frontal assault upon Vicksburg. Bringing his troops down the river from Memphis, Sherman, Grant's ablest lieutenant, attempted to scale the virtually impregnable bluffs on which the city was situated, and the Confederates, commanded by General John C. Pemberton, drove him back. Growing dissatisfied with Grant's management of the campaign, Lincoln authorized former Democratic Congressman

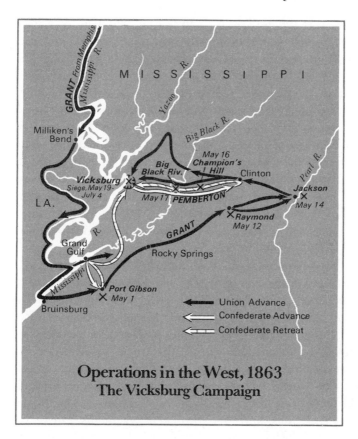

Operations in the West, 1863
The Vicksburg Campaign

John A. McClernand to raise a new army in the Northwestern states for use against Vicksburg.

Grant now reached the turning point in his career. Unwilling to be ousted from command and knowing that he outranked McClernand, he moved his headquarters and his troops down the Mississippi to Young's Point, on the west bank just above Vicksburg. When the Illinois congressman arrived, along with the troops he had raised, Grant quietly took over, informing McClernand that he would be one of his corps commanders. But retaining command of the army did not solve Grant's problem. If he made another frontal attack upon Vicksburg, he would again be defeated. If he withdrew his troops up the river to Memphis for a fresh start overland, Lincoln was sure to remove him from command. Reviewing the situation, Grant saw only one solution. "There was," he concluded, "nothing left to be done but to *go forward to a decisive victory."*

To win that victory, Grant devised, without aid from Washington, a bold plan. Using the navy's gunboats and transports to run his ammunition and supplies past the Vicksburg batteries, he marched his army to a point on the west bank below the city, staged a rapid amphibious crossing, and before the Confederates could recover from their surprise, pushed inland. To the dismay of Washington, he thus abandoned his base of supplies, announcing that he planned to live on the countryside. First he struck at Jackson, the capital of Mississippi, so as to drive back the small Confederate force General Joseph E. Johnston had collected there, and then he turned on Pemberton's army and forced it into Vicksburg. After two ill-advised assaults, the Union army settled down to besiege the city, while from the river the Union gunboats kept up a constant bombardment. As civilians in the city took to caves for safety, and as starvation made mule meat a delicacy, Pemberton fought back as well as he could, but on July 4, 1863—the day after Gettysburg—he had to surrender his army and the city.

When the news reached Washington, Lincoln, who had distrusted Grant's strategy, wrote the general a handsome apology: "I now wish to make the personal acknowledgment that you were right, and I was wrong." The President was happy to be proved wrong, for Grant's success meant that he finally had a general who knew how to plan a campaign and fight it. Putting Grant in command of all the troops in the West. Lincoln directed him to save the army cooped up in Chattanooga. Quickly Grant and Sherman came to the rescue, opened up a line of communication to the starving Union troops in Chattanooga, now commanded by Thomas instead of the inept Rosecrans, and brought in reinforcements. On November 23–25 the combined forces routed Bragg's encircling army and forced it back into Georgia.

This further victory gave Lincoln a solution to the problem of command, which had so long vexed him. Early the next year he brought Grant to Washington, where he received the rank of lieutenant-general, and assigned him to command all the armies of the United States. Initially Washington observers thought the burden might be too much for this "short, round-shouldered man," of whom they now received their first glimpse. R. H. Dana, Jr., reported that the new lieutenant-general "had no gait, no station, no manner, rough, light-brown whiskers, a blue eye, and rather a scrubby look withal . . . rather the look of a man who did, or once did, take a little too much to drink." But appearances were deceiving, for in the next few days Grant set forth a broad strategy for winning the war. Taking advantage of Northern superiority in manpower, he planned a simultaneous advance of all Union armies, so that the Confederates must divide their forces or else leave their territory open to invasion. The idea of involving all the Federal forces at once made sense to Lincoln. "Oh, yes! I can see that," he exclaimed. "As we say out West, if a man can't skin he must hold a leg while somebody else does." Accepting Grant's plan, Lincoln created a modern command system for the United States army, with the President as commander-in-chief, Grant as general-in-chief, and Halleck as essentially a chief of staff, while Stanton as secretary of war ably supported all the others.

Meanwhile the Confederate command system was also evolving through experimentation. The tremendous victories won by Lee and the Army of Northern Virginia obviated the need for constant changing of command in the East, but by 1863 it was evident that there must be a reorganization of Confederate commanders in the West. Davis instituted what was, in effect, a theater command system, with Lee in control of the forces in Virginia, Joseph E. Johnston, now recovered from his wound, in command of the troops between the mountains and the Mississippi River, and Edmund Kirby-Smith in charge of all troops in the vast trans-Mississippi region.

The new system was only partially successful. Made a kind of supercommander of the trans-Mississippi theater, which was becoming increasingly isolated as Union forces captured point after point along the Mississippi, Kirby-Smith did an effective job of recruiting and reorganizing the troops in his region. He stepped up trade with Mexico, so that impressive amounts of European munitions and supplies were brought in by way of Matamoros. So strengthened, "Kirby-Smithdom," as it was popularly called, fared better than most of the South, and the Confederate armies in this area were able to repel General N. P. Banks's invasion up the Red River in 1864 and also to blunt General Frederick Steele's push through Arkansas. But Kirby-Smith linked his fortunes with a group of trans-Mississippi sectionalists, who did not want to see their region bled to help the rest of the South, and he did little to make the vast resources of his command available to the government at Richmond.

In the central theater a strong Confederate command system failed to emerge. Suspicious of Davis and the Confederate war department, aware that his subordinates had the authority to report directly to Richmond, Johnston claimed that he did not know the extent and nature of his duties. Repeatedly he asked whether he was supposed to take field command of the widely separated armies of Bragg, near Chattanooga, and of Pemberton, at Vicksburg, or was merely to serve as adviser to those generals. Knowing that both were protégés of the President, he did not dare give a positive order to either. In consequence, he made only a feeble effort to replace the unpopular Bragg and diverted a few of his troops to support Pemberton. Unable to persuade Pemberton to leave Vicksburg while there was still time, Johnston watched in impotent impatience as the Confederate army was cornered and starved into surrender.

The brilliant successes of Lee and his lieutenants in the Eastern theater allowed the Army of Northern Virginia to operate pretty much as it wished, without much regard for the needs of the Confederacy elsewhere. There were some exceptions to this generalization, as when Lee permitted General James A. Longstreet's corps to join Bragg's army in time to win the Confederate victory at Chickamauga. But mostly Lee, who had direct access to President Davis, resisted any attempt to weaken his force. In mid-1863, rather than attempt to relieve Vicksburg, Lee deliberately chose to stage a new invasion of the North, in the vain hope that it would reduce pressure on Confederate armies elsewhere. The result was the defeat at Gettysburg and the capture of Vicksburg.

Even so, Lee was by 1864 the only Confederate commander who retained the confidence of the country and of his troops. As Southern defeats became more numerous than victories, a strong demand welled up in the Confederate Congress for coordinated direction of all the Southern armies, and men naturally looked to Lee. The general was, however, averse to these broader responsibilities and did all that he could to discourage the plan. When the Congress in January 1865 passed, despite President Davis's disapproval, an act requiring the appointment of a commander-in-chief of all the armies, it clearly had Lee in mind, and Davis named him. In accepting the new position, however, Lee made it clear that he would continue to be essentially a theater commander, responsible only to Davis. Pointedly ignoring Congress, he announced, "I am indebted alone to the kindness of His Excellency, the President, for my nomination to this high and arduous office." The Confederacy thus reached Appomattox without ever developing a truly unified command system, comparable to that of the Union.

⪼ II ⪻

In naval warfare, necessity compelled the Confederates to take the lead in experimentation. Southerners were not a sea-going people, with a tradition of ship-building. Secretary of the Navy Stephen R. Mallory had initially not a single ship at his command. He had to improvise, and he did so with imagination and remarkable success.

In the early months of the war, the long Southern coastline seemed to be at the mercy of the Union fleet, which could pick the most vulnerable points for attack. In November 1861 a Union flotilla commanded by Flag Officer Samuel F. DuPont routed the weak Confederate defenders of Port Royal Sound, and Federal troops occupied Beaufort and the adjacent South Carolina sea islands. The victory gave the vessels in the Atlantic blockading fleet a much needed fueling station, and it also brought freedom to the numerous slaves of the area. In February and March 1862, another Union expedition easily reduced Confederate positions on Roanoke Island and at New Bern, North Carolina, and enabled the Federal blockaders to keep a closer watch on Hatteras Sound. As already mentioned, Farragut's fleet in April 1862 blazed past the forts defending New Orleans and helped capture the Confederacy's largest city.

By this time the Confederacy had greatly strengthened its coastal defenses, and further Union successes came slowly and at great cost. In April 1863 the Confederates repelled a vast Union armada, commanded by DuPont, which tried to capture Charleston. Though a subsequent Federal expedition reduced Fort Sumter to a heap of rubble and repeatedly shelled Charleston itself, that citadel of secession remained in Confederate hands until nearly the end of the war, when Sherman's advance compelled Southern troops to abandon it. Equally effective were the Confederate defenses of Wilmington, North Carolina, which became the main Southern port on the Atlantic through which supplies from Europe were imported. In December 1864 Wilmington's defenders successfully resisted a huge Union naval and military expedition, consisting of sixty-five vessels, and not until January 1865 could Federal troops capture Fort Fisher, its principal de-

FARRAGUT'S MORTAR SCHOONERS ASCENDING THE MISSISSIPPI

From the beginning, Union naval superiority was unquestioned. As early as April 1862 the North was able to demonstrate its mastery by pushing a fleet up the Mississippi and capturing New Orleans. William Waud's drawing shows how David G. Farragut disguised his mortar schooners with boughs of trees. (*Prints Division, The New York Public Library, Astor, Lenox and Tilden Foundations.*)

fense. The powerfully protected harbor of Mobile remained in Southern hands until August 1864, when the sixty-three-year-old Admiral Farragut, lashed in the rigging of his flagship so that he would not fall to his death if wounded, led his fleet past the defending Confederate forts to close the last remaining major Southern port on the Gulf.

To supplement the conventional coastal batteries that protected these and other harbors, the Confederate navy experimented with new weapons. They used torpedoes extensively for the first time in warfare. These "infernal machines," constructed of kegs, barrels, and cans filled with explosives, were sometimes anchored at the entrance of Southern harbors; at other times they were turned loose to float with the tide toward attacking Union vessels or were propelled at the end of a long pole by a small boat, whose crew was willing to undertake the suicidal risk. Even more dangerous were the several Confederate experiments with submarine warfare. The most successful of these novel vessels was the *H. L. Hunley,* propelled underwater by a crank turned by its eight-man crew. After four unsuccessful trials, in which all members of the crews were killed, the *Hunley* in February 1864 sank the Union warship *Housatonic* in Charleston harbor, but the submarine itself was lost in the resulting explosion.

Quickly comprehending that the Confederacy could never build as large a fleet as the Union, Secretary Mallory early in the war urged the construction of iron-armored ships, against which the wooden vessels of the North would stand no chance. Despite shortages of iron and lack of rolling mills, the Confederacy developed a surprising number of these vessels, such as the *Louisiana* and the *Mississippi,* captured just before their completion when New Orleans fell, and the *Tennessee,* which helped defend Mobile Bay. The most famous of these Confederate ironclads was the *Virginia,* originally the United States warship *Merrimack,* which the Federals sank when they abandoned Norfolk navy yard at the beginning of the war. Raised and repaired, the *Virginia* had her superstructure covered with four-inch iron plate, and she carried a cast-iron ram on her prow. On March 8, 1862, just as McClellan began his campaign on the Peninsula, the *Virginia* emerged and began attacking the wooden vessels of the Union fleet at Hampton Roads. In her first day's action she destroyed two of the largest ships in the squadron and ran a third aground. Reappearing the second day, she found her way barred by a curious Union vessel, the *Monitor,* which looked like a tin can on a raft. Belatedly contracted for by the slow-moving Union navy department, the *Monitor,* designed by John Ericsson, was a low-lying ironclad with a revolving gun turret. The battle between the *Virginia* and the *Monitor* proved a draw, but the Confederate ship had to return to Norfolk to repair her defective engines. Two days later, when forced to abandon Norfolk, the Southerners ran the *Virginia* ashore and burned the vessel to prevent its capture. The South's most promising hope for breaking the blockade was lost.

Mallory was equally prompt in purchasing or commissioning conventional vessels for the Confederate navy, ships designed not to combat Union warships but to harass the United States merchant marine. The most successful of these vessels was the C.S.S. *Alabama*, built to Southern specifications at the Laird shipyards in Liverpool and commanded by Raphael Semmes. Ranging over the Atlantic, Indian, and Pacific oceans, the *Alabama* between 1862 and 1864 hunted down and destroyed sixty-nine Union merchantmen, valued at more than $6 million. Not until nearly the end of the war, when the *Alabama* needed general overhauling and its crew was exhausted after twenty-two months of continuous sea duty, could the Union navy corner the raider. On June 19, 1864, the powerful, newly equipped U.S.S. *Kearsarge* engaged the *Alabama* off Cherbourg, France, and sank her. By this time, however, the *Alabama,* along with other Confederate cruisers such as the *Florida,* the *Tallahassee,* and the *Shenandoah,* had virtually exterminated the United States carrying trade.

However imaginative and innovative, Confederate navy officials could not keep pace with the growth of the Union navy, under the slow but honest direction of Gideon Welles. Drawing upon the vast industrial resources of the North and upon the experience of its sea-going population, Welles was able to build up the United States navy from its 42 active vessels in 1861, only 26 of which had steam power, to 671 ships in December 1864, of which 71 were ironclad. Navy personnel rose from 7400 at the start of the war to 68,000 at its end. Superbly equipped and managed, the Union fleet maintained an ever tightening blockade of the Southern coast. According to the best, but not wholly reliable, statistics, the Union fleet captured not more than 1 in 10 blockade runners in 1861, and not more than 1 in 8 in 1862. But by 1864 they caught 1 in 3, and by 1865 every other one. When dispirited by their exhausting but unpublicized duties, Union blockaders could take comfort in the knowledge that they were helping to strangle the Confederacy.

⋗ III ⋖

Inevitably these huge military and naval operations put a heavy strain upon the economic resources of the combatants. In the Confederacy one result was a sharp shift in the nature of Southern agriculture. When the outbreak of war cut off Northern markets, and the blockade increasingly sealed off European outlets for cotton and tobacco, farmers, at the urging of the

Confederate and state governments, turned to the production of grain and other foodstuffs. "We should all plant largely of provisions," wrote a Georgia plantation owner, who restricted his cotton planting to one acre per field hand. "Every bushel of corn and blade of grass will be greatly needed for the support of our armies." Cotton production in the South dropped from 4.5 million bales in 1861 to 300,000 in 1864.

In the North, too, farmers began producing more grain. Partly because of inflation, the price of wheat rose from 65¢ a bushel in December 1860 to $2.26 in July 1864, and farmers, especially in the Middle West, saw a chance to make money. At first the labor shortage kept them from expanding their acreage, for many farm hands enlisted in the Union army at the outbreak of the war, but machines soon made up for the absent men. One of Cyrus Hall McCormick's reapers could replace from four to six farm hands, and McCormick sold 165,000 of his machines during the war.

Industry in both the Union and the Confederacy also grew. The amount and significance of this change has become a matter of controversy among economic historians. Rejecting the traditional view that the Civil War enormously accelerated American economic growth, some scholars, using statistics only recently made available, have concluded that, on the whole, the war years retarded growth. It is difficult to resolve the controversy because statistics from this period are incomplete, because the South is omitted from many of the calculations, and because many factors related to economic growth, such as entrepreneurship and organizational skill, are not readily quantified. It seems safe to conclude, however, that the Civil War years did not witness a dramatic expansion of the American economy but saw a continuation and extension of trends evident before 1861.

However absorbing this controversy over economic growth is to the economist, the historian is more interested in the experimentation and innovation in industry that the war produced and in the striking similarity of these changes in the Union and the Confederacy. In the South, where there had been little manufacturing, the war served as a hothouse for industry. The Union blockade unintentionally served to protect infant Southern manufacturers by cutting off imports, and the demands of the army and the needs of the civilians provided an insatiable market. It is hard to measure Southern industrial growth, both because there was no Confederate census and because inflation affected all prices, yet there are some clues to show that manufacturing could be very profitable. For instance, the 1862 conscription acts exempted the owners of certain basic industries, provided that their annual profits were no more than 75 percent, and the tax records of Virginia that same year show 120 manufacturing establishments, making total profits of $3 million and giving dividends of

375–645 percent. Under the astute management of Joseph Anderson, the Tredegar Iron Works at Richmond, the largest privately owned factory in the South and the primary source for Confederate cannon, made profits of 100 percent in 1861 and of 70 percent in 1862.

Northern manufacturing was equally profitable, especially when it produced items needed for the army. With the demand for uniforms, woolen mills, which had averaged dividends of only 9 percent for the years before the war, by 1865 were able to pay 25 percent dividends, and the number of woolen mills more than doubled. Investors were willing to pour money into such industries more confidently, because Congress raised tariffs to levels that practically excluded competing European products. In 1862 duties were increased to an average of 37.2 percent on all imported goods, and in 1864 they were raised further to a 47 percent level. War demands made the mass production of ready-made clothing profitable, and the army's need for shoes speeded the introduction of Gordon McKay's machine for sewing soles to uppers. Simultaneously, in an unrelated development, the discovery of oil at Titusville, Pennsylvania, in 1859, led to a wartime boom in the new petroleum industry.

If these changes signified no acceleration of American economic growth, they had an important impact on the structure of the economy. The increase in the number of factories, particularly in the Confederacy, encouraged entrepreneurship. In the North, men like John D. Rockefeller and Andrew Carnegie, who started their fortunes during the war, continued to dominate the industrial scene after 1865. When the South began rebuilding its industry in the 1870s and 1880s, it looked for leadership to its wartime entrepreneurs and to the Confederate commanders who likewise had experience in directing the labor of large numbers of men. The war also encouraged the growth of large, rather than small, factories. Obliged to contract for huge shipments, both Union and Confederate governments naturally turned to the manufacturing companies financially and physically able to handle them. The selective process was accelerated because larger firms could pay an agent in Washington or Richmond who understood the requirements of the army and navy—as well as those of influential congressmen and bureaucrats.

Most important of all, the wartime experience changed attitudes toward the role of the national government in the economy. Since the destruction of the second Bank of the United States in the Jackson era, the national government had done little to regulate or control the economy; investment in railroads and canals, regulation of working conditions for certain laborers, and supervision of the quality of milk and other foods were regarded as functions of the state and local authorities. But during the war, both the Union and the Confederate governments took steps that affected every branch of economic life. In passing the Homestead Act of May 20, 1862, which offered any citizen 160 acres of the public domain after five years of continuous residence, the Union Congress signaled its intention henceforth to give more attention to the nation's farmers, as it did in creating a department of agriculture that same year. The Morrill Act of 1862, giving vast tracts of the public domain to endow agricultural (land-grant) colleges, was further evidence of the same purpose.

Both governments found it necessary to regulate transportation, especially railroads, during the war. The Confederates relied upon a loose system of cooperation among railroad officials, under the general supervision of a military railroad coordinator, who had little real power. The Union government passed a stern law in January 1862 authorizing the President "to take possession of any or all the railroad lines in the United States, their rolling stock, their offices, shops, buildings," but its control of railroads depended less upon coercing than upon coopting the leaders of the major rail lines. Davis, despite his strict interpretation of the Confederate Constitution, urged his Congress to finance the construction of some missing links in the Southern rail system. Lincoln in July 1862 signed the Pacific Railroad Act, giving enormous tracts of public land to support the construction of a transcontinental rail route.

In both the United States and the Confederacy, private citizens became aware, often for the first time, of the economic impact of their national governments. When both began to levy excise and income taxes, they had to set up a tax-gathering apparatus that, for the first time in decades, reached down to the pockets of individual citizens. In the Confederacy, the Impressment Act of March 1863 authorized government agents to seize civilians' food, horses, wagons, or other supplies if required for the army and to set an arbitrary price for the confiscated goods. In the Union, the creation of a new national banking system in 1863 (amended and strengthened in 1864) meant, among other things, that a uniform national currency began to replace the dozens of issues by local banks. Citizens, paying national taxes in national currency, grew accustomed to the idea that their national government would henceforth play a positive role in the economic life of the country.

⊰ IV ⊱

During the desperate final years of the Civil War, both Union and Confederate treasury departments had to experiment with new ways to finance the war. Both imposed broad excise duties. The Union Internal Revenue

Act of July 1, 1862, has been fairly characterized as an attempt to tax everything. Duties were imposed upon all sorts of manufactures, with a fresh duty levied each time the raw material underwent a new process. In a carriage, for instance, the leather, the cloth, the wood, and the metal would be taxed; then the manufacturer was taxed for the process of putting them together; the dealer was taxed for selling the carriage; and the purchaser, having paid a sufficient price to cover all these duties, was taxed in addition for ownership. Heavy duties fell upon luxuries, like billiard tables and yachts, and taxes upon professions and occupations covered, as Representative James G. Blaine said, "bankers and pawn brokers, lawyers and horse-dealers, physicians and confectioners, commercial brokers and peddlers." Ultimately these taxes brought in about 21 percent of the total wartime expenditures of the Union government.

The Confederacy moved more slowly, but on April 24, 1863, it too adopted a comprehensive tax measure, which included an income tax, occupational and license taxes ranging from $40 for bowling alleys to $500 for bankers, and what a later generation would call an excess profits tax. A unique feature of the Confederate legislation was the tax-in-kind, which compelled producers of wheat, corn, oats, potatoes, sugar, cotton, tobacco, and other farm products to pay one-tenth of their crop each year to the government. When Southern farmers complained that this tax singled them out for discriminatory treatment, the Confederate Congress in 1864 revised the law, levying a higher duty on business and speculative profits; but by permitting these taxes—in contrast to the tax-in-kind—to be paid in depreciated Confederate notes, it failed to remove the inequity. A last, desperate attempt to tax all coin, bullion, and foreign exchange in March 1865 was made too late to have any effect. All told, the Confederacy raised only about 1 percent of its income from taxes.

The sale of bonds contributed little more to the Confederate treasury. Values were so uncertain in the wartime South that investors were afraid to tie up their money in such rigid investments, and doubts spread as to when and whether the Confederate government would even pay the interest on its obligations. In the Union, on the other hand, bonds became a major source of revenue. Unable initially to sell bonds even at a discount, Secretary Chase appointed his friend, Jay Cooke, the Philadelphia banker who also had an office in Washington, special agent of the treasury department. Using high-pressure advertising, Cooke launched an extensive propaganda campaign, extolling the merits of the "five-twenties" (bonds bearing 6 percent interest, which could be paid off at the expiration of five, and must be redeemed in twenty, years). He was so successful that, as Senator John Sherman said, the bonds were made to stare "in the face of the people

UNION PAPER MONEY: A "GREENBACK"

Secretary of the Treasury Salmon P. Chase said that, in deference to Lincoln's superior position, he put the President's likeness on the $10 Union bill and his own on the $1 note. Enemies claimed that Chase, perennially ambitious for the presidency, knew that more Northerners would become familiar with his face on the less valuable note. (*Courtesy of* Paper Money of the United States *by Robert Friedberg, published by the Coin & Currency Institute, Inc.*)

in every household from Maine to California." Between 600,000 and 1 million citizens were persuaded to invest in the public debt, and the entire loan of half a billion dollars was oversubscribed. But in 1864, as the war stretched on endlessly and victory appeared nowhere in sight, the market for bonds collapsed. Resigning for political reasons, Chase left office at an opportune moment to preserve his reputation as a financier, and Cooke went with him. Chase's successor, William Pitt Fessenden, could only raise money through short-term loans at an exorbitant rate of interest. Not until the very end of the war, when victory was obviously near, did the sale of Union bonds pick up, and Cooke, reappointed special agent, attracted large additional numbers of investors.

Necessarily, therefore, both governments continued to depend upon paper money. The Union treasury, which had cautiously issued its first greenbacks in 1862, continued to print more and more during the rest of that year and during 1863 as well, until most of the $450 million authorized by Congress was in circulation. The value of the greenbacks gradually declined. A Union treasury note with a face value of $1 was worth 99.86¢ in gold in 1862, but by 1864 it was worth only 62.66¢ and, by early 1865, 50.3¢. In the Confederacy, where the printing presses never stopped, paper money had even less value. Perhaps $2 billion in unredeemable paper was issued in all. A Confederate treasury note for $1, worth 82.7¢ in gold in 1862, dropped to 29¢ in 1863 and to 1.7¢ in early 1865. In a desperate attempt to check the slide, the Confederate Congress in February 1864 undertook a partial repudiation of these notes, but the confusing and complex legislation was badly administered and served further to undermine trust in the government and its money. Having lost the confidence of the country, Memminger resigned in the summer of 1864—at about the same time that Chase left the Union treasury department. His successor, the South Carolina banker and businessman, George A. Trenholm, could devise no better solution for the Confederacy's financial woes than to urge citizens to donate to the government their "money, jewels, gold and silver plate, and public securities."

The excessive amount of paper money was only one of many factors that produced runaway inflation in both the North and the South. With importations largely cut off, in the North by the highly protective tariff and in the South by the Union blockade, with the productive labor force sharply reduced because of the number of men in military service, and with a huge portion of all goods required to supply the armies and navies, civilians had to expect shortages and high prices.

In both sections there were some who profited from the wartime economy. War contracts helped pull the Union economy out of a sharp depression, and higher prices spurred on manufacturers, who could now look for higher profits. The demand for grain, along with the Homestead Act, encouraged new settlers to begin farming, and the development of new industries, like petroleum, made for quick fortunes. The wartime boom in the North had a hectic quality about it, and men spent their easily earned money quickly lest it be worth less in the future. Many of the rich were extravagant and hedonistic. Censoriously the *New York Independent* asked in June 1864: "Who at the North would ever think of war, if he had not a friend in the army, or did not read the newspapers? Go into Broadway, and we will show you what is meant by the word 'extravagance.' Ask [A. T.] Stewart [the department-store owner] about the demand for camel's-hair shawls, and he will say 'monstrous.' Ask Tiffany what kinds of diamonds and pearls are called for. He will answer 'the prodigious,' 'as near hen's-egg size as possible,' 'price no object.' What kinds of carpetings are now wanted? None but 'extra.'. . . And as for horses the medium-priced five-hundred-dollar kind are all out of the market. A good pair of 'fast ones' . . . will go for a thousand dollars sooner than a basket of strawberries will sell for four cents."

But not all elements in the North shared in this wartime prosperity.

Wages lagged sadly behind prices, so that in terms of real income a worker between 1861 and 1865 lost 35 percent of his wages. Women, who composed one-fourth of the nation's manufacturing force in 1860, were especially hard hit. As more and more wives and mothers found it necessary to work, since soldiers could only send them a pittance for support, employers actually cut their wages. Even the United States government participated in this practice. At the Philadelphia armory, the government in 1861 paid a seamstress 17¢ for making a shirt; three years later, when prices were at their highest, it cut the wage to 15¢. Meanwhile private contractors paid only 8¢.

Suffering in the North was, however, relatively minor when compared to that in the South. To be sure, residents of some parts of the agricultural South who were never disturbed by Union troops had only minor shortages to complain of. As imported goods disappeared from the grocers' shelves, they resorted to sassafras tea and to "coffee" made of parched rye, okra seeds, corn, and even sweet potatoes, the grounds of which were said to form a remarkable cleaning agent for curtains and carpets. Since salt was in short supply, meat could not be preserved, and Southerners ate more chicken and fish. As clothing wore out, they increasingly turned to homespun, and velvet draperies and brocaded rugs found new use as gowns and overcoats.

The thousands of Southerners in the path of the armies had to think not just of shortages but of survival. Hundreds of families fled before the invading Union armies, often attempting to take their slaves with them, but nowhere could these refugees find assurance of safety. Their lives took on a desperate, nightmarish quality, and merely existing from one day to the next was a struggle. There was never enough of anything, including food. Recalling these unhappy days, one writer declared that "the Confederacy was always hungry."

The greatest destitution appeared in towns and cities, where food and supplies had to be brought in over the rickety, uncoordinated Southern railroad system. White-collar workers, especially those on fixed salaries from the government, were especially hard hit. The celebrated diary of J. B. Jones, a clerk in the Confederate war department at Richmond, is a melancholy record of shortages and high prices. By May 1864 he reported that beans in Richmond were selling for $3 a quart, meal for $125 a bushel, and flour, $400 a barrel. Richmond, he observed, was an astonishingly clean city, for "everything [is] being so cleanly consumed that no garbage or filth can accumulate." The citizens of the Confederate capital were obliged to be "such good scavengers" that there was "no need of buzzards."

Deprivation was the more painful because, as in the North, some made enormous profits from the war. The blockade runner, who preferred to bring in compact, expensive items like silks and jewels rather than bulky supplies for the army, often reaped fantastic profits. Speculators also flourished. As early as the winter of 1862, the governor of Mississippi learned that the families of volunteers in his state were seriously suffering for want of corn and salt, while rich planters, moved by "the *Demon spirit* of speculation which is doing our Government and our people more injury than the Yankees," held back their ample supply of both commodities, waiting for the inevitable rise in prices. Even more remunerative was trading with the enemy, a practice completely illegal but tacitly condoned by both Confederate and Union officials. Southern women and men who were initiated into the mysteries of the trade bought up as much cotton as they could find in their neighborhoods and took it to convenient exchange points like Memphis and Natchez to sell to the Yankees for coffee, clothing, and luxuries. Late in the war they accepted payment in United States greenbacks, which Southerners valued more than their own depreciated money.

❧ V ☙

Along with economic inequity, the unfairness of conscription was the subject of bitter complaints on the part of both Northerners and Southerners during the Civil War. The Confederate conscription act of 1862 ostensibly made all able-bodied white males between the ages of 18 and 35 equally eligible for military service, but the Southern Congress promptly began exempting large categories of men: Confederate and state civil officials, ministers, teachers and professors, miners, industrial workers, and pharmacists. One planter or overseer was exempted for every plantation with more than twenty slaves. Wealthy eligible men who did not want to serve could hire substitutes. Mennonites, Friends, and others with religious convictions against war could escape service by paying $500 or by providing a substitute.

As men rushed to enter "bombproof" occupations and claim exemptions, the outcry against the Confederate conscription system grew louder. One of the most vociferous critics was Governor Joseph E. Brown of Georgia, who protested, "The conscription Act, at one swoop, strikes down the sovereignty of the States, tramples upon the constitutional rights and personal liberty of the citizens, and arms the President with imperial power." After attempting unsuccessfully to induce the Georgia supreme court to declare conscription unconstitutional, Brown proceeded to undermine the policy by naming his supporters to state jobs exempt from military service. According to some estimates, he put 15,000 able-bodied Georgians into this exempt

"THE VOLUNTARY MANNER IN WHICH SOME OF THE SOUTHERN VOLUNTEERS ENLIST"

After the initial enthusiasm wore off, volunteering dwindled in both the Union and the Confederacy. This cartoon suggests that, despite lying propaganda such as the poster announcing the "Suicide of Abe Lincoln," the Confederate volunteer had to be marched to the recruiting office at the point of bayonets. Even so, such recruits were of inferior physical and mental quality, like the drunken figure at the left, too inebriated to notice that a small dog is urinating on him. As volunteering fell off, Union and Confederacy resorted to conscription. (*Library of Congress.*)

category; certainly he created 2000 justices of the peace and 1000 constables, none of whom had to serve in the army. Less prominent than Brown but equally potent were the critics who complained that conscription was class legislation that benefited the educated and the wealthy. They raised especial objection to the so-called "twenty-nigger" provision, which clearly favored planters at the expense of farmers. "Never did a law meet with more universal odium than the exemption of slave owners," wrote Senator James Phelan of Mississippi to President Davis. "It has aroused a spirit of rebellion . . . and bodies of men have banded together to desert."

Despite intense criticism and dubious results, the Davis administration continued conscription, for it saw no other way to raise the needed number of men. Indeed, as the war progressed it was obliged to experiment with even more stringent legislation. In a new conscription act of February 17, 1864, the Confederate Congress declared that all white males between the ages of seventeen and fifty were subject to the draft, with the seventeen-year-old boys and the men above forty-five to serve as a reserve for local defense. As a concession to smaller planters, the act exempted one farmer or overseer for every plantation with fifteen slaves, but it abolished most other exemptions, on the theory that once skilled laborers were in the army the government could detail them to the forges and factories where they were most needed. Total mobilization of manpower was, however, far beyond the competence of the shaky Confederate government, and in practice the industrial-detail system never worked. As the Confederacy scraped the bottom of the barrel, more and more white Southerners began thinking about the one group of able-bodied males who did not serve in the armies: the Negroes.

In the North, too, conscription evoked bitter criticism. The first effective Northern draft act, passed by the Union Congress on March 3, 1863, was patently unfair. Declaring that all able-bodied males between the ages of twenty and forty-five (except for certain high governmental officials and the only sons of widows and infirm parents) were liable to military service, the act promptly contradicted itself by permitting those who could afford to do so to hire substitutes. In an effort to keep the price of substitutes down, it also permitted a man to purchase outright exemption from military service for $300.

As in the South, there was immediate and widespread hostility toward conscription. Since there was a social stigma attached to being drafted, nobody wanted to be forced to serve in the army. This reluctance was magnified when it became evident that the system favored the wealthiest citizens and the most prosperous sections of the country. A well-to-do person like George Templeton Strong of New York, for example, did not dream of serving in the army; he paid $1,100 for a substitute, "a big 'Dutch' boy of twenty or thereabouts," who, as Strong remarked complacently, "looked as if he could do good service." Rich towns and counties raised bounty funds to encourage volunteering, so that none of their citizens would have to be drafted, and as the war progressed, they offered higher and higher bounties. The volunteers they sought were by no means all local residents who needed a little financial inducement; many of them were professional bounty hunters, who went from place to place, enlisting, receiving bounties, and promptly deserting. Perhaps the record for bounty jumping was held by one John O'Connor, who when arrested in March 1865 confessed to thirty-two such desertions.

Part of the outcry against conscription in the North stemmed from the inequity of the quotas the President was authorized to announce for each state, presumably giving credit for the number of volunteers it had previously supplied. The Democratic governor of New York, Horatio Seymour, engaged in acrimonious correspondence with Lincoln and finally forced the President to admit that the quota assigned to the Empire State was excessive. Such concessions, however, came too late to placate those threatened by the draft. In Wisconsin, Kentucky, and Pennsylvania, in Troy, Newark, and Albany, there was outright resistance to the enrolling officers, and in several instances Federal troops had to be brought in to quell the insurgents. None of these outbreaks compared in extent or ferocity to that in New York City, where the drawing of the first draftees' names triggered a three-day riot (July 13–15, 1863) by a mob of predominantly Irish workingmen. Turning first against the enrollment officers and the police, the rioters then exhibited their animus against the rich by plundering fine houses and rifling jewelry stores. Toward Negroes, whom the rioters feared as economic competitors and blamed for the war and hence for conscription, the mob acted with hideous brutality. After sacking and looting a Negro orphan asylum, they chased down any blacks unwary enough to appear on the streets and left those they could capture hanging from lamp-posts. The Union government had to rush in troops from the Gettysburg campaign to stop the rioting and disperse the mob.

Despite all resistance, Lincoln's government continued conscription because, as in the Confederacy, there seemed to be no other source for soldiers. Even so, the draft remained cumbersome and often ineffectual. In 1864, for instance, 800,000 names were drawn, but so many were exempted because of health or occupation and so many others hired substitutes or paid the commutation fee that only 33,000 men were actually inducted into the army. As conscription proved both unfair and ineffective, citizens in the North, like those in the South, began to think of the value of black soldiers.

⩕ VI ⩓

Just as the Negro played a central part in causing the Civil War, so was he to play a major role in determining its outcome. At the outset there was a tacit agreement that the Civil War was to be a white man's fight, and both Union and Confederate governments in 1861 refused to accept black regiments. In the Confederacy during the first two years of the war, virtually nobody questioned the correctness of this decision. After all, as Vice-President Alexander H. Stephens announced, slavery was "the real 'cornerstone'" upon which the Confederate States had been erected, and few Southern whites could even contemplate the possibility of putting arms into the hands of slaves or of freeing blacks who became soldiers.

In the Union, on the other hand, there were from the beginning powerful voices urging the emancipation of slaves and the enlistment of black men in the army. Frederick Douglass, the leading spokesman of blacks in the North, constantly insisted: "Teach the rebels and traitors that the price they are to pay for the attempt to abolish this Government must be the abolition of slavery." Abolitionists, white and black, repeatedly instructed Lincoln that he could win the war only if he emancipated the slaves. Urging the President to make his cardinal rule that *"Nothing against Slavery can be unconstitutional,"* Senator Charles Sumner of Massachusetts visited the White House almost daily in his efforts to persuade Lincoln that emancipation was the *"one way to safety,* clear as sunlight—pleasant as the paths of Peace."

So influential was this antislavery sentiment that several of the President's subordinates who fell into disfavor with the administration tried to appeal to it. When General Frémont was in deep trouble over his maladministration in Missouri, he suddenly announced in August 1861 that the property of all rebels in his region would be confiscated and their slaves freed. Similarly in December 1861 when Secretary of War Cameron came under fire for inefficiency and possible corruption, he surprisingly declared himself in favor of freeing and arming the slaves. In May 1862 General David Hunter, in command of the Union troops occupying the Sea Islands, proclaimed the emancipation of the slaves in Florida, Georgia, and South Carolina. But President Lincoln, aware of the dangerous complexity of the issue, patiently overruled each of these subordinates, declaring that emancipation was a question "which, under my responsibility, I reserve to myself."

Unwillingness to arm or emancipate the slaves did not signify any reluctance to employ blacks in nonmilitary service. Slaves were the backbone of the Confederate labor force. Had blacks not continued to till and harvest the grain, the Confederacy could never have fielded so large an army. Equally important was the role played by blacks, slave and free, in the industrial production of the Confederacy. In the Tredegar Iron Works, for example, half the 2400 employees were blacks; they included not merely unskilled workers but puddlers, rollers, and machinists. Blacks also performed indispensable service for the quartermaster and commissary departments of the Confederacy, serving as teamsters, butchers, drovers, boatmen, bakers, shoemakers, and blacksmiths, and they formed the backbone of the nursing staff of many Confederate hospitals.

So essential was Negro labor to the existence of the Confederacy that President Davis had to ensure that enough blacks were available for this service. From the beginning of the war, Confederate authorities from time to time impressed slaves to work on fortifications, and some states, notably Virginia, moved promptly to require owners to lease their slaves to the government when needed. But the Confederate government itself did not act until the conventional phase of the war was over and the need for experimentation was obvious to all. In March 1863 the Confederate Congress, despite much opposition from planters, authorized the impressment of slaves, whose owners were to receive $30 a month. In February 1864 it permitted military authorities to impress more slaves, with or without the consent of their owners.

Meanwhile the Union was also making full use of the labor of blacks. As slaves fled from their masters to the camps of the Union army, they were put to use as teamsters, cooks, nurses, carpenters, scouts, and day laborers. Perhaps half a million blacks crossed over to the Union lines, and nearly 200,000 of these performed labor for the army. Many of these "contrabands" carried with them valuable information about the disposition of Confederate troops and supplies. Occasionally some brought even more valuable assets. Robert Smalls and his brother, who were slaves in Charleston, South Carolina, in May 1862 daringly seized the Confederate sidewheel steamer, *Planter,* navigated it out of the harbor ringed with Confederate guns, and delivered it to the blockading Union fleet.

When the war appeared to have reached a stalemate, Northern sentiment in favor of freeing and arming the slaves grew. Republican congressmen were ahead of the President on these questions. As early as August 1861 they had passed an act declaring that slaves used to support the Confederate military were free. In March 1862, as already mentioned, Congress forbade the return of fugitive slaves by the military. And on July 17, 1862, in a far-reaching confiscation act, it declared that slaves of all persons supporting the rebellion should be "forever free of their servitude, and not again [to be] held as slaves." These measures were, however, poorly drafted and not readily enforced, so that they had little practical consequence. More effective was the act of April 16, 1862, abolishing slavery in the District of Columbia.

But powerful forces in the North were opposed to emancipation. The border states, where slavery still prevailed, were of such uncertain loyalty that they might try to break away from the Union if emancipation became a Northern war aim. In the free states, anti-Negro prejudice was rampant, and many feared that emancipation would produce a massive migration of blacks to the North, where they would compete with white laborers for jobs. Belief in the inferiority of the Negro race was general, and the experience of Union soldiers in the South often strengthened this stereotype, for the fugitives who fled to their camps were mostly illiterate, ragged, and dirty. "The contrabands are numerous," callously wrote one soldier in Hunter's army in South Carolina, "and ought all to be drowned."

During the initial stages of the war Lincoln, who hated slavery, had to take these racist attitudes into account, and he knew he could move toward emancipation only in a circuitous fashion. In early 1862 he made an earnest, though ultimately unsuccessful, plea to the border states to recognize that the "mere friction and abrasion" of war was certain to put an end to slavery, and he besought them to devise plans of gradual, compensated emancipation, for which he promised federal financial assistance. At the same time, he took anti-Negro sentiment into account by resurrecting a plan he had long cherished of colonizing freedmen in Central America and in Haiti. To a group of black leaders who visited him in the White House, the President explained his position frankly: "You and we are different races. We have between us a broader difference than exists between almost any other two races. Whether it is right or wrong I need not discuss, but this physical difference is a great disadvantage to us both. . . ." "It is better for us both," he concluded, "to be separated."

By the fall of 1862, however, Lincoln felt obliged to act decisively against slavery. By failing to adopt his program of gradual emancipation, the border states had lost their chance. Blacks showed little interest in his plans for colonization, which in any case were poorly thought out and could only lead to disaster. As casualties mounted, Northern soldiers, without necessarily shedding their prejudices against Negroes, came to think it was time to enroll them in the army. Major Charles G. Halpine, who wrote verse in Irish brogue under the pseudonym "Private Miles O'Reilly," caught the change of mood in his popular poem, "Sambo's Right to be Kilt":

> Some tell us 'tis a burnin' shame
>   To make the naygers fight;
> And that the thrade of bein' kilt
>   Belongs but to the white:
> But as for me, upon my soul!
>   So liberal are we here,
> I'll let Sambo be murthered instead of myself
>   On every day in the year.

But most influential in changing Lincoln's mind was his grim recognition after eighteen months of combat that the war could not be ended by traditional means. "We . . . must change our tactics or lose the war," he concluded.

Waiting only for McClellan to check Lee's invasion at Antietam, Lincoln on September 22, 1862, issued a preliminary emancipation proclamation, announcing that unless the rebellious states returned to their allegiance he would on January 1, 1863, declare that "all persons held as slaves" in the territory controlled by the Confederates were "then, thenceforward, and forever free." Since the President justified his action on the ground of military necessity, it was appropriate that the definitive Emancipation Proclamation at the beginning of the new year officially authorized the enrollment of black troops in the Union army.

Promptly the war department began to accept Negro regiments. These were not, to be sure, the first black soldiers to serve in the war, for a few Negroes had been enrolled without permission from Washington in the Federal forces on the Sea Islands, in Louisiana, and in Kansas, but now large numbers of blacks joined the army. They were enrolled in segregated regiments, in nearly all cases with white officers, and they received less pay than did white soldiers. By the end of the war the number of Negroes in the Union army totalled 178,895—more than twice the number of soldiers in the Confederate army at Gettysburg.

At first most Union officials thought black regiments would be useful only for garrison duty, but in bitterly contested engagements such as Fort Wagner and Port Hudson, Miliken's Bend and Nashville, they demonstrated, as Lincoln said, how well, "with silent tongue, and clenched teeth, and steady eye, and well-poised bayonet," they could and would fight. The battle record of these black troops did much to change popular Northern stereotypes of the Negro. In the early stages of the war, cartoonists and caricaturists portrayed blacks as invisible men; their faces were vague and featureless blobs of black, hardly human. But with emancipation and the enrollment of Negroes in the army, war artists began to take a closer look, to depict blacks with distinctive, recognizably human features, and finally, in a kind of perverse tribute to their merit, to sketch them with Nordic profiles.

Meanwhile, and much more slowly, sentiment was growing in the Confederacy for the military employment of blacks. Support for arming the slaves emerged first in those areas scourged by Northern armies. After Grant's successful Vicksburg campaign, the Jackson *Mississippian* boldly called for enrolling slaves as soldiers in the Confederate army. "We must either employ the negroes ourselves," it argued, "or the enemy will employ them against us." Though other Mississippi and Alabama newspapers echoed the call for black recruits, the most powerful voice for arming the slaves was that of General Patrick R. Cleburne, who witnessed how easily the powerful Union army broke the thin Confederate line at Chattanooga. Seeing no other source of manpower, Cleburne, together with his aides, addressed a long letter to General Joseph E. Johnston, who had succeeded Bragg as commander of the Army of Tennessee, urging "that we immediately commence training a large reserve of the most courageous of our slaves, and further that we guarantee freedom within a reasonable time to every slave in the South who shall remain true to the Confederacy in this war."

So drastic a proposal was bound to rouse strong opposition, and President Davis, upon learning of Cleburne's letter, ordered that it be suppressed as "productive only of discouragement, distraction, and dissention." But the subject would not die. As Union armies moved closer to the Confederate heartland, Virginia editors also began to urge arming the blacks, and at an October 1864 meeting Southern governors proposed "a change of policy on our part" as to the slaves.

Finally, on November 7, 1864, President Davis, in a deliberately obscure message to Congress, put himself at the head of the movement. Urging further impressment of blacks "for service with the army," Davis argued that the Confederate government should purchase the impressed slaves. Having state-owned slaves would be, Davis admitted, a "radical modification" of Confederate policy, and he pondered the future of such a bondsman: "Should he be retained in servitude, or should his emancipation be held out to him as a reward for faithful service, or should it be granted at once on the promise of such service . . . ?"

However obscurely phrased, Davis's proposal clearly looked toward the end of slavery, and it at once encountered powerful resistance. Davis, said his enemies, proposed the confiscation of private property; he was subverting the Constitution. His plan would be a confession to the world of the South's weakness. It would deplete the labor force needed to feed the army. And, most frightening of all, it would put arms in the hands of black men who, at best, might desert to the Union armies and, at worst, might use those arms against their masters. "The African is of an inferior race, whose normal condition is slavery," insisted the Charleston *Mercury*. "Prone to barbarism, and incapable of any other state than that of pupilage, he is at his best estate as the slave of the enlightened white man of this country."

Despite all opposition, the Confederate government pushed ahead with the plan, for it had no other reservoir of manpower. In February 1865 the scheme received the backing of General Lee, who wrote that the employment of blacks as soldiers was "not only expedient but necessary" and announced plainly that "it would be neither just nor wise . . . to require them to serve as slaves." Since, as the Richmond *Examiner* declared, "the country will not deny to General Lee . . . *anything* he may ask for," the Confederate Congress the next month passed, by a very close vote, an act calling for 300,000 more soldiers irrespective of color. No provision was made in the act to free blacks who enrolled, but the Confederate war department in effect smuggled emancipation into the measure through the orders it issued for its enforcement. Promptly the recruiting of black troops began, and some black companies were raised in Richmond and other towns. By this time, however, it was too late, even for such a revolutionary experiment, and none of the black Confederate soldiers ever saw service.

≥ VII ≤

Though the Union and Confederate governments moved toward emancipating and arming the blacks because of military necessity, both recognized how profoundly their actions affected the continuing struggle for European recognition and support. Well informed Americans were aware of the intensity of European antislavery sentiment. Repeatedly Carl Schurz, the Union minister to Madrid, told Lincoln that if he freed the slaves no European government would "dare to place itself, by declaration or act, upon the side of a universally condemned institution." Similarly Henry Hotze, the editor of the pro-Confederate London newspaper, *The Index,* and the shrewdest Southern propagandist abroad, warned his government that European repugnance toward slavery was "unanimous and unassailable." But so long as neither government took a bold stand against the South's peculiar institution, European antislavery leaders were puzzled and divided by the war. In Great Britain, for example, some influential spokesmen, like John Bright, Richard Cobden, and John Stuart Mill, from the beginning supported the Union cause, confident that Southern defeat would end slavery. But Lord Russell, on the other hand, predicted that if the South should be conquered and the United States be restored without emancipating the blacks, "slavery would prevail all over the New World. For that reason," he concluded, "I wish for separation."

Lincoln's Emancipation Proclamation ended the confusion. Though some complained that it promised freedom only to slaves whom the Union army could not reach and denied it to those in areas under Union control, European antislavery spokesmen soon recognized that the proclamation marked a new era. Within three months after the final Emancipation Proclamation was issued, fifty-six large public meetings were held in Great Britain to uphold the Northern cause. Resolutions adopted at Sheffield were typical: "*Resolved:* that this meeting being convinced that slavery is the cause of the tremendous struggle now going on in the American States, and that the object of the leaders of the rebellion is the perpetuation of the unchristian and inhuman system of chattel slavery, earnestly prays that the rebellion may be crushed. . . ."

Union diplomacy had need of such popular support, for there still lurked the possibility of European intervention in the war. Though the gravest threat had passed in the fall of 1862, before the full effect of the Emancipation Proclamation could be sensed abroad, the French emperor continued to contemplate the advantages that might come of meddling in American affairs. Hoping that a divided America would assist his mad enterprise of establishing a puppet government under the Emperor Maximilian in Mexico, Napoleon in February 1863, when Northern military fortunes were at their nadir after Fredericksburg, offered to mediate between the two belligerents. Shrewdly judging that Great Britain and Russia were not behind the French move, Secretary of State Seward spurned the offer, declaring "that peace proposed at the cost of the dissolution [of the Union] would be immediately, unreservedly, and indignantly rejected by the American people."

More dangerous to the Union cause than Napoleon's clumsy diplomacy

"MRS. NORTH AND HER ATTORNEY"

This cartoon from the British humor magazine, *Punch,* in September 1864 tells more about the state of British opinion than about American politics, for by this time the war was virtually won and Lincoln's election was assured. It does, however, suggest the difficulties the Lincoln administration had in making its case understood abroad, even after the Emancipation Proclamation. (Punch, *September 24, 1864.*)

MRS. NORTH AND HER ATTORNEY.

Mrs. North. "YOU SEE, MR. LINCOLN, WE HAVE FAILED UTTERLY IN OUR COURSE OF ACTION; I WANT PEACE, AND SO, IF YOU CANNOT EFFECT AN AMICABLE ARRANGEMENT, I MUST PUT THE CASE INTO OTHER HANDS"

were the warships being built for the Confederacy in British shipyards. Supplying either belligerent in a war with armed ships was contrary both to international law and to British statutes, but through a loophole in the law it was legal to sell separately unarmed vessels and the armaments that would convert them into men-of-war. In March 1862 the ship that became the *C.S.S. Florida* sailed from a British shipyard, and in July of that year the more powerful *Alabama* set forth to begin her depredations. Even as these raiders swept the Union merchant marine from the high seas, a more formidable Confederate naval threat, this time to the blockade itself, was being forged in the form of two enormous ironclad steam rams under construction at the Laird yards in Liverpool.

The British government wished to observe its neutrality laws, but the legal machinery was slow and cumbersome. When Union minister Charles Francis Adams called the attention of the foreign office to the rams, Lord Russell replied that he could not act to detain them unless there was convincing evidence of Confederate ownership. Adams and his aides rushed to secure affidavits to prove that the vessels were intended for the Confederacy, but British law officers were unconvinced, since other sworn testimony claimed the rams were being constructed for the French Emperor or the Pasha of Egypt. Finally, in utter exasperation, Adams on September 5, 1863, sent Russell a final warning against permitting the ships to sail, adding: "It would be superfluous in me to point out to your Lordship that this is war." Fortunately, two days before receiving Adams's ultimatum, Russell had already decided to detain the rams, and the Confederates' final hope of breaking the blockade was lost.

With that crisis, the last serious threat of European involvement in the American war disappeared. A few months later Henry Adams, the son of the United States minister, wrote from London: "Our whole question is now old and familiar to every one, so as to have become actually a bore and a nuisance. The enthusiasm for the slaveholders has passed away. . . ." So indifferent, or even hostile, to the Southern cause was the British cabinet that, late in 1863, Confederate Secretary of State Benjamin ordered Mason, his envoy, to leave London on the grounds that "the Government of Her Majesty [Queen Victoria] . . . entertains no intention of receiving you as the accredited minister of this government."

Keenly aware of the influence that emancipation had exerted in uniting European opinion against the South, President Davis sought similarly to capitalize on the actions that the Confederate States took against slavery during the final months of the war. In January 1865 he sent Duncan F. Kenner, one of the largest slaveholders in Louisiana, on a secret mission to Europe, authorizing him to promise the emancipation of the slaves in return for European recognition and aid to the Confederacy. The experiment came too late, for now it was evident that Northern victory was inevitable. Neither the French nor the British government expressed interest in Kenner's proposal.

⩻ VIII ⩻

The military and diplomatic advantages resulting from emancipation were, to a considerable extent, counterbalanced by its political disadvantages. The steps that Lincoln and Davis took toward freeing and arming the slaves enormously increased the opposition to their administrations and provided their domestic enemies a fresh supply of ammunition.

In the Confederacy there had been from the beginning of the war a sizable disloyal element. Unionism was strong in the Upper South, in the mountain regions, and in some of the poorer hill counties. Some white Southerners expressed their hostility toward the Confederate government by enlisting in the Union armies; others, by volunteering information to advancing Union forces; still others, by supplying provisions for the Federal troops. After the war, more than 22,000 Southern Unionists presented claims against the United States government totaling $60 million for supplies they had given the Federal army. As the war progressed, some of these disaffected Southerners joined secret peace societies, such as the Order of the Heroes, which had its following in the Carolinas and Virginia. Disloyalty extended into the ranks of the Confederate army, especially after conscription was initiated, and desertion was widespread. About one out of every nine soldiers who enlisted in the Confederate army deserted. Sometimes these deserters formed guerrilla bands that preyed equally upon Confederate and Union sympathizers. When halted by an enrolling officer and asked to show his pass to leave the army, a deserter would pat his gun defiantly and say, "This is my furlough."

Probably no action of the Davis administration could have won over these actively disloyal citizens, but the policies of the Confederate government alienated also a large number of entirely loyal Southerners. Some of these critics complained that President Davis was timid and tardy. He was sickly, neurasthenic, and indecisive, they said; he could not tolerate strong men around him and relied for advice upon sycophants; he did not know how to rouse the loyalty and the passions of the Southern people; he lacked courage to put himself at the head of the Southern armies and lead the Confederacy to victory. "Oh, for a man at the helm like William of Orange," exclaimed diarist Robert Kean, "a man of steadfast calm temper, heroic character and genius, a man fertile in resources, equal to emergencies. This, it is quite evident, Mr. Davis is not."

A much larger group of Confederates censured their President for exactly opposite reasons. Davis's plan to arm and free the slaves reinforced their conviction that he intended to undermine the principles upon which the Confederacy had been founded. Conscription, they argued, had begun the subversion of state sovereignty, guaranteed by the Constitution. They found evidence of Davis's dictatorial ambitions in his requests that Congress suspend the writ of habeas corpus, so that the disloyal could be arrested and imprisoned without trial. Grudgingly Congress agreed to the suspension for three limited periods, but late in 1864 it rejected Davis's appeals for a further extension on the ground that it would be "a dangerous assault upon the Constitution." Though infringements of civil liberties were infrequent in the Confederacy and no Southern newspaper was suppressed for publishing subversive editorials, critics warned that Davis was reaching after imperial powers. If the South was to have an absolute ruler, announced Yancey, now a senator, he preferred Lincoln, "not a Confederate dictator."

Leading this group of Davis's critics was none other than the Vice-President of the Confederate States, Alexander H. Stephens, who spent most of the final years of the war not in Richmond but in Georgia, stirring up agitation against the President's allegedly unconstitutional usurpation of power and simultaneously complaining of Davis's "weakness and imbecility." The Vice-President was ably supported by his brother, a leader in the Georgia legislature, who believed Davis was "a *little, conceited, hypocritical, sniveling, canting, malicious, ambitious, dogged,* knave and fool," and by Governor Brown, who deplored the President's "bold strides toward despotism." Davis's critics were also powerful in the Congress, where Virginia Senator R. M. T. Hunter was often their spokesman.

The congressional elections of 1863, held after Southerners had begun to realize the gravity of their defeats at Gettysburg and Vicksburg, greatly strengthened the anti-Davis bloc. During the following year, the President was often able to muster a majority in Congress only because of the erratic support of representatives from districts overrun or threatened by advancing Federal armies. In some instances these districts were unable to hold regular elections in 1863, and their incumbent congressmen, chosen in the early days of complete commitment to the Confederate cause, remained in office; in any case, representatives from these occupied regions had little to lose from measures that taxed and bled the rest of the Confederacy.

But by the desperate winter of 1864–1865, not even this support could give Davis control of Congress. Now in a majority, his critics refused his request for control over the state militias and rejected his plea to end all exemptions from conscription. Even as Sherman's army advanced through the Carolinas, Congress endlessly debated his plan for arming the slaves and tried to gut that measure by failing to provide that enrolled blacks would receive their freedom. As has already been mentioned, it passed, over Davis's opposition, an act creating the post of general-in-chief, advising the President to name Lee, and urging him also to give Joseph E. Johnston an important command. Fearful of attacking the President directly, congressional critics began investigations of several of his cabinet officers, and they introduced resolutions declaring that the resignation of Secretary of State Judah P. Benjamin, Davis's closest friend and most trusted adviser, would be "subservient of the public interest." Secretary of War Seddon also came under fire, and when the Virginia delegation in Congress called for his resignation, he felt obliged to leave the cabinet. In January 1865, for the first and only time, the Confederate Congress overrode a presidential veto.

Meanwhile in the North, Abraham Lincoln and his government were subjected to the same kinds of criticism. In the Union as in the Confederacy, there were some who were outright disloyal. Pro-Confederate sympathy was strongest in the states of the Upper South that remained in the Union, in those parts of the Old Northwest originally settled by Southerners, and in cities like New York, where the Irish immigrant population was bitterly hostile to blacks. Relatively few Northerners enlisted in the Confederate army, but many joined secret societies, such as the Knights of the Golden Circle and the Order of American Knights, devoted to bringing about a negotiated peace, which inevitably would entail recognizing Confederate independence. The purposes and, indeed, the very existence of these secret "Copperhead" organizations have become a matter of historical controversy, for it is clear that many members intended nothing more subversive than replacing a Republican administration with a Democratic one. It nevertheless remains certain that a sizable number of Northerners were hostile to the war and were ready to accept a dissolution of the Union. Some idea of the extent of this disaffection can be gained from the figures on desertion. One out of every seven men who enlisted in the Union armies deserted.

Much of the criticism of the Lincoln administration came from those who were entirely loyal to the Union but who deplored the measures the President took to save it. They bitterly complained when Lincoln, without waiting for congressional approval, suspended the writ of habeas corpus, so that suspected subversives could be arrested without warning and imprisoned indefinitely. Though Chief Justice Roger B. Taney protested against the unconstitutionality of these arrests, Lincoln refused to heed his objections, and more than 13,000 persons were thus arbitrarily imprisoned.

Critics also complained when the Lincoln administration curbed the freedom of the press. Because of the publication of allegedly disloyal and incendiary statements, the Chicago *Times,* the New York *World,* the Philadelphia *Evening Journal,* and many other newspapers were required to suspend publication for varying periods of time.

Lincoln's Emancipation Proclamation, followed by the arming of black soldiers, gave his critics further evidence of his ambition to become dictator and of his diabolical plan to change the purpose of the war. As a popular doggerel expressed it:

> "De Union!" used to be de cry—
> For dat we went it strong;
> But now de motto seems to be,
> "De nigger, right or wrong."

The Emancipation Proclamation convinced the Newark *Evening Journal* that Lincoln "is a perjured traitor, who has betrayed his country and caused the butchery of hundreds of thousands of the people of the United States in order to accomplish either his own selfish purpose, or to put in force a fanatical, impracticable idea."

So unpopular was the policy of emancipation that Lincoln's preliminary proclamation, together with the inability of Union generals to win victories, seriously hurt his party in the congressional elections of 1862. In virtually every Northern state there was an increase in Democratic votes. New York, Pennsylvania, Ohio, Indiana, and Illinois, all of which had voted for Lincoln in 1860, went Democratic. The Republican majority in Congress was now paper-thin, and the administration kept that lead only because the army interfered in the Maryland, Kentucky, and Missouri elections. Just as Jefferson Davis's control of the Confederate Congress after 1863 depended upon the votes of border state representatives, so Abraham Lincoln's majority in the Union Congress rested upon the support of representatives from the same region.

If Democrats complained that Lincoln acted arbitrarily and too swiftly, critics within his own party held that he was too slow, too cautious, too indecisive. His attorney general, Edward Bates, who viewed the President somewhat condescendingly as "an excellent man, and, in the main wise," felt that Lincoln had the ability to cope with "neither great *principles* nor great *facts.*" He lacked "practical talent for his important place," concluded Senator Sumner, since in inertia and indecisiveness he resembled "Louis XVI more than any other ruler in history." The President's former law partner, William H. Herndon, angrily berated "Old Abe" for his shameful want of courage: "Does he suppose he can crush—squelch out this huge

LIFE MASK OF ABRAHAM LINCOLN

This life mask, which Clark Mills made in February 1865, suggests how greatly Lincoln had changed during the Civil War years. The face looks a generation older than that of the 1858 politician; its planes and shadows speak of fatigue, of sadness, and of a profound humanity. (*The National Archives.*)

rebellion by pop guns filled with rose water? He ought to hang somebody and get up a name for will or decision. . . . Let him hang some Child or woman, if he has not courage to hang a *man*."

So widespread was dissatisfaction with Lincoln that when Congress reassembled in December 1862, after the fiasco at Fredericksburg, the Senate

Republican caucus tried to force the President to change his cabinet. Just as Davis's critics made Benjamin their target, so Republican senators blamed Secretary of State Seward for the weakness of the Lincoln administration and the mismanagement of the war. By forcing Seward's resignation, they hoped to make Chase, who had fed them stories of Lincoln's incompetence, in effect premier. Deeply distressed by this maneuver, Lincoln thwarted it with great adroitness, by securing Seward's resignation and forcing Chase also to offer his. "I can ride now," he declared, remembering his days on the farm; "I've got a pumpkin in each end of my bag." Announcing that either resignation would leave his cabinet unbalanced, he declined them both. His cabinet remained intact, and the President remained responsible for Union policy.

Such sleight-of-hand was not enough to make dissent within Lincoln's own party disappear, and there gradually emerged two rival Republican factions, the Conservatives (or Moderates) and the Radicals (or "Jacobins," as their enemies called them). Represented by Seward in the cabinet and by Senator James R. Doolittle of Wisconsin in Congress, the Conservatives continued to think the war could be won by conventional means and were opposed to such experiments as emancipation, the arming of slaves, and the confiscation of rebel property. The Radicals, on the other hand, represented by Chase in the cabinet and by Sumner and Thaddeus Stevens in the Congress, were eager to try more drastic experiments; they demanded that the entire Southern social system be revolutionized, that Southern slaveholders be punished and, increasingly, that blacks have not merely freedom but civil and political equality.

Lincoln refused to align himself with either faction and tried to be even-handed in distributing federal patronage to both. He shared the desire of the Conservatives for a speedy peace and a prompt reconciliation between the sections, but he recognized that "in casting about for votes to carry through their plans," they would be "tempted to affiliate with those whose record is not clear," even with persons infected "by the virus of secession." As for the Radicals, he conceded that "after all their faces are set Zion-wards," but he objected to their "petulant and vicious fretfulness" and thought they were sometimes "almost *fiendish*" in attacking Republicans who disagreed with them. For his neutrality the President gained the distrust and abuse of both factions.

The schism within the Republican party was the more serious because the presidential election of 1864 was approaching. In General George B. McClellan the Democrats had a handsome, glorious candidate, and they had a powerful set of issues. They could capitalize upon war weariness. They made much of Lincoln's arbitrary use of executive power and the infringement of civil liberties. They objected to the unfairness of the draft. They showed how the Republican Congress had benefited the Northeast by enacting protective tariffs, handing out railroad subsidies, and creating a national banking system. Democratic Senator Thomas A. Hendricks of Indiana warned his fellow Westerners that Republicans intended them to become "the 'hewers of wood and drawers of water' for the capitalists of New England and Pennsylvania." Endlessly the Democrats rang the changes on the anti-Negro theme, charging that the Lincoln administration had changed a war for Union into a war for emancipation. If Lincoln was reelected, they claimed, Republicans were planning to amalgamate the black and white races; the word *miscegenation* made its first appearance in an 1864 campaign document.

Even in the face of such powerful opposition, the Republicans in the winter of 1863–1864 divided sharply when Lincoln, in December 1863, announced a plan for reconstructing the Southern states. Promising amnesty to all Confederates except a few high government officials, the President proposed to reestablish civilian government in the conquered areas of the South when as few as 10 percent of the number of voters in 1860 took an oath swearing future loyalty to the United States Constitution and pledging acceptance of emancipation. Fearing that this program would replace the antebellum leadership in control of the South and would leave the freedmen in peonage, the Radicals pushed through Congress the Wade-Davis bill, requiring that over half the number of 1860 voters in each Southern state swear allegiance and participate in drafting a new constitution before it would be readmitted to the Union. When Lincoln killed this measure, passed at the very end of the 1864 congressional session, by a pocket veto, Radicals were furious. Thaddeus Stevens declared his action "infamous." Senator Benjamin F. Wade and Representative Henry Winter Davis, the sponsors of the vetoed bill, issued a manifesto, accusing the President of "usurpations" and claiming that he had committed a "studied outrage upon the legislative authority of the people."

Because Lincoln had control of the federal patronage and of the party machinery, he was readily renominated in June 1864 by the Republican national convention, which selected Andrew Johnson of Tennessee as his running mate, but the unanimity of the vote was only a façade. After an unsuccessful attempt to run Chase as a rival to Lincoln, some ultra-Radicals had already thrown their support to a third-party ticket headed by General Frémont, who had been hostile to the President since his removal from command in Missouri. Other Radicals tried, even after Lincoln had been renominated, to persuade the party to pick a new candidate. As late as September 1864, a move was afoot to reconvene the Republican convention for this purpose. A questionnaire sent to Republican governors, leading editors, and prominent congressmen elicited a virtually unanimous response that, if Lincoln could be persuaded to withdraw from the race, Republicans should name another standard-bearer. Massachusetts Governor John A. Andrew expressed the general sentiment that Lincoln was "essentially lacking in the quality of leadership." So bleak was the outlook that the President himself, a few weeks before the elections, conceded that McClellan was likely to win.

⚹ IX ⚹

Until the fall of 1864, then, the wartime history of the United States and of the Confederate States moved in parallel lines as each government improvised experiments that might lead to victory. But, in the final months of the struggle, the course of the two rivals markedly diverged. Increasing dissension and disaffection marked Jefferson Davis's last winter in office, while Abraham Lincoln won triumphant reelection in November 1864. By April 1865 the Confederacy was dead, and a month later Davis was in irons, like a common criminal, at Fort Monroe. The Union was victorious, and Lincoln, killed by the bullet of the mad assassin, John Wilkes Booth, lived in memory as the nation's martyred President who freed the slaves and saved the Union.

Though historians sharply disagree in explaining why the North won the Civil War, it is clear that the very different fates of the Lincoln and Davis administrations were decided, in major part, on the battlefield. When Grant became general-in-chief of the Union armies in 1864, he determined to make his headquarters not in Washington but with the often defeated Army of the Potomac. Working closely with Meade, the actual commander of that army, he developed a plan for pushing Lee back upon the defenses of Richmond. Initially checked in the battle of the Wilderness (May 5–6), Grant did not retreat, as previous Union generals had done, but pushed around Lee's right flank, attempting to get between him and the Confederate capital. Checked again at Spotsylvania (May 8–12), Grant again did not retreat but sent word to Washington: "I propose to fight it out along this line if it takes all summer." In an unwise reversion to Jomini's tactics, he next ordered a direct assault upon Confederate lines at Cold Harbor (June 3). Union soldiers, who had learned the lessons of the war better than their commander, wrote their names on slips of paper and pinned them to their uniforms, so that their corpses could be identified; they knew they were marching to death. In the first month of the campaign, Grant's losses amounted to 60,000—approximately Lee's total strength.

Ignoring charges that he was a mere butcher, Grant again skillfully maneuvered around Lee's right flank, crossed the James River, and joined the Union troops already there under General Butler. He then instituted what became known as the "siege" of Petersburg and Richmond—incorrectly so, since the two cities were not fully invested and supplies continued to come in from the South and West. But as Grant's lines constantly lengthened, he cut these access routes one by one. Pinned down before Richmond, Lee remembered "Stonewall" Jackson's brilliant diversionary campaign of 1862 and sent what men he could spare under Jubal A. Early into the Shenandoah Valley. Though Early achieved initial success and even pushed on to the outskirts of Washington, where President Lincoln himself came briefly under Confederate fire, Grant did not loosen his grip on Richmond. Instead he sent brash, aggressive Philip H. Sheridan to

**Operations in the East
May 1864 - April 1865**

the Shenandoah Valley, ordering him not merely to drive out the Confederates but so to devastate the countryside that thereafter a crow flying over it would have to carry its own rations. Sheridan followed his orders precisely, and Early's army was smashed. More than ever before, the fate of the Confederacy was tied to Richmond and to Lee's army.

Meanwhile, on May 7, 1864, Sherman began his slow progress through northwestern Georgia, opposed by the wily Joseph E. Johnston, who made the Union troops pay for every foot they advanced. But as Sherman neared the railroad hub of Atlanta, President Davis, who had never trusted Johnston, removed the general and put John B. Hood in command. In a series of attacks upon overwhelmingly superior Union forces—just the sort of engagement Johnston had so skillfully avoided—Hood was defeated; and on September 2 Sherman occupied Atlanta. News of the victory reached the North just before the presidential election and made a farce of the Democratic platform's assertion that the war was a "failure."

Next, casually dispatching Thomas to fend off Hood and to hold Tennessee,* Sherman turned his back on the smoking ruins of Atlanta and set out on a march toward Savannah and the sea, where he knew that a Union fleet was waiting with supplies. Meeting only desultory resistance, Sherman's men cut a swath through central Georgia, destroying railroads, military supplies, and even many private houses. Sherman's objective was as much psychological as military. "I can make the march," he had promised Grant, "and make Georgia howl!"

Offering captured Savannah to Lincoln as a Christmas present, Sherman turned his army north, pushing aside the depleted Confederate forces, again under the command of Johnston. His men took Columbia, South Carolina, which was burned either by intention or by accident, and drove on into North Carolina. Grant, meanwhile, clamped down ever tighter on Richmond. At last, on April 2, 1865, Lee found his position untenable and, warning President Davis and his government to flee, tried to lead his ragged troops to join Johnston's dwindling force. Cut off by Grant, he had no alternative but surrender, and on April 9 at Appomattox Courthouse he told his weary, hungry men to lay down their arms. On April 26 Johnston followed by surrendering to Sherman, and when the news reached the trans-Mississippi region, Kirby-Smith capitulated in June. The war had lasted almost a full four years.

The Union cause, and the Lincoln administration, were the beneficiaries

---

* Attempting to force Sherman to turn back, Hood invaded Tennessee but was checked in the battle of Franklin (November 30, 1864) and routed in the battle of Nashville (December 15–16).

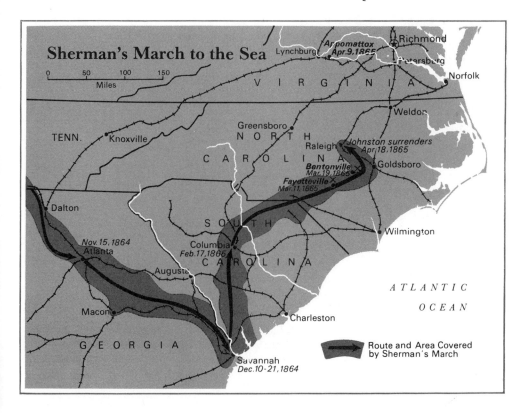

Sherman's March to the Sea

of these victories. The critics of the government had been most vocal, their opposition most powerful, in the heartbreaking summer months of 1864, when Grant seemed to be getting nowhere in Virginia and Sherman appeared unable to bag his enemy in Georgia. Northern morale and support for the President mounted perceptibly at the news of Sherman's success at Atlanta and of Farragut's victory at Mobile Bay. Conversely, support for Davis's administration dwindled, and critical voices became louder as Confederate reverse followed reverse. In a certain sense, then, victory begot victory, and defeat begot defeat.

Yet this is circular reasoning and does not explain the final Union triumph after so many earlier Confederate successes. For a fuller understanding, one must turn to the slow but steady mobilization of the North's infinitely superior economic resources and to the gradual erosion of those in the South. The effect of Northern economic and industrial superiority was not fully felt until after more than two years of war; it took time to award contracts, to expand factories, to recruit skilled laborers, and to deliver the products. By by 1863 observers noted that Lee's veterans invading Pennsylvania looked like a gaggle of "barefooted, ragged, lousy, [but] disciplined, desperate ruffians," so badly supplied and so poorly fed that their line of march was "traceable by the deposit of dysenteric stool the army leaves behind it." By 1863 the Union armies, on the other hand, were so completely equipped that their paraphernalia became a hindrance. When Northern soldiers advanced, they shucked off layers of greatcoats, blankets, and other unnecessary supplies. Nowhere was Northern economic superiority more evident by the end of the war than in its transportation system. By that time Southern railroads simply had worn out because, as the Confederate railroad coordinator, Captain F. W. Sims, reported in February 1865, "not a single bar of railroad iron has been rolled in the Confederacy since [the beginning of] the war, nor can we hope to do better during the continuance." In the Union, on the other hand, some 5000 more miles of railroad were in operation in 1865 than at the start of the war—a figure that does not include the numerous military railroads operated in the

POTOMAC RUN BRIDGE ON THE AQUIA CREEK RAILROAD

The United States military railroad rebuilt and operated Southern rail lines in order to supply advancing Union armies. This bridge was built from standing timber in nine days. It was, Lincoln jocularly remarked, "the most remarkable structure that human eyes ever rested upon . . . about 400 feet long and nearly 100 feet high, . . . and, upon my word, . . . there is nothing in it but beanpoles and cornstalks." (*Library of Congress.*)

South—and, under the necessity of linking up with the newly authorized Union Pacific Railroad, Northern lines all converted to a standard rail gauge.

But supplies do not fight wars, nor do trains; men do. From the start the overwhelming numerical preponderance of the Northern population counted heavily against the Confederacy, and during the conflict that advantage increased. During the four years of war, more than 180,000 male immigrants of military age settled in the North, while there was virtually no immigration to the Confederacy. In addition, the black population of the country became another vast source of Union manpower. Cherishing the institution of slavery and correctly fearing that armed Negroes might point their guns in the wrong direction, Confederates dared not tap this source until their cause was already lost.

But men, no matter how numerous, fight well only if ably led by their military commanders and inspired by their political leaders. It would be hard to argue that Northern generalship was superior to that of the South. While Grant has his admirers, to most students Robert E. Lee is unquestionably the greatest Civil War commander. Nor is it easy to maintain that the political leadership of the North was markedly superior. Later generations, recalling the eloquence of the Gettysburg address and the mystical beauty of the second inaugural address, have found it difficult to remember that, for most of his administration, Lincoln was considered uninspiring and ineffectual. Had Lincoln been defeated for reelection in 1864, he would doubtless be rated as an honest but unsuccessful President. On the other hand, had the Southern states been able to win their independence, Jefferson Davis would undoubtedly rank as the George Washington of the Confederacy.

There were, of course, important differences between the two wartime Presidents, but these were of less significance than the differences in the political systems in which they had to work. Like many more recent emerging nations, the Confederacy tried to present a façade of unity to the world. It was a one-party, or more properly, a no-party state; Southerners blamed the antebellum political parties for encouraging anti-Southern and antislavery sentiment, and they feared that party divisions would suggest they were less than unanimous in seeking independence. The most careful analysis of the voting records of Confederate congressmen has been able to show, at most, only incipient party lines. Senators and representatives were former Whigs or former Democrats, secessionists or opponents of secession, spokesmen for overrun districts or voices from the Southern heartland—but these divisions never coalesced, and small, temporary factions rather than permanent political parties dominated Congress. President Davis's enemies were many, and they were constantly attacking him from all directions, like a swarm of bees; his friends were divided, and he could never rally them into a unified cohort. As with the Congress, so with the people. It is safe to guess that if at any point the voters of the Confederacy had been asked to endorse their President or to topple him, Davis would have received overwhelming support. But, lacking political parties, Southerners had no way of making this sentiment felt.

In the Union, on the other hand, the two-party system remained active. Even at the outbreak of the war when Stephen A. Douglas, who died within a few months, pledged Democratic support for President Lincoln, he reserved the right to lead an opposition to measures he thought wrong. Throughout the war, the Democrats remained a formidable, if not always united, force. They came close to winning a majority in Congress in the 1862 elections. In 1864 their presidential candidate, McClellan, received 45 percent of the popular vote—at a time when the strongest opponents of the Republican party were still out of the Union and, of course, not voting.

The existence of such a powerful opposition party compelled Republicans, however bitterly at odds with each other, to work together. Moderate and Radical Republicans disagreed over slavery, emancipation, and Reconstruction, but they all agreed that their party, and not the Democrats, must control the government. In debates and in preliminary votes on critical issues, Republicans in Congress clashed sharply with each other; but in final roll calls, the need to preserve party solidarity in the face of the Democratic opposition overcame individual and factional preferences. For instance, in December 1862, a Maine representative proposed to give congressional endorsement to Lincoln's preliminary proclamation of emancipation. Though Republicans were badly divided over the propriety and constitutionality of the President's action, they felt obliged to maintain a façade of unity in the light of overwhelming Democratic opposition to this proposal. In the final vote, 76 Republican congressmen, regardless of their personal preferences, voted to endorse Lincoln's policy; only 7, mostly from the border states, opposed.

An astute politician, Lincoln knew how to use party rivalry to strengthen his administration. Every federal employee, down to the lowest grade of postmasters, was made aware that his tenure in office depended on the continued success of the Republican party. As a result, the growing governmental bureaucracy functioned as an efficient machine to harness Northern public opinion behind the administration's policies. Fearing Democratic challengers, Republican war governors looked to the Lincoln administration for encouragement, for favors, and sometimes for financial assistance, and

CONFEDERATE DEAD

Deaths in the Union armies totaled 360,222, of which about one-third were from
battle wounds. The Confederate dead numbered 278,000, of whom 94,000 were
killed or fatally wounded in battle. Such statistics do less to convey the human cost
of the Civil War than does this photograph, all that remains to bear witness
of an unnamed Southern soldier killed near Spotsylvania courthouse in May 1864.
(*Library of Congress.*)

they repaid the President by giving support—even if at times grudging
support—to his policies. Republican congressmen, especially those from
doubtful districts, knew that they had a better chance to defeat Democratic
rivals if they could ride on the coat-tails of a popular Republican presidential candidate. Consequently they swallowed their misgivings about the
administration and worked to reelect Lincoln by a landslide in 1864.

The absence of an organized opposition party in the Confederacy kept
Davis from using such means to rally behind his administration the Southern majority that sympathized with their President, even when they disagreed with some of his policies. Davis was, therefore, never able fully to
mobilize the spiritual and material resources of the Confederacy. On the
other hand, it was the existence of the often-maligned two-party system that
allowed Lincoln, despite impassioned attacks and vitriolic abuse from fellow
Republicans, to experiment boldly and to grow into the most effective wartime leader the United States has ever produced.

FREDERICK DOUGLASS

Born a slave in Maryland, Frederick Douglass escaped to freedom and became one of the most eloquent orators for abolition. During Lincoln's administration he was welcomed to the White House, and a contemporary called him "the greatest black man in the nation." Unswervingly devoted to securing equal rights for Afro-Americans, Douglass believed that the government should play essentially a negative role by not discriminating in favor of either race. (*The National Archives.*)

6

The Limits of
Innovation

"A house divided against itself cannot stand," Abraham Lincoln prophesied in 1858. The Civil War proved that the United States would stand, not as a loose confederation of sovereign states but as one nation, indivisible. Never again would there be talk of secession. The war also ended slavery, the most divisive institution in antebellum America. Weakened by the advances of the Union armies and undermined by Lincoln's Emancipation Proclamation, slavery received its death blow in February 1865, when the Congress adopted the Thirteenth Amendment outlawing slavery and involuntary servitude. Ratified by three-fourths of the states, the amendment became a part of the Constitution in December 1865.

But the Civil War did not settle the terms and conditions on which the several states, sections, races, and classes would live in the firmly united "house." Those problems formed the agenda of the Reconstruction era, one of the most complex and controversial periods in American history. During these postwar years some basic questions had to be answered: What, if any, punishment should be imposed upon Southern whites who had supported the Confederate attempt to disrupt the Union? How were the recently emancipated slaves to be guaranteed their freedom, and what civil and political rights did freedmen have? When, and with what conditions, were the Southern states so recently in rebellion to be readmitted to the Union—that is, entitled to vote in national elections, to have senators and representatives seated in the United States Congress, and, in general, to become once more full-fledged, equal members of the national body politic? In short, the Reconstruction era revolved around the old question of how, in a democratic society, majorities were to treat minorities, whether sectional or racial.

The initial answer to the question came from the President, whose powers had been greatly expanded during the war years. As has been noted in a previous chapter, President Lincoln in December 1863 announced a generous program of amnesty to repentant rebels and inaugurated a plan for reorganizing loyal governments in the South when as few as 10 percent of the voters in 1860 were willing to support them. After the assassination of Lincoln in April 1865, President Andrew Johnson, his successor, continued Reconstruction under a similar plan. Although Johnson required former Confederate leaders and Southerners with estates worth more than $20,000 to make individual applications for pardon—applications that were for the most part promptly granted—he, like Lincoln, expected Southern whites to take the lead in establishing new state governments loyal to the Union. To initiate the process he appointed a provisional governor for each of the former Confederate states (except those where Lincoln had already initiated Reconstruction) and directed them to convene constitutional conventions. These were expected to ratify the Thirteenth Amendment ending slavery, nullify or repeal the ordinances of secession, and repudiate state debts incurred for the prosecution of the war. By early 1866 each of the states that had once formed the Confederacy completed most of these required steps, and the President viewed the process of Reconstruction as concluded. He recommended that the senators and representatives chosen by these reorganized governments be promptly given their rightful seats in Congress.

From the outset this process of presidential Reconstruction had its critics. If, as has been noted, Lincoln's plan met with opposition, Johnson's program was certain to be fiercely attacked. For one reason, Congress, which had jealously watched the executive branch augment its power during the war, was ready to reassert its equality, if not its hegemony. For another, Andrew Johnson, a Tennessee Democrat and former slaveholder, had no popular mandate, as had President Lincoln, nor did the taciturn, inflexible, and pugnacious new occupant of the White House understand that politics is the art of compromise.

After an initial attempt to cooperate with the new President, Republican leaders in 1866 began to devise their own plans for Reconstruction. The first congressional plan was embodied in the Fourteenth Amendment to the Constitution, which made it clear that blacks were citizens of the United States and tried to define the rights and privileges of American citizens. When the Southern states refused to ratify this amendment, congressional Republicans moved in 1867 to a more stringent program of reorganizing the South by requiring Negro suffrage. Under this second plan of congressional Reconstruction, every Southern state (except Tennessee, which had been readmitted to the Union in 1866) received a new constitution that guaranteed to men of all races equal protection of the laws, and between 1868 and 1871 all were readmitted to the Union. Republican governments, which depended heavily upon Negro votes, controlled these states for a period ranging from a few months in Virginia to nine years in Louisiana.

☙ I ☚

Contemporaries called this the period of Radical Reconstruction or, very often, Black Reconstruction, and it is easy to understand why many Americans of the 1860s and 1870s viewed these changes as little short of revolutionary. To their Constitution, which had not been altered since 1804, were added during the five years after the Civil War, the Thirteenth Amendment ending slavery, the Fourteenth Amendment defining the rights of citizens, and the Fifteenth Amendment (1870) prohibiting discrimination in voting on account of race or color. The national government, so recently tottering on the edge of defeat, was now more powerful than in any previous point in American history. The Southern ruling class of whites, lately in charge of their own independent government, were petitioners for pardon. More than 3 million blacks, slaves only a few months earlier, were free men, entitled to the same privileges as all other citizens. Americans fairly gasped at the extent and the speed of the transformation wrought in their society, and it is hardly surprising that most subsequent historians accepted this contemporary view of the Reconstruction era as one of violent, turbulent disorder.

Without denying that real and important changes did occur during the Reconstruction period, it might help to put these into perspective by inventing a little counterfactual history, a recital of conceivable historical scenarios that were never acted out. For instance, it would be easy to imagine how the victorious North might have turned angrily upon the prostrate South. In 1865 Northerners had just finished four years of war that cost the Union army more than 360,000 casualties. To destroy the Confederacy required Americans of this and later generations to pay in taxes at least $10 billion. Northerners had reason to believe, moreover, that their Confederate opponents had prosecuted the war with fiendish barbarity. Sober Union congressmen informed their constituents that the Confederates employed "Indian savages" to scalp and mutilate the Union dead. Reliable Northern newspapers told how in April 1864 General Nathan Bedford Forrest and his Confederates overran the defenses of Fort Pillow, Tennessee, manned by a Negro regiment, and, refusing to accept surrender, deliberately beat, shot, and burned their prisoners. The influential *Harper's Weekly Magazine* carried apparently authentic drawings of a goblet that a Southerner had made from a Yankee soldier's skull, of a Northern veteran's jawbone that served as a Southerner's paperweight, of necklaces made of Yankee teeth that Southern ladies wore. When Union armies liberated Northern prisoners from such hellholes as Andersonville, Georgia, pictures of these half-starved skeletons of men, clad in grimy tatters of their Union uniforms, convinced Northerners that Jefferson Davis's policy had been "to starve and freeze and kill off by inches the prisoners he dares not butcher outright."

When the murder of Abraham Lincoln by the Southern sympathizer, John Wilkes Booth, added to this hyperemotionalism, an outraged North could easily have turned upon the conquered Confederacy in vengeance. The victorious Northerners might have executed Jefferson Davis, Alexander H. Stephens, and a score of other leading Confederates and might have sent thousands more into permanent exile. The triumphant Union might have erased the boundaries of the Southern states and divided the whole region into new, conquered territories. They might have enforced the confiscation acts already on the statute books and have seized the plantations of rebels for distribution to the freedmen. In short, the North could very easily have adopted the policy advocated by the generally cautious, middle-of-the-road senator from Ohio, John Sherman: "We should not only brand the leading rebels with infamy, but the whole rebellion should wear the badge of the penitentiary, so that for this generation at least, no man who has taken part in it would dare to justify or palliate it."

No such drastic course was followed. With the exception of Major Henry Wirtz, commandant of the infamous Andersonville prison, who was hanged, no Confederate was executed for "war crimes." A few Southern political leaders were imprisoned for their part in the "rebellion," but in most cases their release was prompt. To be sure, Jefferson Davis was kept in shackles for two years at Fort Monroe, and he was under indictment for treason until 1869, when all the charges were dropped. His case was, however, as unusual as it was extreme, and one reason for the long delay in bringing him to trial was the certainty that no jury, Northern or Southern, would render an impartial verdict. There was no general confiscation of the property of Confederates, no dividing up of plantations.

Equally conceivable is another scenario—another version of history that did not happen—this time featuring the Southern whites. For four years Confederate citizens, like their counterparts in the Union, had been subjected to a barrage of propaganda designed to prove that the enemy was little less than infernal in his purposes. Many believed the Southern editor who claimed that Lincoln's program was "Emancipation, Confiscation, Conflagration, and Extermination." According to the North Carolina educator Calvin H. Wiley, the North had "summoned to its aid every fierce and cruel and licentious passion of the human heart"; to defeat the Confederacy it was ready to use "the assassin's dagger, the midnight torch, . . . poison, famine and pestilence." Such charges were easy to credit in the many Southern families that had relatives in Northern prison camps, such as the one at Elmira, New York, where 775 of 8347 Confederate prisoners died within three months for want of proper food, water, and medicine. The behavior of Union troops in the South, especially of Sherman's "bummers" in Georgia and the Carolinas, gave Southerners every reason to fear the worst if the Confederate government failed.

It would, therefore, have been perfectly reasonable for Confederate armies in 1865, overwhelmed by Union numbers, to disband quietly, disappear into the countryside, and carry on guerrilla operations against the Northern invaders. Indeed, on the morning of the day when Lee surrendered at Appomattox, Confederate General E. P. Alexander advocated just such a plan. He argued that if Lee's soldiers took to the woods with only their rifles, perhaps two-thirds of the Army of Northern Virginia could escape capture. "We would be like rabbits and partridges in the bushes," he claimed, "and they could not scatter to follow us." The history of more recent wars of national liberation suggests that Alexander's judgment was absolutely correct. But even had his strategy not proved practicable, it would have given time for thousands of leading Southern politicians and planters, together with their families, to go safely into exile, as the Tories did during the American Revolution.

But, once again, no such events occurred. Lee firmly put down talk of guerrilla warfare and reminded his subordinates that they must henceforth think of "the country as a whole." To Virginia soldiers who pressed around him after the surrender, he gave the advice: "Go home, all you boys who fought with me, and help to build up the shattered fortunes of our old state." Following Lee's example, commanders of the other Southern armies also quietly surrendered, and Confederate soldiers promptly became civilians. Some few Confederate leaders did go into exile. For instance, General Jubal A. Early fled to Mexico and thence to Canada, where he tried to organize a Southern exodus to New Zealand; but, finding that nobody wanted to follow him, he returned to his home and his law practice in Virginia. A few hundred Confederates did migrate to Mexico and Brazil. But most followed the advice of General Wade Hampton of South Carolina, who urged his fellow Southerners to "devote their whole energies to the restoration of law and order, the reëstablishment of agriculture and commerce, the promotion of education and the rebuilding of our cities and dwellings which have been laid in ashes."

Still a third counterfactual historical scenario comes readily to mind. Southern blacks, who had been for generations oppressed in slavery, now for the first time had disciplined leaders in the thousands of Negro soldiers who had served in the Union army. They also had arms. Very easily they could have turned in revenge on their former masters. Seizing the plantations and other property of the whites, the freedmen might have made of the former Confederacy a black nation. If the whites had dared to resist, the South might have been the scene of massacres as bloody as those in Haiti at the beginning of the nineteenth century, when Toussaint L'Ouverture and Dessalines drove the French out of that island.

Many Southern whites feared, or even expected, that the Confederacy would become another Santo Domingo. For more than a year after the war, Northern reporters in the South noted "a general feeling of insecurity on the part of the whites," derived from their "vague and terrible fears of a servile insurrection." Whites were much troubled by reports that blacks were joining the Union League, an organization that had originated in the North during the war to stimulate patriotism but during the Reconstruction era became the bulwark of the Republican party in the South. The secrecy imposed by the League upon its members and its frequent nocturnal meetings alarmed whites, and they readily believed reports that the blacks were collecting arms and ammunition for a general uprising. Fearfully, Southern whites read newspaper accounts of minor racial clashes: how freedmen were engaged in vandalism and arson; how a "crew of negro soldiers, aided by some debauched country blacks," assaulted a defenseless Georgia widow; how blacks near Plantersville, South Carolina, were "indulging in the free use of wine and liquors obtained from the houses of former masters" and were "preparing themselves for the commission of crime." Indeed, whites were told, racial tension was so great that blacks "might break into open insurrection at any time."

But no such insurrection occurred. Though the freedmen unquestionably coveted the land of their former masters, they did not seize them. Indeed, black leaders consistently discouraged talk of extralegal confiscation of plantations. With the full approval of the large Negro delegation, the

South Carolina constitutional convention of 1868 announced: "The only manner by which any land can be obtained by the landless will be to purchase it." Nor did freedmen threaten the lives or the rights of whites. One of the earliest black political conventions held in Alabama urged a policy of "peace, friendship, and good will toward all men—especially toward our white fellow-citizens among whom our lot is cast." That tone was the dominant one throughout the Reconstruction period, and in many states blacks took the lead in repealing laws that disfranchised former Confederates or disqualified them from holding office.

The point of these three exercises in counterfactual history is to suggest the inadequacy of traditional accounts of the Reconstruction era as a period of revolutionary change. To those who lived through these years, change did seem to come swiftly and drastically, but in retrospect it is clear that Southern society was transformed only to a quite limited degree. The unprecedented conditions of the Reconstruction era required innovation, but the shared beliefs and institutions of the American people, North and South, black and white, restricted the amount of change that would be tolerated.

☙ II ☙

One set of ideas that sharply curbed social experimentation and political innovation during the Reconstruction period was the continuing constitutionalism of the American people. Despite all the disagreements over the Constitution during the prewar period, despite all the violations of the Constitution (both Confederate and Union) required by the exigencies of war, the national charter was still a document to be revered and followed. Tested in the trial of civil war, the Constitution continued to be the yardstick against which Americans measured the legitimacy of governmental actions during Reconstruction.

Among the most sacrosanct provisions of the Constitution were those that separated the powers of the state and national governments. Although the central government (whether in Richmond or in Washington) greatly expanded its functions during the war years, Americans still tended to think that it should perform only the specific duties enumerated in the Constitution, which granted it almost no authority to act directly upon any individual citizen. The national government could not prevent or punish crime; it had no control over public education; it could not outlaw discrimination against racial minorities; and it could not even intervene to maintain public order unless invited to do so by the state government. Thus virtually everybody agreed that if any laws regulating social and economic life were required, they must be the work of state and local, not of national, government.

Nobody, consequently, even contemplated the possibility that some federal agency might be needed to supervise the demobilization after Appomattox. Everybody simply assumed that after some 200,000 of the Union army volunteers bravely paraded down Pennsylvania Avenue on May 23–24, 1865, and received applause from President Johnson, the cabinet, the generals, and the members of the diplomatic corps, the soldiers would disband and go back to their peaceful homes. This is precisely what they did. Of the more than 1 million volunteers in the Union army on May 1, 1865, two-thirds were mustered out by August, four-fifths by November. Of the 68,000 sailors, artisans, and laborers in the Union navy at the beginning of 1865, only 12,000 remained in active service by December. To the demobilized soldiers and sailors, the United States government offered no assistance in finding jobs, in purchasing housing, or in securing further education. It paid pensions to those injured in the war and to the families of those who had been killed, but beyond that it assumed no responsibility. Nor did anybody think of asking the national government to oversee the transition from a wartime economy to an era of peace. Without notice, the various bureaus of the army and navy departments, by the end of April 1865, simply suspended requisitions and purchases, government arsenals slowed down their production, and surplus supplies were sold off.

Hardly anybody had the thought that the national government might play a role in rebuilding the war-torn South. Everybody recognized that the devastation in the South was immense and ominous. The Confederate dead totaled more than a quarter of a million. In Mississippi, for instance, one-third of the white men of military age had been killed or disabled for life. Most Southern cities were in ruins. The central section of Richmond went up in flames as the Confederate government evacuated that city; Atlanta was a scene of almost total destruction; Columbia, South Carolina, was "a wilderness of ruins," its heart "but a mass of blackened chimneys and crumbling walls." Two-thirds of the Southern railroads were totally destroyed; the rest barely creaked along on worn-out rails with broken-down engines. But none of this was thought to be the concern of the United States government.

The failure of the national government to come to the rescue was not caused by vindictiveness. To the contrary, Union officials often behaved with marked generosity toward Confederates. After the surrender at Appomattox, Grant's soldiers freely shared their rations with Lee's hungry battalions. All over the South, Federal military officials drew from the full Union army storehouses to feed the hungry. In Atlanta alone, in June 1865, some 15,000 recipients received 95,000 pounds of bread and the same amount of meat, plus salt, coffee, sugar, soap, and candles. In distributing these necessities, the Union army made no discrimination; newly freed

RUINS OF THE GALLEGO FLOUR MILLS IN RICHMOND, 1865

When Lee was forced to abandon Richmond and the Confederate government fled, Southern officers began burning supplies that might fall into enemy hands. The destruction got out of control and, after two explosions, flames swept through the business district. When Northern soldiers arrived, they witnessed a scene of ruin and desolation. (*Library of Congress.*)

slaves stood in line with former Confederate soldiers, all with bags to be filled. But beyond these attempts to avert starvation the Federal government did not go, and very few thought that it should. Not until the twentieth century did the United States make it a policy to pour vast sums of money into the rehabilitation of enemies it had defeated in war.

Rebuilding had, therefore, to be the work of the Southern state and local authorities, and this task imposed a heavy tax on their meager resources. In Mississippi, one-fifth of the entire state revenue in 1866 was needed to provide artificial limbs for soldiers maimed in the war. For the larger tasks of physical restoration, the resources of the South were obviously inadequate. Borrowing a leaf from antebellum experience, Southern governments did the only thing they knew how to do—namely, they lent the credit of the state to back up the bonds of private companies that promised to rebuild railroads and other necessary facilities. Since these companies were underfinanced and since the credit of the Southern state governments after Appomattox was, to say the least, questionable, these bonds had to be sold at disadvantageous prices and at exorbitant rates of interest. In later years, when many of these companies defaulted on their obligations and Southern state governments had to make good on their guarantees, these expenditures would be condemned as excessive and extravagant, and Democrats put the blame on the Republican regimes established in the South after 1868. In fact, however, the need for physical restoration immediately after the war was so obvious and so pressing that nearly every government, whether controlled by Democrats or Republicans, underwrote corporations that promised to rebuild the region.

Even in dealing with the freedmen—the some 3 million slaves emancipated as a result of the war—the United States government tried to pursue a hands-off policy. Few influential leaders, either in the North or in the South, thought that it was the function of the national government to supervise the blacks' transition from slavery to freedom. Politicians did not foresee that freedmen would require guidance, counseling, and, most of all, education in order to become free and equal citizens. Even abolitionists, genuinely devoted to the welfare of blacks, were so accustomed to thinking of the Negro as "God's image in ebony"—in other words, a white man in a black skin—that they had no plans for assisting him after emancipation. In 1865 William Lloyd Garrison urged the American Anti-Slavery Society to disband, since it had fulfilled its function, and he suspended the publication of *The Liberator.* Sharing the same point of view, the American Freedmen's Inquiry Commission, set up by the Union war department in 1863, unanimously opposed further governmental actions to protect the blacks. "The negro does best when let alone," argued one member of the commission, Samuel Gridley Howe, noted alike for his work with the deaf, dumb, and blind and for his hostility to slavery; "we must beware of all attempts to prolong his servitude, under pretext of taking care of him. The white man has tried taking care of the negro, by slavery, by apprenticeship, by colonization, and has failed disastrously in all; now let the negro try to take care of himself."

But the problem of the care of the freedmen could not be dismissed so easily. Wherever Union armies advanced into the South, they were "greeted by an irruption of negroes of all ages, complexions and sizes, men, women, boys and girls . . . waving hats and bonnets with the most ludicrous caperings and ejaculations of joy." "The poor delighted creatures thronged upon us," a Yankee soldier reported, and they insisted: "We'se gwin wid you all." "What shall be done with them?" commanders in the field plaintively wired Washington.

The administration in Washington had no comprehensive answer. Initially it looked to private philanthropic organizations to rush food, clothing, and medicine to the thousands of blacks that thronged in unsanitary camps around the headquarters of each Union army. The New England Freedmen's Aid Society, the American Missionary Association, and the Philadelphia Society of Friends promptly responded, but it was soon clear that the problem was too great for private charity.

Slowly, and without much guidance from Washington, Union commanders in the field began to improvise plans to assist the blacks clustered about their camps. In Louisiana, General N. P. Banks told freedmen that they had to support themselves, either by working on the levees or at other public employment or by returning to labor on the plantations, "where," Banks said, "they belong." Farther north, Grant named Chaplain John Eaton general superintendent of all freedmen in his military department, which consisted mostly of Mississippi and Tennessee, and directed him to supervise the freedmen's camps, to provide for their education and health, and to set them to work picking cotton on abandoned plantations.

As such piecemeal and often inconsistent programs for dealing with the freedmen got underway, sentiment grew in the North for the creation of a general "Emancipation Bureau" in the federal government—only to conflict directly with the even stronger belief that the national government had limited powers. Out of this conflict emerged the Freedmen's Bureau Act of March 3, 1865. Congress established, under the jurisdiction of the war department, a Bureau of Refugees, Freedmen, and Abandoned Lands and

CONTRABANDS COMING INTO CAMP

Everywhere slaves fled to the advancing Union armies and to freedom. Alfred R. Waud's sketch captures one group of "contrabands"—as the runaways were called—who came into the Union camp after learning of the Emancipation Proclamation. "I ran away," declared one woman, " 'cause master too bad; couldn't stay no longer." (*Library of Congress.*)

entrusted to the new agency, for one year after the end of the war, "control of all subjects relating to refugees and freedmen." To head the new organization, Lincoln named Oliver O. Howard, a Union general less conspicuous for military skill than for devotion to Christianity and for paternalistic views toward blacks.

At first glance, the Freedmen's Bureau seems to have been a notable exception to the rule that the national government should take only a minor, passive role in the restoration of the South. Howard had a vision of a compassionate network of "teachers, ministers, farmers, superintendents" working together to aid and elevate the freedmen, and, under his enthusiastic impetus, the bureau appointed agents in each of the former Confederate states. The most urgent task of the bureau was issuing food and clothing, mostly from surplus army stores, to destitute freedmen and other Southern refugees. During the twelve months beginning September 1, 1865, the bureau issued nearly 30,000 rations a day and unquestionably prevented mass starvation in the South. The bureau also took the initiative in getting work for freedmen. Fearful, on the one hand, that Southern planters would attempt to overwork and underpay the freedmen, and troubled, on the other, by the widespread belief that blacks, once emancipated, were not willing to work, the bureau agents brought laborers and landlords together and insisted that workers sign labor contracts.

No part of the bureau's work was more successful than its efforts in the field of education. The slow work of educating the illiterate Southern blacks had already begun under the auspices of army chaplains and Northern benevolent societies, and Howard's bureau cooperated with these agencies, providing housing for black schools, paying teachers, and helping to establish normal schools and colleges for the training of black teachers. All these educational efforts received an enthusiastic welcome from the freedmen. During the day, classrooms were thronged with black children learning the rudiments of language and arithmetic; in the evenings they were filled with adults who were "fighting with their letters," learning to read so that they would not be "made ashamed" by their children. "The progress of the scholars is in all cases creditable and in some remarkable," reported one of the teachers. "How richly God has endowed them, and how beautifully their natures would have expanded under a tender and gentle culture."

Even more innovative was the work of the bureau in allocating lands to the freedmen. During the war, many plantations in the path of Union armies had been deserted by their owners, and army commanders like Grant arranged to have these tilled by the blacks who flocked to his camp. The largest tract of such abandoned land was in the Sea Islands of South

NOON AT THE PRIMARY SCHOOL FOR FREEDMEN, VICKSBURG, MISSISSIPPI

One of the principal efforts of the Freedmen's Bureau was to help establish schools for the former slaves. Ultimately nearly 10,000 teachers worked in these schools. The freedmen exhibited what one observer called a "greed for letters." (*Harper's Weekly, June 23, 1866.*)

Carolina, which were overrun by Federal troops in the fall of 1861. Though speculators bought up large amounts of this land during the war, sizable numbers of black residents were able to secure small holdings. When General W. T. Sherman marched through South Carolina, he ordered that the Sea Islands and the abandoned plantations along the river banks for thirty miles from the coast be reserved for Negro settlement and directed that black settlers be given "possessory titles" to tracts of this land not larger than forty acres. The act creating the Freedmen's Bureau clearly contemplated the continuation of these policies, for it authorized the new bureau to lease confiscated lands in tracts no larger than forty acres to freedmen and to "loyal refugees." The bureau could also sell the land to these tenants and give them "such title thereto as the United States can convey."

But if the Freedmen's Bureau was an exception to the policy of limited federal involvement in the reconstruction process, it was at best a partial exception. Though the agency did invaluable work, it was a feeble protector of the freedmen. Authorized to recruit only a minimal staff, Howard was obliged to rely heavily upon Union army officers stationed in the

South—at just the time when the Union army was being demobilized. Consequently the bureau never had enough manpower to look after the rights of some 3 million freedmen; toward the end of its first year of operation, it employed only 799 men, 424 of whom were soldiers on temporary, assigned duty. Important as was the work of the bureau in Negro education, its chief function was to stimulate private philanthropy in this field. In providing land for the freedmen, the bureau was handicapped because it controlled only about 800,000 acres of arable land in the entire South, enough at best for perhaps one black family in forty. Moreover, its efforts to distribute lands to the Negroes were repeatedly undercut both by the Congress and the President. The very wording of the act creating the bureau suggested congressional uncertainty as to who actually owned deserted and confiscated lands in the South; General Sherman announced that the "possessory titles" he had issued were valid only so long as the war lasted; and President Johnson issued pardons to Southerners that explicitly included the "restoration of all rights of property." In October 1865, the President directed Howard to go in person to the Sea Islands to notify blacks there that they did not hold legal title to the land and to advise them "to make the best terms they could" with the white owners. When blacks bitterly resisted what they considered the bureau's betrayal, Union soldiers descended upon the islands and forced blacks who would not sign labor contracts with the restored white owners to leave. Elsewhere in the South, the record of the bureau was equally dismal.

In short, belief in the limited role to be played by the national government affected the rehabilitation of the freedmen, just as it did the physical restoration of the South and the demobilization in the North. In all these matters, as Americans read the Constitution, the United States government was supposed to play the smallest possible part, and its minimal activities were to be of the briefest duration.

It is certain that most whites in the North and in the South fully approved these stringent limitations on the activities of the national government. What the masses of freedmen thought is harder to determine. On the one hand stands the protest of Sea Island blacks when they learned they were about to be dispossessed: "Why, General Howard, why do you take away our lands? You take them from us who have always been true, always true to the Government! You give them to our all-time enemies! That is not right!" On the other is Frederick Douglass's reply to the question, "What shall we do with the Negroes?" The greatest black spokesman of the era answered: "Do nothing with them; mind your business, and let them mind theirs. Your *doing* with them is their greatest misfortune.

They have been undone by your doings, and all they now ask and really have need of at your hands, is just to let them alone."

ᨆ III ᨇ

Along with the idea of limited government went the doctrine of laissez-faire ("let things alone"), which sharply limited what the government could do to solve economic problems that arose after the Civil War. Except for a handful of Radical Republicans, such as Charles Sumner and Thaddeus Stevens, most congressmen, like most academic economists, adhered to an American version of laissez-faire. As has been noted in an earlier chapter, objections to governmental intervention in the economy during the antebellum era had been largely pragmatic. But after the war, practice hardened into dogma. Now government inspection, regulation, or control of business was thought to violate the inexorable laws of economics. "You need not think it necessary to have Washington exercise a political providence over the country," William Graham Sumner, the brilliant professor of political and social science, told his students at Yale. "God has done that a great deal better by the laws of political economy."

In the Reconstruction years, as in the antebellum era, no violation of economic laws was deemed more heinous than interference with the right of private property—the right of an individual or group to purchase, own, use, and dispose of property without any interference from governmental authorities. Since Americans' attachment to property was so deeply rooted in the national character, there was never a chance that congressmen would support Thaddeus Stevens's radical program to confiscate all Southern farms larger than 200 acres and to divide the seized land into forty-acre tracts among the freedmen. "No man in America," announced the *Nation,* a journal that spoke for educated Republicans, "has any right to anything which he has not honestly earned, or which the lawful owner has not thought proper to give him." Stevens's plan could lead only to socialism, or worse. "An attempt to justify the confiscation of Southern land under the pretense of doing justice to the freedmen," declared the New York *Times,* "strikes at the root of all property rights in both sections. It concerns Massachusetts quite as much as Mississippi."

Informed opinion in the North held that the best program of Reconstruction was to allow the laws of economics to rule in the South with the least possible interference by the government. Behind this theory lay the judgment, which Republicans had accepted long before the Civil War, that slavery had blighted the South. The war served as drastic surgery to remove the cancer of slavery. Now it was reasonable to expect that, though there might be some soreness and subsequent healing, Southerners, white and black, should, without further governmental meddling, set about making money and acquiring property just like the free men in the Northern and Western states.*

Obsessed by laissez-faire, Northern theorists left out of their calculations the physical devastation wrought in the South by the war, and they did not recognize how feeble were the section's resources to rebuild its economy. Even excluding the loss of property in slaves, the total value of assessed property in the Southern states shrank by 43 percent between 1860 and 1865.

Northern pundits also failed to take into account the psychological dimensions of economic readjustment in the South. For generations, Southern whites had persuaded themselves that slavery was the natural condition of the black race, and they truly believed that their slaves were devoted to them. But as Union armies approached and slaves defected, they were compelled to recognize that they had been living in a world of misconceptions and deceits. They grew bitter toward the blacks, particularly toward the house servants who were usually among the first to flee the plantations. "My life long," complained the mistress of three coastal plantations in Georgia, "I have been laboring and caring for them, and . . . expended everything I had upon their support, directly or indirectly; and this is their return." She was, she announced, "thoroughly disgusted with the whole race."

So shattering was the idea that slaves were free that many Southern whites simply refused to accept it. Even after the Confederate surrender, some owners refused to inform their slaves of their new status. Others did so grudgingly. When Union army officers required a South Carolina matron to tell her servants of the Emancipation Proclamation, she did it but refused to release them, saying that "it was not at all certain that they would be freed." As late as July 1865, according to officials of the Freedmen's Bureau, planters in Mississippi were resorting to "whipping and the most severe modes of punishment . . . to compel the Freedmen to remain at the old plantations and the negro [was] kept in ignorance of his real condition." A few planters angrily announced they were so disillusioned that they would never again have anything to do with blacks, and they sought, vainly, to persuade European immigrants and Chinese coolies to work their fields.

---

* Discussion of economic changes and problems in the North is reserved for the following chapter.

Even those whites who overtly accepted the reality of emancipation betrayed the fact that, on a deeper emotional level, they still could only think of blacks as performing forced labor. "The general interest both of the white man and of the negroes requires that he should be kept as near to the condition of slavery as possible, and as far from the condition of the white man as is practicable," explained Edmund Rhett of South Carolina. "Negroes must be made to work, or else cotton and rice must cease to be raised for export." The contracts that planters in 1865, under pressure from the Freedmen's Bureau, entered into with their former slaves were further indications of the same attitude. In some of these contracts, according to an irate bureau agent, "the negro promises to work for an indefinite time for nothing but his board and clothes, and the white man agrees to do nothing." Even the more generous of these contracts provided that blacks were "not to leave the premises during work hours without the consent of the Proprietor," that they would conduct "themselves faithfully, honestly and civilly," and that they would behave with "perfect obedience" toward the land owner.

Blacks, too, had difficulties in adjusting to their new status that were never anticipated by the devotees of laissez-faire. *Freedom*—that word so often whispered in the slave quarters—went to the heads of some blacks. A few took the coming of "Jubilo," with the promise to put the bottom rail on top, quite literally. At Brokenburn plantation in northeastern Louisiana, Webster, the family coachman and diningroom attendant who was considered a most trusted servant, suddenly announced that he owned the plantation. More typical was the reaction of a Charleston black woman when her former owner, now her employer, told her to scour some pots: "You betta do it yourself. Ain't you smarter an me? You think you is— Wy you no scour fo you-self."

Many blacks had an initial impulse to test their freedom, to make sure it was real. As Patience Johnson, a former slave in the Laurens District of South Carolina explained when her mistress asked her to continue working for wages: "No, Miss, I must go, if I stay here I'll never know I am free." During the first months after the war there was, then, much movement among Southern blacks. "They are just like a swarm of bees," one observer noted, "all buzzing about and not knowing where to settle."

Much of this black mobility was, however, purposeful. Thousands of former slaves flocked to Southern towns and cities where the Freedmen's Bureau was issuing rations, for they knew that food was unavailable on the plantations. Many blacks set out to find husbands, wives, or children, from whom they had been forcibly separated during the slave days. A good many freedmen joined the general movement of Southern population away from

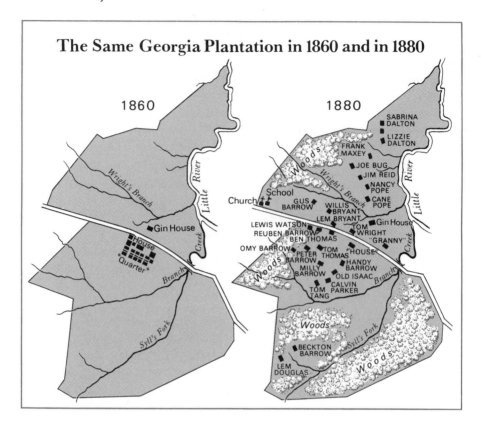

the seaboard states, devastated by war, and migrated to the Southwestern frontier in Texas. Most blacks, however, did not move so far but remained in the immediate vicinity of the plantations where they had labored as slaves.

The reluctance of freedmen in 1865 to enter into labor contracts, either with their former masters or with other white landowners, was also generally misunderstood. Most blacks wanted to work—but they wanted to work on their own land. "We all know that the colored people want land," declared a member of the South Carolina constitutional convention. "Night and day they think and dream of it. It is their all in all." Freedmen knew that the United States government had divided up some abandoned plantations among former slaves, and many believed that on January 1, 1866—the anniversary of their freedom under Lincoln's Emancipation Proclamation —all would receive forty acres and a mule. With this prospect of having their own farms, they were unwilling to sign contracts to work on somebody else's plantation.

Even when the hope of free land disappeared, freedmen were averse to signing labor contracts because, as has been noted, so many white landowners expected to continue to treat them like slaves. Especially repugnant was the idea of being again herded together in the plantation slave quarters, with their communal facilities for cooking and washing and infant care, and their lack of privacy. Emancipation did much to strengthen the black family. Families divided by slave sales could now be reunited. Marital arrangements between blacks, which had had no legal validity during slavery, could be regularized. Freedmen's Bureau officials performed thousands of marriage ceremonies, and some states passed general ordinances declaring that blacks who had been living together were legally man and wife and that their children were legitimate. This precious new security of family life was not something blacks were willing to jeopardize by returning to slave quarters. Before contracting to work on the plantations, they insisted on having separate cabins, scattered across the farm, each usually having its own patch for vegetables and perhaps a pen for hogs or a cow.

When these conditions were met, freedmen in the early months of 1866 entered into labor contracts, most of which followed the same general pattern. Sometimes these arrangements called for the payment of wages, but landowners were desperately short of cash and freedmen felt that a wage system gave planters too much control over their labor. The most common

PLANTING SWEET POTATOES ON JAMES HOPKINSON'S PLANTATION

After the Civil War most freedmen continued to be agricultural workers, usually on or near the plantations where they had always lived. As this South Carolina photograph indicates, they worked, as under slavery, with awkward and inefficient implements. (*Courtesy of The New-York Historical Society, New York City.*)

system was sharecropping. Though there were many regional and individual variations, the contracts usually called for the dividing of the crop into three equal shares. One of these went to the landowner; another went to the laborer—usually black, though there were also many white sharecroppers in the South; and the third went to whichever party provided the seeds, fertilizer, mules, and other farming equipment. For the planter this system had several advantages. At a time when money was scarce, he was not obliged to pay out cash to his laborers until the crop was harvested. He retained general supervision over what was planted and how the crop was cultivated, and he felt he was more likely to secure a good harvest because the freedmen themselves stood to gain by a large yield. Blacks, too, found the sharecropping system suited to their needs. They had control over how their crops were planted and when they were cultivated and harvested. They could earn more money by working harder in the fields. And, best of all, they could live in individual family units scattered over the plantation, each cabin having some privacy.

To some observers, the disappearance of the slave quarters and the resettling of families in individual, scattered cabins seemed to mark a revolution in the character of Southern agriculture. According to the United States census, the number of Southern landholdings doubled between 1860 and 1880 and their average size dropped from 365 acres to 157 acres. To the Southern poet Sidney Lanier, this "quiet rise of the small farmer" seemed "the notable circumstance of the period, in comparison with which noisier events signify nothing." In Lanier's view, "Small farming means . . . meat and bread for which there are no notes in [the] bank; pigs fed with homemade corn . . . yarn spun, stockings knit, butter made and sold (instead of bought); eggs, chickens . . . products of natural animal growth, and grass at nothing a ton." In fact, both Lanier's vision and the census figures were misleading, because the census takers failed to ask farmers whether they owned their land or were sharecroppers. An examination of tax records, which show land ownership, in the representative state of Louisiana helps correct the distortion of the census. Between 1860 and 1880 in Louisiana, the number of independently owned farms of less than 100 acres actually dropped by 14 percent, while during the same period the number of plantations increased by 287 percent. By 1900 plantations of 100 acres or more encompassed half the cultivated land in the state, and more than half of all the farmers were not proprietors.

If the postwar period did not see the breakup of large plantations, it did bring some significant changes in ownership and control of the land. Hard hit by debt, by rising taxes, and by increasing labor costs, many Southern planters had to sell their holdings, and there was an infusion of Northern capital into the region after the war. More tried to cling to their acres by going heavily into debt. Since the banking system of the postwar South was inadequate, the principal source of credit was the local merchant, who could supply both the landowner and his sharecroppers with clothing, shoes, some food, and other necessities to tide them over the lean months between the planting of the tobacco or cotton crop and its harvest. On each sale the merchant charged interest, to be paid when the crop was sold, and he also charged prices ranging from 40 percent to 110 percent higher for all goods sold on credit. It is hardly surprising that those planters who could afford to do so set up their own stores and extended credit to their own sharecroppers, and quite soon they discovered they were making more profits on their mercantile enterprises than from farming. Planters who could not make such arrangements frequently had to sell their lands to the neighborhood merchant. It is not accidental that in William Faulkner's fictional saga of Southern history, the power of planter families like the Compsons and the Sutpens diminished during the postwar years, while the Snopes family of storekeepers, hard-trading, penny-pinching, and utterly unscrupulous, emerged prosperous and successful.

It would, however, be a mistake to accept the novelist's hostile characterization of the Southern merchant without reservation. If the storekeeper insisted on a crop-lien system, which required the farmer legally to pledge that the proceeds from his crop must go first to pay off his obligation to the merchant, it was because he was aware that, as in both 1866 and 1867, crops throughout the South could fail. And if the merchant urged farmers to forget about soil conservation, diversification, and experimentation with new crops, it was because he knew that the only way to pay his own debts was to demand that his debtors raise cotton and tobacco, for which there was a ready cash market.

Thus merchants, landowners, and sharecroppers, thus white Southerners and black Southerners, became locked into an economic system that, at best, promised them little more than survival. At worst it offered bankruptcy, sale of lands, and hurried nocturnal migrations in an attempt to escape from a set of debts in one state but with little more than the hope of starting a new set in another.

By the 1880s, then, the South had become what it remained for the next half-century, the economic backwater of the nation. In 1880 the per capita wealth of the South was $376; that in the states outside the South, $1,086. Yet it was this impoverished region that had to deal with some of the most difficult political and racial problems that ever have confronted Americans. In attacking these problems, Southerners, black and white, could expect no assistance from the government, since such intervention would violate the immutable laws of laissez-faire economics. Even the most humane national leaders could discover no way to help this backward region. They could only agree with Whitelaw Reid, editor of the influential New York *Tribune,* who concluded after his tour of the South in 1879 that "manifestly something is wrong," and gave as his diagnosis: "Economic laws are violated in some way."

❧ IV ❦

Of the institutions that checked radical change during Reconstruction, none were more influential than the national political parties. The return of the South to the Union meant the end of purely sectional politics. In order to gain control of the national government, both the Republicans and the Democrats—like the Whigs and the Democrats in the Jacksonian era—had to seek national constituencies. Both parties became conglomerates of disparate and often competing sectional and class interests, and party policy had to be arrived at through compromise and concession. In that process, extreme and drastic measures were nearly always screened out.

Nationally the Democratic party during the postwar years was torn by two conflicting interests. On the one hand, Democrats sought the immediate readmission of the Southern states under the governments President Johnson had set up. Controlled by whites hostile to the Republican party, these states would surely send Democrats to Congress and support Democratic candidates in a national election. Even during the 1850s the South had increasingly become a one-party region; now the goal of a solidly Democratic South appeared within reach. On the other hand, too enthusiastic advocacy of the Southern cause could hurt Democrats in the North by reviving talk of disloyalty and the Copperhead movement during the war. Throughout the Reconstruction era, Democrats remained vulnerable to charges like those brought by Governor O. P. Morton of Indiana during the 1868 campaign: "Every unregenerate rebel . . . every deserter, every sneak who ran away from the draft calls himself a Democrat. . . . Every man who labored for the rebellion . . . , who murdered Union prisoners by cruelty and starvation . . . calls himself a Democrat. . . . In short, the Democratic party may be described as a common sewer and loathsome receptacle, into which is emptied every element of treason North and South, every element of inhumanity and barbarism which has dishonored the age." To minimize the effectiveness of such attacks, Northern Democrats had no choice but to mute their defense of the South and to urge restraint on their colleagues in the former Confederacy.

Among Republicans, similar constraints operated to dampen any ideas of taking vengeance on the South or of encouraging blacks to seize control of that region. From its inception the Republican party had been an uneasy admixture of antislavery men, former Whigs, disgruntled Democrats, and Know-Nothings, united mainly by opposition to further expansion of slavery. How tenuous were the ties that bound these groups together became evident in the factional disputes that racked Lincoln's administration, and for the party it was a bad omen that the sharpest area of disagreement between Radical and Conservative Republicans concerned Lincoln's plan to reorganize the Southern states.

During the first year after Lincoln's death, quarrels between the Radicals and the Conservatives were somewhat muted because most Republicans could join in opposing President Johnson's program of Reconstruction. Followed only by Secretary of State Seward, Navy Secretary Gideon Welles, and a handful of other very cautious Republicans, Johnson began to work closely with the Democrats of the North and South. He announced that the Southern states had never been out of the Union. "Their life-breath has only been suspended," the President maintained, and after the Confederate surrender at Appomattox it had been his duty to administer the necessary artificial respiration. Once resuscitated, the Southern states, under the provisional governments he set up, were ready to assume their equal places in the Union, and he insisted that Congress seat their duly elected senators and representatives.

It is easy to understand why both Radical and Conservative Republicans rejected the President's argument. Regardless of faction, they were outraged when the Southern elections in 1865, held at the direction of the President, resulted in the choice of a Confederate brigadier-general as governor of Mississippi, and they were furious when the new Georgia legislature named Alexander H. Stephens, the Vice-President of the Confederacy, to represent that state in the United States Senate.

What made these newly elected Southern officials more threatening to Republicans was the fact that (though many had been Whigs before the war) they clearly contemplated allying themselves with the Democratic party. However much Republicans disagreed among themselves, they all agreed that their party had saved the Union. They believed, with Thaddeus Stevens, "that upon the continued ascendency of that party depends the safety of this great nation." Now that ascendency was threatened, for, ironically, when the Southern states were readmitted to the Union they would receive increased representation in Congress. Before the ratification of the Thirteenth Amendment, only three-fifths of the slave population of the South had been counted in apportioning membership in the House of Representatives; but now that the blacks were free men, all would be counted. In short, the Southern states, after having been defeated in the

THADDEUS STEVENS

Sardonic and grim, the Radical Thaddeus Stevens was recognized as one of the ablest men in Congress. "He was sturdy, well built, with dark-blue and dull-looking eyes, overhanging brow, thin, stern lips, and a smooth-shaven face," a reporter noted, "and he wore a dark-brown wig." (*Library of Congress.*)

most costly war in the nation's history, would have about fifteen more representatives in Congress than they had had before the war. And under the President's plan, all of the Southern congressmen unquestionably would be Democrats.

Equally troubling to Republicans of all factions was the fear of what white Southerners, once restored to authority, would do to the freedmen. The laws that the Southern provisional legislatures adopted during the winter of 1865–1866 gave reason for anxiety on this score. Not one of these governments considered treating black citizens just as they treated white citizens. Instead, the legislatures adopted special laws, known as the Black Codes, to regulate the conduct of freedmen. On the positive side, these laws recognized the right of freedmen to make civil contracts, to sue and be sued, and to acquire and hold most kinds of property. But with these rights went restrictions. The laws varied from state to state, but in general they specified that blacks might not purchase or carry firearms, that they might not assemble after sunset, and that those who were idle or unemployed should "be liable to imprisonment, and to hard labor, one or both, . . . not exceeding twelve months." The Mississippi code prohibited blacks from renting or leasing "any lands or tenements except in incorporated cities or towns." That of South Carolina forbade blacks from practicing "the art, trade or business of an artisan, mechanic or shopkeeper, or any other trade, employment or business (besides that of husbandry, or that of a servant)." So clearly did these measures seem designed to keep the freedmen in quasi-slavery that the Chicago *Tribune* spoke for a united, outraged Republican party in denouncing the first of these Black Codes, that adopted by the Mississippi legislature: "We tell the white men of Mississippi that the men of the North will convert the state of Mississippi into a frog-pond before they will allow any such laws to disgrace one foot of soil over which the flag of freedom waves."

Unwilling, for all these reasons, to recognize the regimes Johnson had set up in the South, all Republicans easily rallied in December 1865, when Congress reassembled, to block the seating of their senators and representatives. All agreed to the creation of a special Joint Committee on Reconstruction to handle questions concerning the readmission of the Southern states and their further reorganization. In setting up this committee, congressional Republicans carefully balanced its membership with Radicals and Moderates. If its most conspicuous member was the Radical Stevens, its powerful chairman was Senator William Pitt Fessenden, a Moderate.

Congressional Republicans found it easier to unite in opposing Johnson's plan of Reconstruction than to unite in devising one of their own. Nevertheless, they recognized the necessity of remaining undivided. If all Republicans voted together, they could not only pass legislation but could enact it over President Johnson's anticipated vetoes. But if they divided, the President's negatives would be sustained. In that event the Republican party would be a laughingstock in the next election, for Democrats could show how, even with its huge majorities in both houses of Congress, it had been unable to agree upon any Reconstruction program.

Throughout the winter of 1865–1866, the joint committee met to consider various plans for reorganizing the South. With its evenly balanced membership, the committee dismissed, on the one side, the President's theory that the Southern states were, in reality, already reconstructed and back in the Union. On the other side, it discarded the theory of Thaddeus Stevens that the Confederacy was conquered territory over which Congress could rule at its own discretion, and it rejected Charles Sumner's more elaborate argument that the Southern state governments had committed suicide when they seceded, so that their land and inhabitants now fell "under the exclusive jurisdiction of Congress." More acceptable to the majority of Republicans was the "grasp of war" theory advanced by Richard Henry Dana, Jr., the noted Massachusetts constitutional lawyer, who was also the author

"OH! PONDER WELL, BE NOT SEVERE"

President Andrew Johnson, here depicted as a schoolmaster who understands the ways of errant students, instructs the "janitor," Thaddeus Stevens, and his barking Radical dog to re-admit the Southern states to the Union. (*American Antiquarian Society.*)

of *Two Years before the Mast*. Dana argued that the Federal government held the defeated Confederacy in the grasp of war for a brief and limited time, during which it must act swiftly to revive state governments in this region and to restore promptly the constitutional balance between national and state authority. Dana's theory was an essentially conservative one, in that it called for only a short period of federal hegemony and looked toward the speedy restoration of the Southern states on terms of absolute equality with the loyal states.

Finding in Dana's theory a constitutional source of power, the joint committee after much travail produced the first comprehensive congressional plan of Reconstruction in a proposed Fourteenth Amendment to the Constitution, which was endorsed by Congress in June 1866 and submitted to the states for ratification. Some parts of the amendment were noncontroversial. All Republicans recognized the need authoritatively to overturn the Supreme Court decision in the Dred Scott case, which had declared that Negroes were not citizens of the United States, and consequently accepted the opening statement of the amendment: "All persons born or naturalized in the United States, and subject to the jurisdiction thereof, are citizens of the United States and the State wherein they reside." There was also no disagreement about the provision declaring the Confederate debt invalid.

All the other provisions, however, represented a compromise between Radical and Moderate Republicans. For instance, Radicals wanted to keep all Southerners who had voluntarily supported the Confederacy from voting until 1870, and the arch-Radical Stevens urged: "Not only to 1870 but 18070, every rebel who shed the blood of loyal men should be prevented from exercising any power in this Government." Moderates favored a speedy restoration of all political rights to former Confederates. As a compromise, the Fourteenth Amendment included a provision to exclude high-ranking Confederates from office but one that did not deny them the vote.

Similarly, the Fourteenth Amendment's provisions to protect the freedmen represented a compromise. Radicals like Sumner (who was considered too radical to be given a seat on the joint committee) wanted an unequivocal declaration of the right and duty of the national government to protect the civil liberties of the former slaves. But Moderates drew back in alarm from entrusting additional authority to Washington. The joint committee came up with a provision that granted no power to the national government but restricted that of the states: "No State shall make or enforce any law which shall abridge the privileges and immunities of citizens of the United States; nor shall any State deprive any person of life, liberty, or property, without due process of law; nor deny to any person within its jurisdiction the equal protection of the laws."

Finally, another compromise between Radicals and Moderates resulted in the provision of the amendment concerning voting. Though Sumner and other Radicals called Negro suffrage "the essence, the great essential," of a proper Reconstruction policy, Moderates refused to give to the national government the power to interfere with state requirements for suffrage. The joint committee thereupon devised a complex and, as it proved, unworkable plan to persuade the Southern states voluntarily to enfranchise blacks, under threat of having reduced representation in Congress if they refused.

The efficacy of the Fourteenth Amendment as a program of Reconstruction was never tested because of the deterioration of relations between Congress and the President. While the joint committee was deliberating, Johnson further alienated the Republicans, who were already distrustful of his policy. Recognizing that a constitutional amendment would take time for ratification, congressional leaders early in 1866 tried to pass interim legislation to protect the freedmen. One bill extended the life and expanded the functions of the Freedmen's Bureau, and a second guaranteed minimal civil rights to all citizens. Contrary to expectations, Johnson vetoed both these measures. Incorrectly terming these bills the work of Radical Republicans who wanted "to destroy our institutions and change the character of the Government," the President publicly announced that he intended to fight these enemies of the Union just as he had once fought secessionists and traitors in the South. Congress sustained Johnson's veto of the Freedmen's Bureau bill (a later, less sweeping measure extended the life of that agency for two years), but it passed the Civil Rights Act over his disapproval.

From this point, open warfare existed between the President and the majority of the Republican party that had elected him Vice-President in 1864. During the summer of 1866, Johnson and his friends tried to create a new political party, which would rally behind the President's policies Conservative Republicans, Northern Democrats, and Southern whites. With the President's hearty approval, a National Union Convention held in Philadelphia in August stressed the theme of harmony among the sections. The entry into the convention hall of delegates from Massachusetts and South Carolina, arm in arm, seemed to symbolize the end of sectional strife. The President himself went on a "swing around the circle" of leading Northern cities, ostensibly on his way to dedicate a monument to the memory of another Democrat, Stephen A. Douglas. In his frequent public speeches, he defended the constitutionality of his own Reconstruction program and berated the Congress, and particularly the Radical Republicans, for attempting to subvert the Constitution. In a final effort to consolidate sentiment against the Congress, he urged the Southern states not to ratify the proposed Fourteenth Amendment. With the exception of Tennessee, which was controlled by one of Johnson's bitterest personal and political enemies, all the former Confederate states rejected the congressional plan.

When Congress reassembled in December 1866, the Republican majority had, therefore, to devise a second program of Reconstruction. Cheered by overwhelming victories in the fall congressional elections, Republicans were even less inclined than previously to cooperate with the President, who had gone into political opposition, or to encourage the provisional regimes in the South, which had unceremoniously rejected their first program. Republican suspicion that Southern whites were fundamentally hostile toward the freedmen was strengthened by reports of a race riot in Memphis during May 1866, when a mob of whites joined in a two-day indiscriminate assault upon blacks in that city, and of a more serious affair in New Orleans four months later, when a white mob, aided by the local police, attacked a black political gathering with what was described as "a cowardly ferocity unsurpassed in the annals of crime." In New Orleans, 45 or 50 blacks were killed, and 150 more were wounded.

Once again, however, the Republican majority in Congress found it easier to agree on what to oppose than what to favor in the way of Reconstruction legislation. Stevens urged that the South be placed under military rule for a generation and that Southern plantations be sold to pay the national debt. Sumner wanted to disfranchise large numbers of Southern whites, to require Negro suffrage, and to create racially integrated schools in the South. Moderate Republicans, on the other hand, were willing to retain the Fourteenth Amendment as the basic framework of congressional Reconstruction and to insist on little else but ratification by the Southern states.

The second congressional program of Reconstruction, embodied in the Military Reconstruction Act of March 2, 1867, represented a further compromise between the demands of Radical and Moderate Republican factions. It divided the ten former Confederate states that had not ratified the Fourteenth Amendment into five military districts. In each of these states, there were to be new constitutional conventions, for which black men were allowed to vote. These conventions must draft new constitutions that had to provide for Negro suffrage, and they were required to ratify the Fourteenth Amendment. When thus reorganized, the Southern states could apply to Congress for readmission to the Union.

The radical aspects of this measure, which were pointed out by Democrats during the congressional debates and were denounced by President Johnson in his unsuccessful veto of the act, were easy to recognize. In particular, the requirement of Negro suffrage, which Sumner sponsored, seemed to Radicals "a prodigious triumph."

In fact, however, most provisions of the Military Reconstruction Act were more acceptable to Moderate than to Radical Republicans. The measure did nothing to give land to the freedmen, to provide education at national expense, or to end racial segregation in the South. It did not erase the boundaries of the Southern states, and it did not even sweep away the provisional governments Johnson had established there, though it did make them responsible to the commanders of the new military districts. So conservative was the act in all these respects that Sumner branded it as "horribly defective."

Intent on striking some kind of balance between the Radical and Conservative wings of the Republican party, the framers of the Military Reconstruction Act drafted the measure carelessly, and it promptly proved to be, as Sumner had predicted, "Reconstruction without machinery or motive power." Facing the acceptance of military rule or Negro suffrage, the provisional governments in the South chose the former, correctly believing that army officers were generally in sympathy with white supremacy. To get the Reconstruction process under way, Congress had, therefore, to enact a supplementary law (March 23, 1867), requiring the federal commanders in the South to take the initiative, when the local governments did not, in announcing elections, registering voters, and convening constitutional conventions. During the summer of 1867, as the President, the attorney-general, and Southern state officials tried by legalistic interpretations to delay the Reconstruction program, Congress had to pass two further supplementary acts, explaining the "true intent and meaning" of the previous legislation.

With these measures, the fabric of congressional Reconstruction legislation as it affected the South was substantially completed. Both the first and the second congressional plans of Reconstruction were compromises between the Radical and the Moderate factions in the Republican party. The Radicals' insistence on change was essential in securing the adoption of this legislation, but the Moderates blocked all measures that would have revolutionary social or economic consequences in the South.

The same need to compromise between the factions of the Republican party shaped the relationships between Congress and the other two branches of the national government during the Reconstruction era. Many Republicans in both factions were profoundly suspicious of the Supreme Court, because of its decision in the Dred Scott case before the war. Not even Lincoln's appointment of Salmon P. Chase in 1864, to succeed Taney as chief justice, removed their doubts about the judiciary. They grew alarmed when the Court in 1866 handed down its decision in *ex parte* Milligan, a landmark case in the history of American civil liberties, which denied the power of a Civil War military tribunal to try the Indiana Copperhead conspirator Lambdin P. Milligan, and held that he should have been brought before a civil tribunal. Some Republicans in Congress feared —quite incorrectly—that the Court was getting ready to invalidate military rule in the South and thus destroy the main protection for the freedmen's rights. Thaddeus Stevens protested that the decision placed "the knife of the rebel at the throat of every man who now or ever had declared himself a loyal Union man" in the South, and Moderate John A. Bingham of Ohio favored "annihilating the usurpers" on the Supreme Court bench by a constitutional amendment providing for "the abolition of the tribunal itself."

Timorous Republicans watched in something approaching panic as the provisional governments in both Georgia and Mississippi brought suit to test the constitutionality of the Military Reconstruction Act, and they were relieved when the Supreme Court refused to hear these cases. When, however, William H. McCardle, a Mississippi editor arrested and tried by military commission for publishing criticism of the congressional Reconstruction policy, succeeded in bringing his case before the Court, Republicans in Congress acted swiftly to deprive the Court of jurisdiction in such cases.

This step was highly exceptional, and Republican fulminations against the Court were largely a matter of Radicals' letting off steam. Moderate Republicans were always numerous enough to block Radical proposals to hobble the judiciary. Congress did reduce the number of justices from ten to seven, but this was a nonpartisan move, approved by President Johnson himself, which was designed to increase the efficiency of the Court, not to undermine its authority. Even the Radical success in the McCardle case was of little significance. The Court promptly demonstrated in *ex parte* Yerger (1869), another case involving a Mississippian, that its jurisdiction derived not from an act of Congress but from the Constitution itself, and it freed Yerger from the prison to which a military court had sentenced him. Radicals stewed impotently, while Moderates prevented them from taking further measures against the Court.

The same balance between Radical and Moderate Republican factions dictated the policy of Congress toward the President during the Reconstruction years. Most Republicans were suspicious of the President and were fearful that he intended turning the South over to Confederate rule. Most were angered by Johnson's repeated veto messages, which assailed carefully balanced compromise legislation as the work of Radicals and attacked the Congress itself as an unconstitutional body, since it refused to seat congressmen from all the states. Republicans of both factions were, therefore, desirous of keeping a close eye on the President and were willing to curb executive powers that had grown during the war. In 1867, fearing that Johnson would use his power as commander-in-chief to subvert their

Reconstruction legislation, Republican factions joined to pass an army appropriations bill that required all military orders to the army, including those of the President himself, to go through the hands of General Grant. Suspecting that Johnson wanted to use the federal patronage to build up a political machine of his own, they adopted at the same time the Tenure of Office Act, which obliged the President to secure the consent of the Senate not merely when he appointed officials but when he removed them.

Up to this point the Republicans in Congress were prepared to go in striking unanimity—but no further. When Radical Republican James M. Ashley in January 1867 moved to impeach the President, he was permitted to conduct a seriocomic investigation of Johnson's alleged involvement in Lincoln's assassination, his purported sale of pardons, and other trumped-up charges, but when Ashley's motion reached the floor of the House of Representatives, Moderate Republicans saw that it was soundly defeated.

A subsequent attempt at impeachment fared better, but it also revealed how the Radical and Moderate factions checked each other. In August 1867 President Johnson suspended from office Secretary of War Edwin M. Stanton, whom he correctly suspected of having collaborated closely with the Radicals in Congress, and, as required by the Tenure of Office Act, he asked the Senate to consent to the dismissal. When the Senate refused, the President removed Stanton and ordered him to surrender his office. News of this seemingly open defiance of the law caused Republicans in the House of Representatives to rush through a resolution impeaching the President, without waiting for a list of specific charges against him to be drawn up.

The trial of President Johnson (who was not present in court but was represented by his lawyers) was a test of strength not only between Congress and the Chief Executive, but also between the Radical and the Moderate Republicans. Impeachment managers from the House of Representatives presented eleven charges against the President, mostly accusing him of violating the Tenure of Office Act but also censuring his repeated attacks on Congress. With fierce joy, Radical Thaddeus Stevens, who was one of the managers, denounced the President: "Unfortunate man! thus surrounded, hampered, tangled in the meshes of his own wickedness—unfortunate, unhappy man, behold your doom!"

But Radical oratory could not persuade Moderate Republicans and Democrats in the Senate to vote for conviction. Though Sumner, like a handful of other Radicals, was prepared from the outset of the trial to pronounce that Johnson was "guilty of all, and infinitely more," most senators were open-minded. They listened as Johnson's lawyers challenged the constitutionality of the Tenure of Office Act, showed that it had not been intended to apply to cabinet members, and proved that, in any case, it did not cover Stanton, who had been appointed by Lincoln, not Johnson. When the critical vote came, Moderate Republicans like Fessenden voted to acquit the President, and Johnson's Radical foes lacked one vote of the two-thirds majority required to convict him. Several other Republican senators who, for political expediency, voted against the President were prepared to change their votes and favor acquittal if their ballots were needed.

Nothing more clearly shows how the institutional needs of a political party prevented drastic change than did this decision not to remove a President whom a majority in Congress despised, hated, and feared. The desire to maintain the unity of the national Republican party, despite frequent quarrels and incessant bickering, overrode the wishes of individual congressmen. Moderate Republicans felt that throughout the Reconstruction period they were constantly being rushed from one advanced position to another in order to placate the insatiable Radicals. With more accuracy, Radical Republicans perceived that the need of retaining Moderate support prevented the adoption of any really revolutionary Reconstruction program.

➢ V ➣

A final set of beliefs that limited the nature of the changes imposed upon, and accepted by, the South during the Reconstruction period can be labeled racism. In all parts of the country, white Americans continued, after the war as before it, to look with suspicion and fear upon those whose skin was of a different color. For example, in California white hatred built up against the Chinese, who had begun coming to that state in great numbers after the discovery of gold and who were later imported by the thousands to help construct the Central Pacific Railroad. White workers resented the willingness of the Chinese to work long hours for "coolies' " wages; they distrusted the unusual attire, strange diet, and peculiar habits of the Chinese; and they disliked all these things more because the Chinese were a yellow-skinned people. Under the leadership of a recent Irish immigrant, Dennis Kearney, white laborers organized a significant Workingman's party, with the slogan, "The Chinese must go."

The depression of 1873 gave impetus to the movement, for day after day thousands of the unemployed gathered in the sand lots of San Francisco to hear Kearney's slashing attacks on the Chinese and on the wealthy corporations that employed them. In the summer of 1877 San Francisco hoodlums, inspired by Kearney, burned twenty-five Chinese laundries and destroyed dozens of Chinese houses. Politically the movement was strong enough to force both major parties in California to adopt anti-Chinese platforms, and California congressmen succeeded in persuading their colleagues to pass a bill limiting the number of Chinese who could be brought into the United States each year. Since the measure was clearly in conflict with treaty arrangements with China, President Rutherford B. Hayes vetoed it, but he had his secretary of state initiate negotiations leading to a new treaty that permitted the restriction of immigration. Accordingly, Congress in 1882 passed the Chinese Exclusion Act, which suspended all Chinese immigration for ten years and forbade the naturalization of Chinese already in the country.

If white Americans became so agitated over a small number of Chinese, who were unquestionably hardworking and thrifty and who belonged to one of the most ancient of civilizations, it is easy to see how they could consider blacks an even greater danger. There were more than 3 million Afro-Americans, most of them recently emancipated from slavery. The exploits of black soldiers during the war—their very discipline and courage—proved that Negroes could be formidable fighters. The fact that blacks were no longer portrayed as invisible men but now, in photographs and caricatures, had sharply etched identities exacerbated, rather than allayed, white apprehensions. More clearly than ever before Negroes seemed distinctive, alien, and vaguely menacing.

Most American intellectuals during the Reconstruction era unquestioningly accepted the dogma that blacks belonged to an inferior race. Though a few reformers like Sumner vigorously attacked the notion, a majority of even philanthropic Northerners accepted the judgment of the distinguished Harvard scientist Louis Agassiz that, while whites during antiquity were developing high civilizations, "the negro race groped in barbarism and never originated a regular organization among themselves." Many also accepted Agassiz's conjecture that Negroes, once free, would ultimately die out in the United States. Others reached the same conclusion by studying the recently published work of Charles Darwin, *Origin of Species* (1859), and they believed the Darwinian argument that in the desperate struggle for survival "higher civilized races" must inevitably eliminate "an endless number of lower races." Consequently, the influential and tender-hearted Congregational minister Horace Bushnell could prophesy the approaching end of the black race in the United States with equanimity. "Since we must all die," he asked rhetorically, "why should it grieve us, that a stock thousands of years behind, in the scale of culture, should die with few and still fewer children to succeed, till finally the whole succession remains in the more cultivated race?"

When even the leaders of Northern society held such views, it is hardly

WHAT MISCEGENATION IS!

WHAT WE ARE TO EXPECT

Now that Mr. Lincoln is Re-elected.

By L. SEAMAN, LL. D.

WALLER & WILLETTS, Publishers,
NEW YORK.

"WHAT MISCEGENATION IS!"

Miscegenation was a word introduced into the English language during the 1864 presidential campaign in order to discredit the Republicans, who were supposed to favor it. L. Seaman's pamphlet shows how crudely the worst racial fears were appealed to during the Reconstruction years. (*Library of Congress.*)

surprising that most whites in the region were overtly anti-Negro. In state after state, whites fiercely resisted efforts to extend the political and civil rights of blacks, partly because they feared that any improvement of the condition of Negroes in the North would lead to a huge exodus of blacks from the South. At the end of the Civil War, only Maine, New Hampshire, Vermont, Massachusetts, and Rhode Island allowed Negroes to have full voting rights, and in New York blacks who met certain property-holding qualifications could have the ballot. During the next three years, in referenda held in Connecticut, Wisconsin, Kansas, Ohio, Michigan, and

Missouri, constitutional amendments authorizing Negro suffrage were defeated, and New York voters rejected a proposal to eliminate the property-holding qualifications for black voters. Only in Iowa, a state where there were very few blacks, did a Negro suffrage amendment carry in 1868, and that same year Minnesota adopted an ambiguously worded amendment. Thus at the end of the 1860s most Northern states—and all of the Northern states that had substantial numbers of Negro residents—refused to give black men the ballot.

In words as well as in votes, the majority of Northerners made their deeply racist feelings evident. The Democratic press constantly stirred up the racial fears of its readers; editors regularly portrayed the Republicans as planning a "new era of miscegenation, amalgamation, and promiscuous intercourse between the races." From the White House, denouncing Republican attempts "to Africanize the [Southern] half of our country," President Andrew Johnson announced: "In the progress of nations negroes have shown less capacity for self-government than any other race of people.... Whenever they have been left to their own devices they have shown an instant tendency to relapse into barbarism." Even Northern Republicans opposed to Johnson shared many of his racist views. Radical Senator Timothy O. Howe of Wisconsin declared that he regarded "the freedmen, in the main ... as so much animal life," and Senator Benjamin F. Wade of Ohio, whom the Radical Republicans would have elevated to the presidency had they removed Johnson, had, along with a genuine devotion to the principle of equal rights, an incurable aversion to blacks. Living in Washington was a nightmare for him, for, he wrote to his wife, the food was horrible, all "cooked by Niggers until I can smell and taste the Nigger ... all over." Representative George W. Julian of Indiana, one of the few Northern congressmen who had no racial prejudice, bluntly told his colleagues in 1866: "The real trouble is that *we hate the negro*. It is not his ignorance that offends us, but his color.... Of this fact I entertain no doubt whatsoever."

Both personal preferences and the wishes of constituents inhibited Northern Republicans from supporting measures that might alter race relations. When Sumner sought to expunge federal laws that recognized slavery or to prohibit racial discrimination on the public transportation in the District of Columbia, his colleagues replied: "God has made the negro inferior, and ... laws cannot make him equal." Such congressmen were hardly in a position to scold the South for racial discrimination or to insist on drastic social change in that region.

If racism limited the innovation that Northerners were willing to propose during the Reconstruction period, it even more drastically reduced the amount of change that white Southerners were prepared to accept. The note of racial bigotry runs through both the private correspondence and the public pronouncements of Southern whites during the postwar era. "Equality does not exist between blacks and whites," announced Alexander H. Stephens. "The one race is by nature inferior in many respects, physically and mentally, to the other. This should be received as a fixed invincible fact in all dealings with the subject." A North Carolina diarist agreed: "The Anglo-Saxon and the African can never be equal. . . . One or the other must fall." Or, as the Democratic party of Louisiana resolved in its 1865 platform: "We hold this to be a Government of white people, made and to be perpetuated for the exclusive benefit of the white race; and . . .

"RE-CONSTRUCTION, OR 'A WHITE MAN'S GOVERNMENT' "

Up to 1868 Grant's position on Reconstruction was so ambivalent that both Democrats and Republicans talked of nominating him for the presidency. In that year, however, he made his views clearly known and, as this 1868 Currier & Ives cartoon indicates, advised Southern whites to accept Negro suffrage. (*American Antiquarian Society.*)

that people of African descent cannot be considered as citizens of the United States, and that there can, in no event, nor under any circumstances, be any equality between the white and other races." The Black Codes were the legal embodiment of these attitudes.

These racist views shaped the attitude of most Southern whites toward the whole process of Reconstruction. They approved of President Johnson's plan of Reconstruction because it placed government in the Southern states entirely in the hands of whites. They rejected the Fourteenth Amendment primarily because it made blacks legally equal to whites. They watched with incredulity bordering on stupefaction as Congress passed the 1867 Military Reconstruction Act, for they simply could not believe that the freedmen were to vote. Stunned, they looked on as army officers supervised the process of voter registration, a process that excluded many prominent whites who had participated in the Confederate government but included more than 700,000 blacks, who formed a majority of eligible voters in South Carolina, Florida, Alabama, Mississippi, and Louisiana. Knowing that these Negro voters were well organized by the Union League, often with the assistance of agents of the Freedmen's Bureau, whites were more apathetic than surprised when the fall elections showed heavy majorities in favor of convening new constitutional conventions.*

With hostile and unbelieving eyes, most Southern whites observed the work of these conventions, which between November 1867 and May 1868 drafted new constitutions for the former Confederate states. To Southern whites unaccustomed to seeing blacks in any positions of public prominence, the presence of freedmen in these conventions meant that they were Negro-dominated. In fact, except in the South Carolina convention, in which blacks did form a majority, only between one-fourth and one-ninth of the delegates were Negroes. Whites ridiculed the Negro members' ignorance of parliamentary procedures, and they laughed sardonically when they read how the "coal black" temporary chairman of the Louisiana convention put a question by asking those who favored a motion "to rise an stan on der feet" and then directing "all you contrary men to rise."

The reactions of Southern whites to the constitutions these conventions produced were also determined by their racial prejudice. Generally they denounced these new charters as "totally incompatible with the prosperity and liberty of the people." In reality the constitutions, often copied from Northern models, were generally improvements over the ones they super-

---

* The Texas election was not held until February 1868. Tennessee had no election, because it had already been readmitted to the Union.

seded. In addition to requiring Negro suffrage (as Congress had directed), they promised all citizens of the state equality before the law. They reformed financial and revenue systems, reorganized the judiciary, improved the organization of local government, and, most important of all, they instituted a state-supported system of public education, hitherto so notably lacking in most Southern states.

Because these constitutions guaranteed racial equality, Southern whites tried, without great success, to block their ratification. In Alabama, whites boycotted the ratification election; in Mississippi, they cast a majority of votes against the new constitution. In Virginia, ratification was delayed because the conservative army commander of that district discovered that there was no money to hold an election, and in Texas all moves toward the creation of a new government lagged several months behind those in the Eastern states. Despite all the foot-dragging, new governments were set up, and in June 1868 Congress readmitted representatives and senators from Alabama, Arkansas, Florida, Georgia, Louisiana, North Carolina, and South Carolina. Two years later the reconstruction of Virginia, Mississippi, and Texas was completed, and in early 1870 these states were also readmitted. Meanwhile

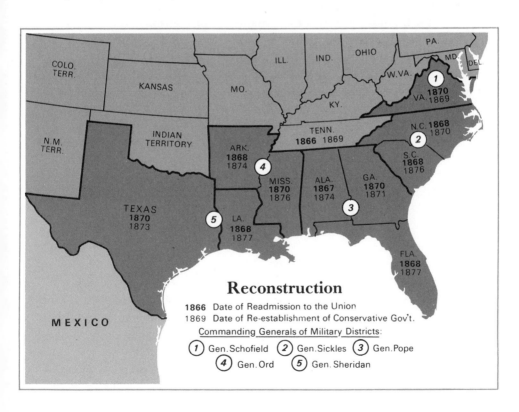

Reconstruction

1866 Date of Readmission to the Union
1869 Date of Re-establishment of Conservative Gov't.
Commanding Generals of Military Districts:
(1) Gen. Schofield (2) Gen. Sickles (3) Gen. Pope
(4) Gen. Ord (5) Gen. Sheridan

Georgia underwent one further reorganization after the legislature of that state attempted to exclude Negroes who had been elected to that body. But by 1871, when Georgia senators and representatives again took their seats in Congress, all the states of the former Confederacy had undergone the process of Reconstruction and had been readmitted to the Union.

With bitter hostility, most Southern whites witnessed this reorganization of their state governments, and the name Black Reconstruction, which they gave to the ensuing period of Republican ascendency in the South, reveals the racial bias behind their opposition. Actually these Southern state governments were not dominated by Negroes, and the proportion of offices held by blacks was smaller than the percentage of blacks in the population. Only in South Carolina did the legislature have a black majority. No Afro-American was elected governor, though there were black lieutenant-governors in South Carolina, Louisiana, and Mississippi. Only in South Carolina was there a black state supreme court justice. During the entire Reconstruction period, only two blacks, Hiram R. Revels and Blanche K. Bruce, both from Mississippi and both men of exceptional ability and integrity, served in the United States Senate, and only fifteen blacks were elected to the House of Representatives.

Even to the most racist Southern whites it was obvious that most of the leaders of the Republican party in that section, and a large part of the Republican following as well, were themselves white. To those white Republicans born in the North, they gave the label "Carpetbaggers," because they allegedly came South with no more worldly possessions than could be packed into a carpetbag, or small suitcase, ready to live on and to exploit the prostrate region. The term, with its implication of corruption, was applied indiscriminately to men of Northern birth who had lived in the South long before the war as well as to newly arrived fortune hunters, many of them recently discharged Union army officers. It was used to brand both Henry Clay Warmoth, who at the age of twenty-six became governor of Louisiana and helped loot that state, openly declaring that he was a corruptionist, and Adelbert Ames, the incorruptible Maine-born governor of Mississippi, who entered politics as part of a mission to secure "exact and equal justice" to men of all races.

Southern-born white Republicans were called "scalawags," a term that cattle drovers applied to "the mean, lousy and filthy kine that are not fit for butchers or dogs." Again the term was used indiscriminately. Southern racists applied it to poor hill-country whites, who had long been at odds with the planters in states like North Carolina and Alabama and now joined the Republican party as a way of getting back at their old enemies. But other scalawags were members of the planter, mercantile, and industrial classes of the South; many of these were former Whigs who distrusted the Democrats, and they felt at home in a Republican party that favored protective tariffs, subsidies for railroads, and appropriations for rebuilding the levees along the Mississippi River. A surprising number of Southern-born white Republicans were former high-ranking officers in the Confederate army, like General P. G. T. Beauregard and General James Longstreet, who knew at first hand the extent of the damage wrought by the war and were willing to accept the victor's terms without procrastination.

Bitterly as they attacked these white Republicans, Southern Democrats reserved their worst abuse for Negroes, and they saw in every measure adopted by the new reconstructed state governments evidence of black incompetence, extravagance, or even barbarism. In truth, much that these state governments did supplied the Democrats with ammunition. The postwar period was one of low political morality, and there was no reason to expect that newly enfranchised blacks would prove any less attracted by the profits of politics than anybody else. Petty corruption prevailed in all the Southern state governments. Louisiana legislators voted themselves an allowance for stationery—which covered purchases of hams and bottles of champagne. The South Carolina legislature ran up a bill of more than $50,000 in refurbishing the state house with such costly items as a $750 mirror, $480 clocks, and 200 porcelain spittoons at $8 apiece. The same legislature voted $1,000 to the speaker of the house of representatives to repay his losses on a horse race.

Bad as these excesses were, Southern Democrats were angered less by them than by the legitimate work performed by the new state governments. Unwilling to recognize that Negroes were now equal members of the body politic, they objected to expenditures for hospitals, jails, orphanages, and asylums to care for blacks. Most of all they objected to the creation of a public school system. Throughout the South, there was considerable hostility to the idea of educating any children at the cost of the taxpayer, and the thought of paying taxes in order to teach black children seemed wild and foolish extravagance. "It is worse than throwing money away to give it to the education of niggers," announced the Livingston (Louisiana) *Herald* in 1870. To many, Negro education seemed positively harmful. Tennessee planters told an agent of the Freedmen's Bureau that "the more ignorant they [the freedmen] are the better they work; that in proportion as they increase in intelligence the more insolent, lazy and worthless they become." The fact that black schools were mostly conducted by Northern whites, usually women, who came South with a reforming mission, did nothing to increase popular support; too many of the teachers stated plainly and publicly their intention to use "every endeavor to throw a ray of light here and there, among this benighted race of ruffians, rebels by nature." Adding to all these hostilities was a fear that a system of public education might some day lead to a racially integrated system of education. These apprehensions had little basis in fact, for during the entire period of Reconstruction in the whole South there were significant numbers of children in racially mixed schools only in New Orleans between 1870 and 1874.

Not content with criticizing Republican rule, Southern Democrats organized to put an end to it. Theirs was a two-pronged attack. On the one hand, they sought to intimidate or to drive from the South whites who cooperated politically with the Republican regimes; on the other, they tried to terrorize and silence blacks, especially those active in politics. Much of this pressure was informal and sporadic, but much was the work of racist organizations that sprang up all over the South during these years. The most famous of these was the Ku Klux Klan, which originated in 1866 as a social club for young white men in Pulaski, Tennessee. As the Military Reconstruction Act went into effect and the possibility of black participation in Southern political life became increasingly real, racists saw new potential in this secret organization with its cabalistic name and its mysterious uniforms of long flowing robes, high conical hats that made the wearers seem preternaturally tall, and white face masks. In 1867 the Klan was reorganized under a new constitution that provided for local dens, each headed by a Grand Cyclops, linked together into provinces (counties), each under a Grand Titan, and in turn into realms (states), each under a Grand Dragon. At the head of the whole organization was the Grand Wizard, who, according to most reports, was former Confederate General Nathan Bedford Forrest, who had been responsible for the slaughter of black Union troops at Fort Pillow. Probably this elaborate table of organization was never completely filled out, and certainly there was an almost total lack of central control of the Klan's activities. Indeed, at some point in early 1869, the Klan was officially disbanded. But even without central direction its members, like those of the Order of the White Camellia and other racist vigilante groups, continued in their plan of disrupting the new Republican regimes in the South and terrorizing their black supporters.

Along with other vigilante organizations, the Klan was an expression of the traditional racism of Southern whites. They were willing to accept the defeat of the Confederacy, and they were prepared to admit that slavery was dead; but they could not bring themselves to contemplate a society that would treat blacks and whites as equals. As a group of South Carolina whites protested to Congress in 1868: "The white people of our State will never quietly submit to negro rule. . . . We will keep up this contest until we have regained the heritage of political control handed down to us by honored ancestry. That is a duty we owe to the land that is ours, to the graves that it contains, and to the race of which you and we alike are members—the proud Caucasian race, whose sovereignty on earth God has ordained."

The appeal was shrewdly pitched, for the Southern racist knew how to reach his Northern counterpart. Joined together, their fears of men with darker skins helped to undercut the Reconstruction regimes in the South and halted any congressional efforts at further innovative Reconstruction legislation.

FRANCIS LIEBER

This photograph of Lieber in his old age suggests his Germanic thoroughness, his deep seriousness of purpose, that enabled him to become adviser to Presidents and the leading political philosopher of his day. It does not, however, do justice to the human side of Lieber or reflect his warmth of friendship, his enthusiasm for learning, and his sometimes elephantine gaiety of spirits. (*Library of Congress.*)

7

The American Compromise

An exclusive focus on the Southern states during the postwar years obscures the fact that Reconstruction was a national, not just a sectional, process. In all regions the nationalistic impulses unleashed by the war portended revolutionary consequences. Just as some Radical Republicans sought to overturn the entire Southern social system, so other postwar nationalists yearned to expand the role of the federal government and to integrate the imperfectly articulated American economy. But many Northerners considered the changes that occurred in their section during the Civil War and Reconstruction as offensive and unacceptable as most white Southerners found the program of the Radical Republicans. In the South, as has been shown in the previous chapter, plans for drastic social and economic change ran headlong into long-established institutions and values, so that the amount of innovation tolerated was limited. A similar fate met schemes to transform the ideas, the society, and the economy of the North and the West. Here, too, deeply rooted local and parochial interests resisted the majority force of nationalism.

The resolution of this tension between the nation and its constituent parts, between the majority will and the desires of minorities, was what can be called—for want of a better phrase—"The American Compromise."

213

The term does not refer to formal agreements or legislative enactments embossed on parchment. Instead, it embraces a whole series of loose, informal and frequently tacit understandings that by the end of the 1880s legitimated the broader role played by the national government and the extension of the national economy, but also protected the states and the local or regional economic interests. To an observer from Bismarck's recently reunited Germany, these arrangements would doubtless have seemed chaotic and incomprehensible, for, like most American solutions to difficult problems, they were entirely pragmatic and not always logical or consistent. But, like many other such informal American agreements, the American Compromise rested on a broad popular consensus, and it worked. This uneasy equilibrium between national power and local interests, between majority rule and minority rights, achieved by the end of the 1880s, served for a generation as the basis for the country's social and political order.

⋊ I ⋉

The Civil War strongly encouraged the sentiment of nationalism among Northerners. The primary Northern war aim was not to guarantee equal rights to all men nor even to end slavery; it was to preserve the Union. By that often repeated phrase, men and women of the war years meant something more than merely maintaining the country as a territorial unit. Attached to the idea of Union was an almost mystical sense of the wholeness of the American people. Americans viewed themselves as a chosen people, selected to conduct an experiment in self-government, to be a test of the viability of democratic institutions.

Faith in the special destiny of the United States gave courage and hope to Northerners during the darkest hours of the war. Defeats on the battlefield, properly understood, were the fire that served to burn away the dross and impurities in American life. As the Reverend Marvin R. Vincent of Troy, New York, announced: "God has been striking, and trying to make us strike at elements unfavorable to the growth of a pure democracy; and . . . he is at work, preparing in this broad land a fit stage for a last act of the mighty drama, the consummation of human civilization." A similar inspiration moved Mrs. Julia Ward Howe to draw upon the imagery of the Book of Revelation in composing the most powerful and popular battle hymn ever written:

> Mine eyes have seen the glory of the coming of the Lord:
> He is trampling out the vintage where the grapes of wrath are stored;
> He has loosed the fateful lightning of his terrible swift sword:
> His truth is marching on.

Northerners believed that the Union would emerge from the war more powerful, more cohesive than ever before. They expected that the United States would no longer be a confederation or a union of states but, in the fullest sense, a nation. A small shift in grammar tells the whole story. Before the Civil War many politicians and writers referred to the United States in the plural, but after 1865 only a pedant or the most unreconstructed Southerner would dream of saying "the United States *are*."

The word *nation* came easily now to American lips. Unlike his predecessors who generally avoided the term, Lincoln regularly referred to the United States as a nation. For example, he used the word no fewer than five times in his brief Gettysburg address, most eloquently in the concluding pledge "that this nation, under God, shall have a new birth of freedom." In 1865, when Republicans agreed to establish a weekly journal that would reflect their views, they called it, as a matter of course, *The Nation*, and it became, as it has remained, one of the most influential periodicals in the country. In 1867, when Sumner took to the lecture circuit to supplement his senatorial salary, he chose for his topic, "Are We a Nation?" The answer, he believed, was obvious. Americans were "one people, throbbing with a common life, occupying a common territory, rejoicing in a common history, sharing in common trials." Never again should any "local claim of self-government" be permitted "for a moment [to] interfere with the supremacy of the Nation." He concluded: "Such centralization is the highest civilization, for it approaches the nearest to the heavenly example."

Political theorists as well as public men in the postwar generation exalted American nationalism. In 1865 Orestes Brownson, the former Jacksonian spokesman, published the first book-length contribution to the bibliography of American nationalism, *The American Republic: Its Constitution, Tendencies, and Destiny*. "Nations are only individuals on a larger scale," Brownson argued, and his treatise was designed to resolve the identity crisis of the Civil War by persuading the American nation to "reflect on its own constitution, its own separate existence, individuality, tendencies, and end." Even more soaring were the claims of the Reverend Elisha Mulford's *The Nation: The Foundations of Civil Order and Political Life in the United States* (1870). The nation, Mulford argued in terms of Hegelian philosophy, was a mystic body, endowed with a spirit and a majesty of its own. "The Nation," he concluded, "is a work of God in history. . . . Its vocation is from God, and its obligation is only to God."

It would be easy to conclude from such statements that Americans of the post–Civil War generation, rejoicing in the newly restored unity of their country, were swept up into an ultranationalistic frenzy comparable to that of the Germans, who almost simultaneously achieved national unity under

Four score and seven years ago our fathers brought forth, upon this continent, a new nation, conceived in Liberty, and dedicated to the proposition that all men are created equal.

Now we are engaged in a great civil war, testing whether that nation, or any nation so conceived, and so dedicated, can long endure. We are met on a great battlefield of that war. We have come to dedicate a portion of it, as a final resting place for those who here gave their lives, that that nation might live. It is altogether fitting and proper that we should do this.

But in a larger sense, we can not dedicate—we can not consecrate—we can not hallow, this ground. The brave men, living and dead, who struggled here, have consecrated it, far above our poor power to add or detract. The world will little note, nor long remember, what we say here, but can never forget what they did here. It is for us, the living, rather to be dedicated here to the unfinished work which they have, thus far, so nobly carried on. It is rather

for us to be here dedicated to the great task remaining before us—that from these honored dead we take increased devotion to that cause for which they here gave the last full measure of devotion—that we here highly resolve that these dead shall not have died in vain; that this nation shall have a new birth of freedom; and that government of the people, by the people, for the people, shall not perish from the earth.

ABRAHAM LINCOLN'S GETTYSBURG ADDRESS

Lincoln's brief address, delivered at the dedication of the national cemetery at Gettysburg on November 19, 1863, is a basic document in the history of American nationalism. Contrary to legend, Lincoln did not write his address on the back of an envelope or on a sheet of brown paper while on the train to Gettysburg. There are several slightly varying versions of the address in Lincoln's own handwriting. This is the second draft, the manuscript of which is in the Library of Congress. (Library of Congress.)

Bismarck, or of the Italians, who were being reunited under Cavour. But a moment's reflection shows the weakness of these historical parallels. After all, the federal structure of the American government survived the Civil War. The national government continued to consist of three separate centers of power, which often checked each other. If there was no further talk of secession, there was frequent invocation of states' rights, and regionalism and localism did not disappear from American life. The very fact that the Reconstruction policies imposed upon the conquered South were so limited in scope and so brief in duration is the best evidence that the high priests of American nationalism did not have things their own way.

Indeed, if the works of these nationalistic writers are read carefully, they convey an ambivalent message. These theorists of nationalism were really addressing the same problem so often discussed before the war by the theorists of sectionalism: the relationship of the individual to the group, of minority rights to majority power. For instance, Brownson, even while rejoicing in the growth of American nationality, warned that this could lead to "consolidation"—the same term Robert Y. Hayne and John C. Calhoun had used—and the result might be "socialism, or centralized democracy." Because the history of the United States since 1845 demonstrated that the proper check on nationalism was not state sovereignty—for that had led to the disintegration of the Union—Brownson proposed instead reliance on states' rights. One of Brownson's admirers, the able lawyer J. C. Hurd, warned even more vigorously against the dangers from a despotic national government. In *The Theory of Our National Existence* (1881), Hurd strongly endorsed national sovereignty, but he also sought liberty, under the national aegis, for the growth of localism and particularism. Too much concentration of power in Washington, he feared, might lead to another civil war; and the next time it would be truly internecine, not a contest between sections but a war of interest groups and classes that would divide the American people "as the constituent members of States, cities, towns, communes, families, and even households."

The most successful attempt to work out a political theory that would at once safeguard the gains made by American nationalism during the Civil War and also recognize the wide diversity of regional, class, and ethnic interests in American society was that of Professor Francis Lieber, whose career, appropriately enough, was a kind of epitome of the American national experience. As a lad this Prussian-born savant had wept when he saw the troops of Napoleon overrun his native land, and he had been old enough to fight against the French at Waterloo. But he had also experienced the repressive side of nationalism when the Prussian government arrested him for harboring dangerous, liberal ideas. After a disillusioning experience in the war for Greek independence, Lieber came to the United States, where he founded and edited the *Encyclopaedia Americana* (13 volumes, 1829–1833). Unable to find an academic or literary position in New England, he accepted a professorship at South Carolina College (now the University of South Carolina), where he taught history and political economy. Suspected by Southerners because of his friendship with Charles Sumner and other abolitionists and distrusted by Northerners because he did not speak out against the South's peculiar institution—indeed, he even owned slaves—Lieber felt caught in the middle, and he found no escape until 1857, when he was appointed professor at Columbia College (later Columbia University) in New York. When war broke out, one of Lieber's sons joined the Confederate army and was killed in action; the other two fought for the Union, and one lost an arm at Fort Donelson.

A passionate American nationalist, Lieber did all he could to sustain the Union government during the war. Highly respected in Washington, he became an adviser to the war department, and he drafted for the guidance of the Union army General Orders No. 100, the first codification of military law ever published. Alarmed at the lack of popular support for the national government, he helped found the Union League; he was also instrumental in setting up the Loyal Publication Society, for which he and other nationalists prepared pamphlets to promote the Union cause. Lieber's wartime message was consistent: "The people are conscious that they constitute and ought to constitute a nation, with a God appointed country, the integrity of which they will not and must not, give up, cost what it may."

But along with Lieber's exaltation of nationalism went warnings against excess. He opposed efforts of the Radical Republicans, like his friend Sumner, to permit the national government to supervise the daily activities of citizens in the South. These attempts would "run the [national] cart into such a mire that we shall be able to extricate it only by sacrificing a good deal of our best baggage." Lieber's concern became greater when he observed how Bismarck's triumphant reuniting of Germany was followed by curbs on civil liberty. The United States, he feared, might face a similar danger.

To forestall this threat, Lieber reverted to arguments that he had earlier developed in his influential book *On Civil Liberty and Self-Government,* which had gone through two editions before the war. Without disavowing his nationalism, he sought to distinguish it from centralism. "Centralization is the convergence of all the rays of power into one central point," Lieber wrote; "nationalization is the diffusion of the same life-blood through a system of arteries, throughout a body politic." Nationalism was to be encouraged; centralism, to be avoided. The most effective restraint upon despotism, toward which centralism tended, lay in what Lieber called

"Institutional Liberty." Having closely examined Calhoun's proposals for mechanical checks and balances between the various branches of government, all of which had proved themselves ineffectual limits on power, Lieber looked instead to organically related institutions—the family, the churches, the scientific community, the business community, the literary world, and the like—to provide "a union of harmonizing systems of laws instinct with self-government." Such "self-evolving," "interlimiting," and "inter-guaranteeing" institutions could supply "the negation of absolutism" and thus lead to "the only self-government, or self-government carried out in the realities of life." Thus he would simultaneously preserve majority rule and protect minority rights.

Lieber's theory of Institutional Liberty was, then, a doctrine of compromise, one very congenial to the postwar generation. So popular was it that when Lieber died in 1872, President Theodore Dwight Woolsey of Yale willingly undertook the preparation of a new edition of *On Civil Liberty*, for he enthusiastically endorsed both Lieber's high nationalism and his fear of "a more centralized government." That ambivalence, indeed, was the special attraction of Lieber's theory. He exalted American nationalism—but encouraged autonomy for local and particularistic interests. He upheld the Union—but sought to prevent its powers from becoming despotic. His solution for the theoretically unresolvable antagonism between liberty and authority was pragmatic; he allowed Americans to eat their cake and have it.

⊰ II ⊱

American diplomacy during the post–Civil War generation followed a pattern that Lieber undoubtedly would have approved. On the one hand, it was vigorously nationalistic, even at times bellicose; on the other, it drew back from conflict with foreign powers, and it refrained from pursuing goals strongly opposed by influential interest groups. In short, American foreign policy showed how Lieber's Institutional Liberty worked.

During the decade after Appomattox, hardly a year passed without some significant American diplomatic initiative. With President Johnson's willing acquiescence, Secretary of State Seward maneuvered skillfully to force the withdrawal of French troops from Mexico, and he tried unsuccessfully to persuade Queen Victoria's government to pay for the damages British-built Confederate cruisers inflicted upon Union shipping during the war. Seward also promoted the construction of a canal across the isthmus of Panama, the annexation of all or part of Santo Domingo, the acquisition of the Danish West Indies, and the purchase of Russian North America. There was no diminution of America's outward thrust during the first five years of President Grant's administration. His able secretary of state,

Hamilton Fish, succeeded in settling the Alabama claims (as the whole group of shippers' claims against Great Britain came to be called), in adjudicating the long-standing controversy between Canadians and Americans over fisheries in the North Atlantic, and in demarcating the disputed boundary between British Columbia and the state of Washington. The President himself took a deep interest in the efforts of Cuban insurgents to oust their Spanish rulers, and at one point Spain and the United States came close to war. Grant also took the lead in seeking the annexation of the Dominican Republic.

These foreign policy initiatives received considerable popular support. After Appomattox there was a general feeling that the United States, with a million seasoned veterans under arms, was in a position to humiliate the French Emperor Napoleon III, to have a showdown with John Bull, and to pick up any adjacent territory that it pleased. The old spirit of manifest

"A PEEP INTO THE FUTURE—THE MONROE DOCTRINE TRIUMPHANT"

A manifestation of postwar nationalism, this cartoon shows a stern Uncle Sam—looking remarkably like Abraham Lincoln—protecting Canada, Mexico, and Central America from the unwanted advances of European powers. (*American Antiquarian Society.*)

destiny, quiescent during the war, sprang to life again. Even those who feared it anticipated its triumph. Referring to the recently completed dome of the United States Capitol, one of Herman Melville's wartime poems predicted the outcome:

> Power unanointed may come—
>> Dominion (unsought by the free)
> And the Iron Dome,
>> Stronger for stress and strain,
>> Fling her huge shadow athwart the main....

The more optimistic rejoiced in the prospect. Advocating the annexation of both Haiti and the Dominican Republic and hoping for the future acquisition of the Kingdom of Hawaii, President Johnson's 1868 annual message to Congress concluded: "The conviction is rapidly gaining ground in the American mind that with the increased facilities for intercommunication between all portions of the earth the principles of free government, as embraced in our Constitution, if faithfully maintained and carried out, would prove of sufficient strength and breadth to comprehend within their sphere and influence the civilized nations of the world."

Despite both fears and hopes, the accomplishments of American foreign policy during the Reconstruction years were few. From the point of view of national security, the most important feat was Seward's success in getting French troops removed from Mexico. Introduced into Mexico during the Civil War, ostensibly to compel the bankrupt Mexican government of President Benito Juarez to pay its debts, French troops in 1864 provided the support for the installation of the Archduke Maximilian of Austria as Emperor of Mexico. Unable to do more than protest against this violation of the Monroe Doctrine while the war was going on, Seward adopted a more vigorous tone after Appomattox. Yet, knowing the French emperor was a proud and volatile man, he refrained from direct threats and allowed Napoleon to discover for himself how expensive, unpopular, and unsuccessful his Mexican adventure was proving. By 1867 Napoleon finally decided to cut off further financial support for Maximilian's shaky regime and, under steady American pressure, withdrew his troops. Captured by Juarez's troops, Maximilian was shot by a firing squad on June 19, 1867. Never again would a European power so openly challenge the Monroe Doctrine.

A second diplomatic achievement of the Reconstruction years was the settlement of the Alabama claims. Immediately after the war it probably would have been possible to clear up this controversy speedily and inexpensively, had not the British government haughtily denied that it had violated international law in permitting Confederate raiders to be built in its shipyards. With delay, American grievances festered. Sumner, the powerful chairman of the Senate Committee on Foreign Relations, began to argue that the British owed not merely repayment for actual damages done by the *Alabama* and other vessels; they were also responsible for protracting the war, for the "immense and infinite" cost of the entire last two years of the conflict. The failure of Reverdy Johnson, Seward's special envoy to Great Britain, to secure an apology or expression of regret from the stubborn British government further exacerbated American feelings. Not until after Hamilton Fish took charge of the American state department and not until after there was a change of government in Great Britain could a settlement be worked out. In the Treaty of Washington of 1871, Great Britain admitted negligence in permitting the Confederate cruisers to escape and expressed regret for the injury they had caused; and the United states tacitly abandoned the extravagant claims put forward by Sumner and agreed that the amount of damages should be assessed by a commission of arbitration representing five nations. Ultimately losses in American shipping were estimated at $15.5 million, and the British government paid this amount. More important than any monetary settlement was the precedent set for arbitration of international disputes, and the Treaty of Washington paved the way for the rapprochement of the two greatest English-speaking nations. Not until the two world wars of the twentieth century would the full consequences of this development emerge.

Apart from the almost unnoticed American occupation of the Midway Islands in August 1867, the sole territorial acquisition of the United States during the Reconstruction era—and it was a very considerable addition—was the purchase of Alaska. There was little public enthusiasm for Seward's 1867 treaty to buy Russian America for $7.2 million. Newspapers called the territory "a barren, worthless, God-forsaken region," "a national icehouse" consisting of nothing but "walrus-covered icebergs." Congressmen were equally unenthusiastic. Senator Fessenden declared that he would vote for the treaty only on condition that Seward "be compelled to live there, and the Russian government be required to keep him there." Yet after much grumbling, the Senate finally ratified the treaty and the House reluctantly appropriated the money for the purchase. Seward's success was due in part to his ability to convince Sumner and other senators that Alaska had vast, hidden natural resources; in part it was due to the judicious payments of money to American congressmen by the Russian minister in Washington. More influential than either of these factors, however, was the general feeling that rejecting the treaty would alienate Czar Alexander II, who alone of the European rulers had been sympathetic to the Union cause during the Civil War.

Nothing came of the other postwar plans for expansion. Each of them ran into snags that made American diplomats draw back. For instance, the desire of many United States politicians, including Grant, Fish, and Sumner, to annex Canada had to be abandoned when it became clear that the British would not withdraw without a fight, and the United States was clearly not prepared to wage another major war. Grant's plan to acquire the Dominican Republic aroused the opposition of Sumner, who considered himself the senatorial voice of the black race and wanted the island of Santo Domingo to become not an American possession but the center of "a free confederacy [of the West Indies], in which the black race should predominate." Seward's treaty for the purchase of the Danish West Indies was pigeonholed by the Senate when those unfortunate islands were visited by a hurricane, a tidal wave, and a series of earthquake shocks.

It would, however, be a mistake to put too much stress upon these idiosyncratic factors that stopped American expansion, for there were broader forces at work. The American people, exhausted by four years of fighting, were not prepared to support a vigorously nationalistic foreign policy if it threatened another war. Northern businessmen felt that it was more important to reduce taxes and to return to a sound monetary policy than to engage in foreign adventures. Because of the difficulties of racial adjustment in the South, increasing numbers of politicians hesitated before agreeing to annex additional populations of dark-skinned inhabitants. During Johnson's administration, many Republicans opposed all of Seward's plans for expansion because they might bring credit to that unpopular President. During Grant's tenure, disaffected Republicans, who by 1872 joined the Liberal Republican party and opposed Grant's reelection, had similar motives for blocking his diplomatic schemes. So powerful were these combined elements of opposition that after 1874 there was little further talk of a vigorously nationalistic foreign policy or of American expansionism.

American foreign policy during the Reconstruction generation, then, illustrates the operation of the evolving American Compromise. On issues that clearly touched the national security, those that affected the existence of the nation itself, such as the presence of French troops in Mexico and the difficulties with Great Britain that might have resulted in war, there was a consensus sufficiently strong to permit the national government to act. Even the purchase of Alaska, which seemed to involve the friendship between the United States and the powerful Russian empire, fell into this category. But where there was no clear, overriding national interest, local, sectional, racial, and class objections to expansion prevailed. Though Presidents and secretaries of state might fume, there was a tacit agreement that the wishes of these minorities must be respected. To use Lieber's phraseology, American foreign policy during the postwar years was an expression of nationalism but a rejection of centralism.

❧ III ❦

The years immediately following the Civil War witnessed an enormous boom in the American economy. Except for the South, still recovering from the ravages of war, every region of the country prospered during the eight years after Appomattox. Except for the merchant marine, which never recovered from the damages inflicted by Confederate raiders, every branch of commerce, industry, and agriculture flourished.

The age was an expansive one, and Americans rushed to settle vast tracts of hitherto uninhabited land in the West. In 1860 the western frontier of settlement lay near the Missouri River, and between eastern Kansas and California there were hardly any white inhabitants except in the Mormon settlement in Utah and in the Spanish-speaking community at Santa Fe. Thirty years later, immigrants, pushing west into the Great Plains and Rocky Mountain region and pushing east from California, formed a virtually uninterrupted pattern of settlement across the continent. In 1890 the superintendent of the United States census announced—a bit prematurely—that the frontier was gone: "Up to and including 1880 the country had a frontier settlement, but at present the unsettled area has been so broken into by isolated bodies of settlement that there can hardly be said to be a frontier line."

To some extent the peopling of the West was triggered by the passage in 1862 of the Homestead Act, which offered free of charge to any citizen who was over 21 or was head of a family 160 acres of public lands if he resided on them for five continuous years. As an alternative, a homesteader could purchase his land from the government for $1.25 an acre after six months' residence. Between 1862 and 1900 about 400,000 families received free homesteads under this program, but the dream that free public land would siphon off industrial workers from the overcrowded cities of the East was not realized. Very few urban artisans could afford to transport themselves and their families to the frontier, to pay the necessary fees at the land office, to construct a cabin, to purchase the necessary tools and seeds, and to buy food during the long growing season before the wheat or corn was harvested. Even fewer knew how to farm. Consequently the great majority of homesteaders were men and women who had spent all their earlier years on the land. Even experience was no guarantee of success, for fully two-thirds of all homestead claimants before 1890 failed at the venture.

Most settlers in the West did not stake claims under the Homestead

Act but continued, as they had always done, to purchase land directly from the government. Thousands more bought land from the railroad companies, which received from state and national governments enormous tracts of land, equal to more than twice the acreage made available to homesteaders. For instance, Congress gave the Union Pacific and the Central Pacific lines ten square miles of public land for every mile of track completed in the states, and twenty square miles for every mile built in the territories.

However Western settlers secured their land titles, they looked to the national government to protect their farms from the Indians, about 225,000 of whom roamed the Great Plains and Rocky Mountains. In the north the Sioux, Arapaho, Cheyenne, and Nez Percé were the most powerful tribes; to the south the most warlike were the Comanches, Apaches, and Utes. Intrepid and hardy, the braves of all these tribes were fine horsemen and superb marksmen; they were exceedingly dangerous foes of the whites who penetrated their territory to build railroad lines, to mine for gold, or to farm. Hostilities between white settlers and Plains Indians, which broke out during the Civil War, continued almost without interruption for a quarter of a century, with the most barbarous atrocities committed by both sides. After the war, the army slowly but ineluctably forced the tribes into ever smaller reservations. Some desperately resisted, as did the Sioux led by Sitting Bull and Crazy Horse, who tried to keep the Black Hills, tribal holy grounds, from spoliation by gold miners. In 1876, when the army attempted to disperse the Sioux, the Native Americans succeeded in massacring the whole force of 264 officers and men commanded by the dashing, golden-haired Civil War hero, George A. Custer, at Little Big Horn. Such Indian successes were, however, at best temporary, for the army ultimately subdued such great tribal leaders as Chief Red Cloud of the Sioux, Chief Joseph of the Nez Percé, and Geronimo of the Apaches. The final victory of the white settlers was symbolized in the Dawes Act of 1887, which allotted the lands within the still further restricted Indian reservations in 160-acre parcels to Native American residents and thus anticipated the end of the traditional Indian tribal relationship. The West, it was clear, would belong to the white settlers, whose numbers were mounting astronomically.

Indeed, the whole country was growing at a fantastic pace. During the decade from the end of the Civil War to 1876, when the Republic celebrated its centennial year, the population of the United States, despite all the losses in the war, jumped by 30 percent, from 35.7 million to 46.1 million. During these same years more than 3 million immigrants, mostly from Europe, poured into the country. Railroad mileage increased by 111 percent during the decade, from 35,000 miles in 1865 to 74,000 in 1875. The number of bushels of corn produced in the United States increased by 100 per-

MOHAVE BRAVE

The isolation, the stillness, of this Mohave brave suggests the desolate fate
that lay ahead for most Native Americans in the post–Civil War era. A courageous
fighting tribe, the Mohave were removed to a reservation in the Southwest in
1865. (*Library of Congress.*)

cent in the first decade after the war. Almost no American steel was manufactured at the end of the war; 390,000 tons were made ten years later.
Production of bituminous coal increased by 163 percent during the same
decade.

This phenomenal rate of growth fostered a tendency to consolidate the
American economy into one huge functional unit. This had been the dream
of some businessmen long before the war, but after 1865 for the first time
the necessary preconditions for economic integration existed. Never before

had the United States had a national currency, and earlier businessmen had been obliged to settle their obligations with an assortment of state bank notes, local script, and coin. But the National Banking Act of 1864 created a uniform circulating medium. Banks chartered by the national government were allowed, in return for purchasing government bonds, to issue the new national bank notes supplied by the federal comptroller of the currency. A tax placed on state bank notes in 1865 ensured that these national bank notes would thereafter have no competition.

For the first time, too, the United States after 1865 was bound together by a modern communications network. Before the Civil War, a number of rival telegraph companies had been constructing lines but their efforts had been sporadic and uncoordinated. Thanks in part to the extensive military use of the telegraph during the war, the Western Union Telegraph Company grew strong enough to absorb smaller rivals, extended a line across the continent to San Francisco, and, after a sharp fight with Jay Gould's Atlantic & Pacific Telegraph Company in the 1870s, secured a virtual monopoly in the field. Western Union made it possible for a citizen in almost any part of the country to communicate almost instantaneously with his fellows in any other part of the reunited nation. After Alexander Graham Bell invented the telephone in the 1870s, and particularly after he demonstrated the miraculous ability to transmit the human voice by electrical current at the great Centennial Exhibition in Philadelphia in 1876, a second communications network appeared. By the 1880s most city physicians had telephones, and during President Hayes's administration an instrument was installed in the White House. The telephone was still such a novelty that when it rang, the President himself was likely to pick up the receiver.

An improved transportation network also cemented the nation together. A transcontinental railroad, long advocated but repeatedly postponed because of sectional controversies, received the support of Congress in 1862, when it incorporated the Union Pacific Railroad Company. Financed by vast tracts of public lands, the Union Pacific began constructing a line from western Iowa to join with the Central Pacific Railroad, which was pushing eastward from San Francisco. In 1869 the two roads met at Promontory Point, Utah, and it became possible to move passengers and freight by rail from the Atlantic to the Pacific. Less dramatic but more economically significant was the simultaneous coordination and consolidation of rail lines in more settled areas. Before the Civil War there had been eleven different rail gauges in use on Northern roads; President Lincoln's choice of the 4-foot 8½-inch gauge for the Union Pacific led to the standardization of all roads at this width. Before the war, rail travel from New York to Chicago had been barely possible by using eight or ten independent lines, with re-

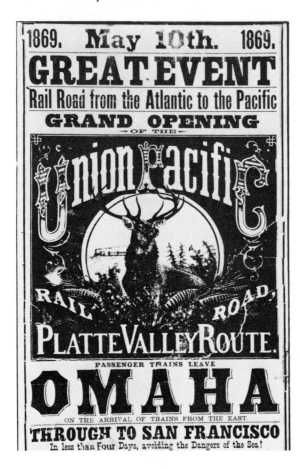

COMPLETION OF
THE UNION PACIFIC RAILROAD

On May 10, 1869, the rails of
the Union Pacific and Central
Pacific Railroads met at Promontory Point, Utah, and the first
transcontinental railroad was
completed. (*Library of Congress.*)

peated transfers. But in 1869 Commodore Vanderbilt consolidated the
New York Central and the Hudson River Railroads to give continuous
service from New York to Buffalo, and five years later he completed arrangements with Western railroads to offer through service to Chicago. At
about the same time the Pennsylvania Railroad, under J. Edgar Thompson,
who dominated the Pennsylvania legislature, and the Erie Railroad, controlled by the unscrupulous financier Jay Gould, completed connections
with Chicago. In 1874, when the Baltimore & Ohio Railroad also reached
the Illinois metropolis, there were four through routes connecting West
and East.

A national communications and transportation network encouraged businessmen to seek national markets for their products. Business consolidation,
already under way before the war, proceeded rapidly, and a striking number
of new entrepreneurs—"robber barons," as later critics called them—were

men whose wartime experience had taught them the advantages of techno-
logical innovation and large-scale management. For instance, Andrew Carnegie, who came to the United States as a poor Scottish immigrant and
trained himself to become a skilled telegraph operator, served during the
war as aide to Thomas A. Scott, the vice-president of the Pennsylvania
Railroad who became assistant secretary of war in charge of all government railroads and transportation lines. From this vantage point, Carnegie
shrewdly foresaw the postwar expansion and reorganization of the railway
system, and he invested his early savings in the company that owned the
patents for Pullman sleeping cars. When these cars became standard equipment on railroads, Carnegie was on his way to acquiring his huge fortune,
with which he subsequently helped build the steel industry in the United
States.

John D. Rockefeller, the pious young Baptist from Cleveland, Ohio, was
not so close to the seat of power in Washington, but he got his start through
handling wartime government contracts for hay, grain, meat, and other
commodities. Quickly he learned how a company managed with order and
enterprise could drive inefficient competitors out of business, and he decided to apply this lesson to the new petroleum industry. Before the Civil
War, the "rock oil" that bubbled to the surface of covered streams in western Pennsylvania had been valued only as a quack medicine, reputedly discovered by the Indians and having miraculous curative powers. But the
discovery that petroleum was a superb lubricant for the machines of the
modern world and that, when refined as kerosene, it provided an efficient
and inexpensive source of illumination made a business out of a craze. In
1859 Edwin L. Drake bored the first well at Titusville, Pennsylvania, and
five years later oil derricks spread over a district of more than 400 square
miles and produced more than 1.1 million barrels of petroleum a year.

Astutely recognizing that the way to dominate the petroleum industry
was to control the refining process, Rockefeller in 1863 constructed the
largest refinery in Cleveland, and two years later he built a second one.
His brother, William, developed the Eastern and the export markets for
their products. Enlisting Harry M. Flagler as a partner in 1867, Rockefeller
worked systematically to cut costs and to rationalize an industry hitherto
unstandardized and intensely competitive. By 1870 Rockefeller's company,
Standard Oil of Ohio, made its own barrels, built its own warehouses, and
owned its own fleet of tankers. Because of the volume of his business,
Rockefeller was able to force the railroads to give his firm lower rates, or
rebates, upon all his shipments. Then, as his power grew, he compelled the
railroads to turn over to Standard Oil "draw-backs," or a portion of what
other oil companies had to pay in the way of freight. As a result of these

business practices, which were at once shrewd and unscrupulous, Standard Oil by 1880 controlled 95 percent of the refining business of the country and practically all the transportation of oil in the United States, whether by pipeline or railroad.

While businesses that operated on a nationwide scale were emerging, so was a national labor movement. There were several attempts to organize labor on a national scale. One of the earliest was the eight-hour movement, led by Ira Steward, a Boston machinist, who sought legislation to limit the work day to eight hours without reduction of wages. Under this pressure the United States established an eight-hour day for its employees in 1868, and legislatures in six states passed acts to make eight hours "a legal day's work." In private industry these laws proved ineffectual because they instituted the eight-hour restriction only "where there is no special contract or agreement to the contrary." Consequently, most businessmen required employees to agree to work longer hours as a condition of employment.

EARLY DAYS IN THE PETROLEUM CENTER OF PENNSYLVANIA

These crowded oil derricks on the west side of Triumph Hill, near Tidionta, Pennsylvania, suggest how rapidly and how wastefully the nation's petroleum resources were exploited. Not more than one out of twenty wells was properly sunk and carefully managed. (*Brown Brothers.*)

The National Labor Union, created in 1866 at a Baltimore conference of delegates from various unions, proved little more successful. It was headed by William H. Sylvis, a dedicated propagandist and a superb speaker, whose interests, however, were not in conventional labor issues, like hours and wages, but in cooperatives and currency reform. Sylvis recruited many members for the National Labor Union—it claimed 640,000 in 1868—but whether these were actual workingmen is questionable. A scornful observer remarked that the National Labor Union was headed by "labor leaders without organizations, politicians without parties, women without husbands, and cranks, visionaries, and agitators without jobs." After Sylvis's death in 1869 the organization began to decline, and it disappeared during the depression of 1873.

A more successful labor movement was the Knights of Labor, founded in 1869 by Uriah Stevens and other garment workers of Philadelphia. It grew slowly at first and, like the National Labor Union, received a serious setback in the depression. By the 1880s, however, its membership increased in a spectacular fashion as it attempted to create a broad union of all workingmen, skilled and unskilled. But its leadership, like that of the National Labor Union, was averse to discussing hours, wages, and working conditions and was reluctant to call strikes. After 1879 the General Master Workman of the Knights of Labor was the idealistic, eloquent, and neurasthenic Irishman Terence V. Powderly, who preferred to think of himself as the head of a national educational institution rather than of a labor union. Indeed, Powderly never behaved like a labor leader but, as an analyst has said, "acted more like Queen Victoria at a national Democratic convention." In consequence, size failed to bring strength to the Knights of Labor and, until the organization of the American Federation of Labor in 1886, there was no national organization that could legitimately claim to speak for the labor movement.

While industry was expanding to reach a national market, other segments of the economy were becoming integrated into the national system. In the post-Civil War years, a huge Western range cattle industry became the prime supplier of beef for the East and also for Europe. Even before the Civil War, cattle raising had become a major occupation in the Great Plains area stretching from Texas to Canada. There tough, hardy cattle, descendants of Mexican longhorns, fed upon open ranges. At yearly roundups, calves were branded so that their owners could identify them, and cowboys selected the strongest steers for the long drive East. When the war cut off markets for Texas cattle, herds became uncomfortably large, and as soon as peace was restored Texas cattlemen renewed their annual drive of cattle on an unprecedented scale.

Initially these vast herds headed for the railroad at Sedalia, Missouri, where they could be transported to Chicago, St. Louis, and other Eastern markets, but Missouri farmers were bitterly opposed to having their crops trampled by thousands of cattle, and town residents did not want their peaceful community disrupted by the "butcher-knife boys, flat-footed boys, huge-pawed boys," who drove the herds. When the Kansas Pacific Railroad reached Abilene, Kansas, in 1867, cattlemen found a shorter, safer route to market. From Texas alone 35,000 head of cattle came to the new railhead in its first year of operation; 350,000 in 1869; 700,000 in 1871. Thereafter, as the national rail network extended farther West, Wichita and Dodge City came to rival, if not to replace, Abilene. These were wild, rowdy frontier towns, where the cowboys, black as well as white, lonely after long months on the range, could let off steam in the dance halls, the saloons, and the red light districts. But these cattle towns also served a basic economic function by tying the range cattle industry into the national economy.

Farmers, too, became part of that national network in the postwar era. The first few years after the war were boom times for Northern and Western farmers. With the repeal of the Corn Laws in 1846 (a repeal that became fully effective in 1849), Great Britain became increasingly dependent on American foodstuffs. By the time of the Civil War, British need for American wheat was great enough to counter, in some measure, British dependence on Southern cotton, and English friends of the Union warned pointedly that recognition of the Confederacy would cut the lifeline of Northern foodstuffs. After the war European, and particularly English, importation of American grain increased to the point that an Austrian observer predicted "hereafter England's wheat fields will lie in America." By 1880, for the first time, the value of American wheat and flour exports nearly equalled that of exported cotton.

Heartened by rising prices, Northern and Western farmers expanded their operations. Using new and improved farm machinery, such as Cyrus Hall McCormick's reaping machine, they were able to cultivate and harvest large crops with less manpower. Since this machinery was expensive and since it operated best on large, level tracts of land, small, self-sufficient farmers, chronically short of cash, were at a disadvantage. The future seemed to belong to large producers, and confident Western farmers went heavily into debt to purchase more land and better machines. More than in any previous era, they were now tied into a national market economy, for their fortunes depended not alone on the land, the weather, and their own efforts, but on the grain elevators, the railroads, and the national and international markets.

≥ IV ≤

The movement toward a national economy in the post–Civil War decades encountered opposition. It rapidly became evident that complete integration could be achieved only at enormous economic, social, and psychological costs. Not even the business interests of the Northeast, which tended to be the primary beneficiaries of a national economic system, were unanimously in favor of all the changes consequent to integration. If New York City grew because of the increasingly centralized financial and transportation networks, that growth was at the expense of such rivals as Boston and Philadelphia. If Standard Oil benefited by Rockefeller's rationalization of the refining industry, hundreds of less successful oil men were forced into failure. If mass production of nails at Andrew Carnegie's massive J. Edgar Thompson steel mill made building construction cheaper and safer, it also cost local blacksmiths and ironmongers their markets.

These tensions within the business community rarely surfaced as issues of public policy to be settled in the political arena. During the Gilded Age —so called from the novel by Mark Twain and Charles Dudley Warner depicting the boom-and-bust speculative mentality of businessmen of the post–Civil War era and the willing complaisance of the politicos who served their interests—almost everybody agreed that the role of government, and especially of the national government, in economic life should be minimal. In only two principal fields was it considered proper for the national government to act in a way that affected the economy: the tariff and the currency. Disagreements among business interests were, therefore, usually voiced in connection with these two endlessly troublesome, highly technical questions, so complex that only a handful of congressmen fully understood them.

The tariff issue was seldom debated in terms of free trade versus protection. Except for a few doctrinaire economic theorists, everybody recognized that some tariff barrier was required to protect some American industries. The debates in Congress revolved about which industries and how much protection. At the end of the Civil War, the high tariffs of the war period, enacted in part to protect heavily taxed American industry from untaxed foreign competition, were clearly anachronistic. Even the protectionist Justin S. Morrill, who had managed the wartime tariff legislation in the House of Representatives, warned fellow congressmen: "It is a mistake of the friends of a sound tariff to insist upon the extreme rates imposed during the war, if less will raise the necessary revenue."

Seeking some reasonable compromise, the New England economist David A. Wells, who was appointed Special Commissioner of the Revenue in 1866, drafted a bill to reduce duties on imported raw materials, such as scrap iron, coal, and lumber, to eliminate arbitrary and unnecessary duties on items like chemicals and spices, and to lower slightly duties on most manufactured articles. Virtually all lawmakers admitted the theoretical excellence of Wells's bill—and virtually all opposed its provisions that lessened or removed protection for their own constituents' businesses. Consequently Wells's bill was defeated, and during the next fifteen years there was no general revision of the tariff legislation.

The absence of general tariff acts did not mean that discussion of tariff rates was at an end. To the contrary, there was throughout the period an endless pulling and hauling between economic interests that stood to gain or lose from changes in duties on specific imported items. For example, during the war a considerable copper industry had grown up in Boston and Baltimore that smelted and refined Chilean ore, which paid a very low tariff duty. But in the late 1860s, the great copper mines around Lake Superior began to be worked on a large scale, and their owners asked Congress to protect their product by raising duties on imported ore. After sharp disagreement, in which President Johnson took the side of the refiners and most congressional Republicans supported the ore producers, the tariff on copper ore was increased in 1869 to the point where most of the Eastern smelting firms had to go out of business.

Other tariff changes were the consequence of combined efforts by the producers and processors of raw materials. An 1867 act revising the duties on raw wool and on woolen cloth was drafted at a convention of wool producers and manufacturers in Syracuse, and it was lobbied through Congress by the indefatigable and effective secretary of the Wool Manufacturers' Association, John L. Hayes. The act accomplished its purpose by a kind of sleight of hand. First came some highly technical and little understood provisions that, as congressmen discovered after voting for them, effectually raised the duty on imported wool; foreign wool was reclassified so that practically all fell into the highest-duty category. Hayes then persuaded congressmen that these new rates on raw materials would substantially increase the cost of woolens manufactured in the United States, so that in all fairness duties on woolen cloth had to be raised too.

Some of the minor adjustments made in the tariff during the postwar years reflected political pressures. In a general way Republicans, with some notable exceptions, tended to favor high protective tariffs, and Democrats, especially those in the South who needed foreign markets for their cotton, wanted to reduce duties. But the issue was rarely clear-cut, for Democrats in manufacturing states like Pennsylvania were high-tariff men. Moreover, both parties tinkered with the tariff issue at election time. In 1872, for instance, the Republican party faced a split, when many tariff reformers in the Liberal Republican movement were preparing to join the Democrats. Attempting to check the bolt, the Republican-dominated Congress rushed through a bill reducing all duties by 10 percent. Once Grant was triumphantly reelected, the Congress promptly repealed the reduction. Again in 1883, when it seemed likely that in the next election Democrats would elect Grover Cleveland President and would win majorities in both Houses of Congress, Republicans hurriedly enacted the first general tariff act since the Civil War. They claimed that it reduced duties by an average of 5 percent, but in fact the measure was so complex and so contradictory that nobody could predict its impact. John L. Hayes, now president of the United States Tariff Commission, gave the secret away when he explained, shortly after the passage of the 1883 act: "In a word, the object was *protection through reduction. . . .* We wanted the tariff to be made by our friends."

The whole complex history of tariff legislation during the Gilded Age, then, demonstrates the continuing strength of the highly nationalistic impulse toward protectionism. At the same time it shows how powerful regional and economic interests adversely affected by excessively high duties were able to secure concessions that gave relief without compromising the general protective framework.

The debate over currency during the post-Civil War generation was more complex, but in general it illustrates the same point. Unless a historian is prepared to write a book about these monetary issues, perhaps he ought to confine his account to two sentences: During the generation after the Civil War, there was constant controversy between those who wished to continue, or even to expand, the inflated wartime money supply and those who wanted to contract the currency. Most debtors favored inflation, since it would allow them to pay debts in money less valuable than when they borrowed it, and creditors favored contraction, so that the money they received in payment of debts would be more valuable than when it was loaned.

But those two sentences, accurate enough in a general way, fail to convey the full dimensions of the controversy. They make the whole argument seem a purely economic question of profit and loss. In fact, for many people the resumption of specie payments—that is, the redemption of the paper money issued by the United States government in gold, at face value—involved the sanctity of contracts, the reliability of the government's pledges, and the rights of private property. Indeed, the return to the gold standard seemed to have almost a religious significance. Probably most economists of the period shared the conviction of Hugh McCulloch, Johnson's secretary of the treasury, that there was something fundamentally wrong, even immoral, about paper money. "By common consent of the nations," McCulloch announced, "gold and silver are the only true measure of value. They are the necessary regulators of trade. I have myself no more doubt that these metals were prepared by the Almighty for this very purpose, than I have that iron and coal were prepared for the purposes for which they are being used." On the other hand, the advocates of so-called "soft" money argued that it was downright un-American to drive greenbacks out of circulation and return to the gold standard. "Why," asked the promoter Jay Cooke, "should this Grand and Glorious Country be stunted and dwarfed—its activities chilled and its very life blood curdled by these miserable 'hard coin' theories—the musty theories of a bygone age?"

That two-sentence summary also ignores the fact that the currency controversy involved economic interests falling into more sophisticated categories than debtors and creditors. Merchants engaged in foreign trade were ardent supporters of resumption, because fluctuations in the gold value of United States paper money made the business of these importers and exporters a game of chance. For example, a merchant who imported silk from France had to pay for his purchase in gold, yet when he sold the silk in the United States he received treasury notes (that is, greenbacks) for it. Since the gold value of greenbacks varied from day to day, the importer had no way of predicting whether his sales price would really equal his purchase price. The profits of foreign commerce were, therefore, so uncertain that, as the New York Chamber of Commerce reported, "prudent men will not willingly embark their money or their merchandise in ventures to distant markets." On the other hand, many American manufacturers, especially iron makers, were stanch foes of resumption, because they needed an inflated currency to keep their national markets expanding. Furthermore, they reckoned that greenback currency served as an additional protective tariff against competing imported iron, which had to be paid for in gold.

Finally, that two-sentence summary does not indicate that attitudes toward these monetary policies changed over time. Throughout the postwar period, farmers were mostly debtors, but they were primarily concerned with such issues as railroad regulation and, until the 1870s, showed little interest in the currency. Creditor interests of the Northeast were indeed mostly supporters of resumption, but when the depression began they unsuccessfully urged President Grant to sign a so-called Inflation Bill of 1874, which would have slightly increased the amount of paper money in circulation. In other words, they preferred mild inflation to economic collapse. Moreover, by the late 1870s inflationists were no longer calling for additional greenbacks; instead, they joined forces with Western mining interests to demand that the government expand the currency by coining silver dollars. When they discovered that, partly by oversight, partly by plan, the Coinage Act of 1873 had discontinued the minting of silver, they were outraged. Protesting the "Crime of '73," they demanded a return to bimetallism (both gold and silver being accepted in lawful payment of all debts) and the free and unlimited coinage of silver dollars.

With so many opposing forces at work, it is scarcely surprising that the history of currency policy and financial legislation in the postwar years is one of sudden fits and starts. Right after the war, Secretary McCulloch assumed that everybody wanted to return to specie payments promptly and, as a means of raising the value of the paper currency, he quietly sequestered greenbacks paid into the United States treasury for taxes and for public lands. His mild contraction of the currency checked business expansion, and Congress forced him to desist. Subsequently these greenbacks were reissued, and in the total amount of $382 million they remained in circulation for the next decade.

In an indirect fashion, the currency became an issue in the presidential election of 1868. During the previous year, what became known as the "Ohio Idea" gained popularity in the Middle West. Critics of hard money objected to the government's practice of paying interest on the national debt in gold—which was, of course, much more valuable than greenbacks. Since the bonds had been purchased with greenbacks, they argued, it would be entirely legal and proper to pay their interest in the same depreciated currency. In this way the crushing burden of the national debt on the taxpayer would be reduced. So attractive was this proposition that the Democratic national convention incorporated a version of the Ohio Idea in its 1868 platform, but it negated this move by nominating Governor Horatio Seymour of New York, an earnest hard-money man, for President. The Republican national convention, against the wishes of many Western delegates, sternly rejected the Ohio Idea, and Grant was nominated with a pledge to reject "all forms of repudiation as a national crime."

Despite this commitment, Grant's administrations witnessed the completion of a series of compromises on currency. The new President announced that he favored a return to the gold standard; but at the same time he warned: "Immediate resumption, if practicable, would not be desirable. It would compel the debtor class to pay, beyond their contracts, the premium on gold . . . and would bring bankruptcy and ruin to thousands." But, lest anyone think that this last statement meant he desired further issues of paper money, Grant, as has been mentioned, vetoed the Inflation Bill of 1874, against the advice of many of his advisers.

It was within this broad policy of affirmation checked by negation that John Sherman, the Senate expert on finance, persuaded Congress in 1875 to pass the Resumption Act, announcing the intention of the United States government to redeem its paper money at face value in gold on or after January 1, 1879. Ostensibly a victory for hard-money interests, the act was, in fact, a brilliant compromise. It did commit the United States to resumption—but only after a delay of four years. Sherman sweetened this pill for the silver mining interests by providing that "as rapidly as practicable" silver coins would be minted to replace the "fractional currency"—notes of postage-stamp size in 3, 5, 10, 15, 25, and 50-cent denominations—issued during the war. To placate the greenback interests in the South and West, Sherman's measure made it easier to incorporate national banks, which had the right to issue treasury notes, in those regions.

Though attempts were made after 1875 to repeal the Resumption Act, it was such a carefully constructed compromise that they all failed. Sherman, who became secretary of the treasury in President Hayes's cabinet, skillfully managed the transition in 1879 so that resumption took place without fanfare and without economic disturbance. The whole controversy over currency during the Gilded Age was thus another illustration of the kind of compromises Americans of this generation hammered out. The national policy of resumption, desired by most businessmen and needed if the United States was to play a part in world trade, was sustained; but local business interests were able to delay and modify implementation of the policy so that it did not impose too sudden or heavy a burden on groups adversely affected by hard money.

⋊ V ⋉

If the emergence of a national economy produced strains within the business community, it created severe problems for farmers and laborers, who felt that they were not fairly sharing its rewards. Discontent became vocal first among farmers. Even in the buoyant years immediately after the Civil War, the life of the Northern and Western farmer was often lonely and dull. On the Western plains, where farmers lived miles from stores, schools, and churches, where there were often no near neighbors, and where there was no regular mail service, even the prosperous lived stunted lives. Perhaps farm women felt the isolation even more deeply than the men.

In an effort to remedy these problems, Oliver Hudson Kelley, a clerk in the United States department of agriculture, in 1867 founded a secret society called the "Patrons of Husbandry." Kelley, who had resided in Massachusetts, Iowa, and Minnesota and who had traveled extensively through the South after the war, knew at first hand the bleakness and the deprivation of rural living, and he wanted to give farmers all over the country a broader vision and a livelier social and intellectual life. The Patrons of

THE PURPOSES OF THE GRANGE

This lithograph features a not very convincing farmer leaning on his shovel. It seems doubtful that his exertions would sustain the Granger's motto, "I Pay For All." But the artist has accurately captured the idealistic objectives of the Patrons of Husbandry. (*Library of Congress.*)

Husbandry was intended to stimulate farmers' thinking through lectures, debates, and discussions, and it was designed to promote a sense of social solidarity through group singing, picnics, and other family entertainment. Each local unit of Kelley's society was called a "Grange," and women as well as men belonged as equal members. So new was the whole idea to American farmers that the organization got off to a slow start, and at the end of 1868 only ten Granges had been established.

In the following year, when the price of farm commodities dropped sharply, agrarian discontent mounted, and by the mid-1870s about 800,000 farmers, mostly in the Middle West and the South, joined the Granger movement. Though the Granges never abandoned their social and intellectual objectives, the meetings came increasingly to focus on economic issues important to farmers, such as the declining price of wheat and the mounting costs of railroad transportation. Forbidden by the constitution of the Patrons of Husbandry to engage in politics, the Grangers found it easy after the recital of the Grange litany and the standard literary or musical program to move that the meeting be adjourned; then, technically no longer Grangers but simply farmers gathered together, they discussed politics and endorsed candidates who favored the farmers' cause.

That cause embraced a variety of discontents with the operations of the national economy. Farmers in Iowa, Nebraska, and Kansas complained that it took the value of one bushel of corn to pay the freight charges for shipping another bushel to Eastern markets; farmers in Minnesota and Dakota said the same of wheat. Middle Western farmers protested the policy of the grain elevators, used to store their wheat and corn until it could be picked up for rail shipment. Elevator operators frequently misgraded grain, offering the farmer with superior produce only the price for a lower grade, and the farmer usually had to accept, for he could not dump his grain on the ground. Southern and Western farmers also objected to the limited bank credit available in their regions. When the national banking system was set up, the war was still going on, and no provision was made for establishing national banks in the South. In the West there were few national banks, because Congress required a minimum capital of $50,000, which few Western towns could raise. In consequence, the circulation of national bank notes, and hence the availability of loans, was grossly inequitable. Connecticut alone had more national bank notes in circulation than Michigan, Wisconsin, Iowa, Minnesota, Kansas, Missouri, Kentucky, and Tennessee.

Farmers' dissatisfaction with the national economy blended into a more general pattern of Middle Western discontent. It was not farmers alone who objected to high and discriminatory railroad rates; businessmen in Middle Western cities and towns, especially those served by only one rail line, also protested. Because the railroads set rates that favored large grain terminals, wheat produced twenty miles from Milwaukee might be diverted to Chicago. Because the railroads gave special preference to long-distance shippers, lumber merchants in Clinton, Iowa, found that Chicago lumber dealers could undersell them; trainloads of lumber rumbled in from Chicago on the way to central and western Iowa without even slowing down at Clinton. The inequities in the national banking system affected Western businessmen at least as much as they did farmers, for the absence of credit crippled business expansion.

Out of these general Western grievances emerged what came to be known, somewhat inaccurately, as the Granger laws. Between 1869 and 1874, legislatures in Illinois, Iowa, Wisconsin, and Minnesota set maximum charges for grain elevators and railroads, and some of these states established regulatory commissions with broad powers. Though farmers supported this legislation, it was actually framed by Western lawyers and pushed by Western businessmen; only in Wisconsin were the Grangers the principal advocates of regulation. Promptly the railroad and grain elevator companies challenged the constitutionality of these acts, but the United States Supreme Court, in *Munn* v. *Illinois* (1877), upheld the right of states to regulate railroads, even to the point of setting maximum rates.

In the long run, state regulation of railroads and grain elevators proved ineffectual, and the Granger laws were repealed or seriously modified. Nevertheless, their temporary success marked a victory for the forces of localism injured by a national economy. The Supreme Court's decision, in effect, endorsed and legitimated the American Compromise: Middle Western farmers and businessmen made no attempt to dismantle the national system of transportation, communications, and marketing, but that system was required to concede a degree of autonomy to localities and interests adversely affected by economic consolidation.

Far different was the outcome of labor protests against a national economic system during these same years. Labor discontent became articulate and forceful when the panic of 1873, precipitated by the failure of Jay Cooke and Company, led into the longest and most severe depression Americans had yet experienced. As business activity declined by about one-third between 1873 and 1879 and the number of bankruptcies doubled during the same period, workers were laid off. During the winter of 1873–1874, about one-fourth of all laborers in New York City were unemployed, and during the following winter the number increased to one-third.

While private charities did what they could to relieve distress, nobody seemed to know how to end the depression. Informed opinion tended to view the panic and the subsequent unemployment and suffering as part of the natural workings of the national economic order, necessary to purge unsound businesses and speculative practices. Economists warned that "coddling" laborers would only retard this inevitable and necessary process. Blaming the depression on the wartime habit of looking to the federal government for leadership, Democratic Governor Samuel J. Tilden of New York called for a return to "government institutions, simple, frugal, meddling little with the private concerns of individuals . . . and trusting to the people to work out their own prosperity and happiness."

Labor leaders were little more helpful. For one reason, the national labor movement collapsed during the depression, and many local unions disappeared as well. In New York City, for example, membership in all unions dropped from 45,000 in 1873 to 5000 in 1877. Those labor spokesmen who remained active tended to advocate panaceas. A writer in the *Radical Review* found the cause of the depression in the private ownership of land, "which begets ... ground rent, an inexorable, perpetual claim for the use of land, which, like air and light, is the gift of Nature." In 1879 Henry George made that proposition the basis for the economic reforms proposed in *Progress and Poverty*. Other labor voices supported the Socialist Labor movement, founded in 1874, which anticipated the ultimate overthrow of the capitalist system through a socialist revolution but, as interim measures to combat the depression, advocated federal aid for education, industrial accident compensation, and women's suffrage. The movement attracted a minuscule following.

Some labor spokesmen sought the way out of the depression by supporting independent political parties pledged to protect labor's position in the national economy. There was considerable labor support for the Greenback, or National Independent, party, which was organized in 1874 in Indianapolis. The party's national platform opposed the resumption of specie pay-

THE GREAT STRIKE—THE WORK OF
DESTRUCTION IN PITTSBURGH

After the panic of 1873, labor unrest led to violence in a number of areas. The most serious riots occurred in 1877, the worst year of the depression. During the great railroad strike of that year, laborers seized and set fire to the roundhouse of the Pennsylvania Railroad in Pittsburgh. Federal troops were sent to quell the disturbance. (*Harper's Weekly, 1877.*)

ments and advocated further issues of paper money "to furnish relief to the depressed industries of the country." That the Greenback party was not a labor movement exclusively is attested by the fact that its presidential candidate in 1876 was the eighty-five-year-old New York iron manufacturer, Peter Cooper. The 80,000 votes Cooper received came mostly from Middle Western farm states. In the congressional elections two years later, however, more laborers supported the National Independent party as it campaigned for government regulation of the hours of labor and for the exclusion of Chinese immigrants. Like other advocates of inflation, the party by this time had moved beyond favoring greenbacks and urged expansion of the currency through silver coinage. Candidates endorsed by the National Independent party received more than 1 million votes in the 1878 congressional elections.

Other laborers during the depression rejected politics in favor of direct action. With the collapse of the trade union movement, the "Molly Maguires," a secret ring that controlled the popular fraternal society, the Ancient Order of Hibernians, gained power in the anthracite coal region of Pennsylvania. Soon mine owners reported a "crime wave" in collieries, as

the "Mollies" allegedly intimidated and even murdered bosses and superintendents they considered unfair. Eventually, on the rather dubious testimony of a paid infiltrator, a number of the ringleaders were arrested, and when twenty-four of them were convicted in late 1876, the disturbances ended.

Labor unrest reached its peak in 1877, the worst year of the long depression. Railroad managers precipitated a crisis when, without warning, they cut wages on most railroads east of the Mississippi River by 10 percent. On July 17, the day after the cut became effective, workers on the Baltimore & Ohio Railroad went on strike, took possession of the railyards at various points, and refused to let any freight trains depart. Promptly employees of other Eastern railroads also went on strike, and traffic on the four trunk lines connecting the Atlantic coast and the Middle West was paralyzed. Shortly afterward, the strike spread to some of the roads beyond the Mississippi and in Canada.

Local and state governments proved unable or unwilling to cope with the crisis. The governor of Maryland called out the state militia, but these civilian soldiers fraternized with their friends and relatives among the strikers. In Pittsburgh, the strikers had the sympathy of the local government, for the city fathers had long felt that the Pennsylvania Railroad was discriminating against their city. Employees of nearby ironworks joined the railroad men in blocking all traffic on the Pennsylvania. When the governor sent in state militia companies from Philadelphia to clear the tracks, they succeeded in dispersing a large mob by killing twenty-six persons, but their action roused so much additional hostility that the troops were obliged to retreat into the roundhouse, which the mob promptly surrounded and set on fire. The next morning the Philadelphia soldiers fought their way out of the roundhouse and retreated from the city, leaving it in control of a mob of strikers, sympathizers, and looters, who proceeded to destroy railroad property worth some $5 million.

To protect the national system of transportation so essential to the national economy, President Hayes sent in regular army troops. This was the first time in American history that the army had been used on any extensive scale to crush labor disturbance. Promptly the army restored order, and the strike collapsed. Deeply disturbed members of the business community took steps to prevent any recurrence of such labor violence. State legislatures began passing conspiracy laws directed against labor organizations, and the courts began to invoke the doctrine of malicious conspiracy to break strikes and boycotts. Throughout the North, the state militia, which had so often proved untrustworthy during the 1877 crisis, was reorganized and given stricter training. Cyrus Hall McCormick personally purchased equipment for the Second Regiment of Illinois militia because it had "won great credit for its action during . . . disturbances and can be equally relied on in the future."

Thus labor protests against the national economy failed at just the time that farm protest movements largely succeeded. This different outcome is attributable, in part, to the fact that there was a long history of agrarian discontent in the United States, and the Granger movement seemed as American as apple pie. Urban labor, labor unions, and massive strikes were, on the other hand, something novel to most Americans, and no doubt all three seemed the more dangerous, since so many industrial laborers were immigrants with strange-sounding names and alien ways of behavior. In part, too, the differences stemmed from the fact that farmers and their allies lived in a distinct region of the United States, where they were strong enough to control local and state governments in the South and Middle West; scattered through states that had many competing economic interests, industrial laborers nowhere had similar political power.

More important than either of these differences was the fact that agrarian discontent did not pose a basic threat to the structure of the national economy. The imposition of limits on the power of railroads and of a few other monopolies was an idea that a good many businessmen thought desirable. Labor unrest, on the other hand, appeared to strike at the heart of the national economic system. A popular Boston minister declared that the rioting of "the lawless classes at the bottom of our cities" had been instigated by "secret socialistic societies." The prominent financial editor, W. M. Grosvenor, spoke for much of the business community when he announced that "the light of the flame at Pittsburgh" portended "a terrible trial for free institutions in this country." He warned: "The Communist is here."

In short, the American Compromise worked, but only within limits. Advocates of a national economy could accept compromise when various segments of the business community differed over particular legislative issues, such as the tariff or the currency. They could coexist with the local autonomy demanded by the Granger movement. But they could not tolerate the fundamental threat that insurrectionary labor seemed to pose to the capitalist system.

PRESIDENT ULYSSES S. GRANT

Only forty-seven when inaugurated President, Grant had lost the air of seedy indecisiveness that had misled so many during the Civil War. Now portly and self-contained, with a countenance "hard, small and expressionless," he played politics with a skill that confused his critics—and some subsequent historians as well. Grant's inaugural plea, "Let us have peace," became the motto of the age of reconciliation. (*Library of Congress.*)

8

Reconciliation

It is evident, then, that the nationalistic impulse stimulated during the Civil War lost much of its momentum during the Reconstruction years. In both the North and the South, long-established institutions, deeply rooted interests, and ingrained American values limited innovation and slowed down the tendency toward centralization. By the end of the postwar period, the forces of nationalism and localism reached equilibrium. The American Compromise between these forces guaranteed, within a sphere much broader than before the war, the supremacy of the national government and the primacy of a nationally integrated economy. It also protected, though within limits more constricted than in 1860, the minority rights of regions and states and localities.

So long as this American Compromise was simply the result of a balance between opposing forces, it was a fragile arrangement. Any fluctuation in the business cycle, any significant shift of voters, could easily upset it and again set North against South, East against West, hard-money advocate against inflationist, businessman against farmer, white against black. In order to endure, the American Compromise had to be legitimated. Politicians of both national parties had to agree not to consider these informal arrangements as issues in elections. Equally important, these agreements had to find a place in the minds and hearts of the American people. A lasting compromise had to rest not on calculation but on consensus. The times called for reconciliation.

❧ I ❦

In this process of reconciliation during the final years of Reconstruction, politicians played a vital part. On first thought this may seem an odd idea to advance, since the 1870s and 1880s are generally considered a singularly uninteresting period in American political history, when the holders of public office appeared as interchangeable as Tweedledum and Tweedledee. Many historians have written of the Gilded Age as a time of mediocre Presidents, uninspired congressmen, and unimportant legislation.

That verdict fails to take into account the fact that these politicians most effectively gave legitimacy to the American Compromise by not upsetting the balance. Their most useful role was the one W. S. Gilbert attributed to the British peers:

> The House of Lords throughout the war
> Did nothing in particular,
> And did it very well.

It must be conceded that the achievement of the politicos of the Gilded Age was, in large measure, inadvertent. Many of them professed to have policies they wished to pursue, but fortunately they failed ever to receive a popular mandate to act. Most of the Presidents of the period barely squeaked into office. Grant's success in 1868 was a tribute to a great military leader, not an endorsement of the Republican party that nominated him. Even so, he received only 53 percent of the popular vote. Grant's reelection by a huge popular margin in 1872 was due chiefly to his opponents' willingness to commit political suicide. Dissatisfied members of Grant's own party joined the Liberal Republican movement, which agitated for lower tariffs and for reconciliation with the South—and then proceeded to nominate for President the erratic New York *Tribune* editor, Horace Greeley, famed as a protectionist and hated for his prewar denunciations of slaveholders. Holding its nose, the Democratic party also endorsed Greeley, but thousands of Democrats and Liberal Republicans stayed away from the polls. In 1876 Republican Rutherford B. Hayes received a minority of the popular vote and, after prolonged controversy, was elected by a majority of only one vote in the electoral college. Hayes's successor, James A. Garfield, had a plurality of only 9000 votes over his Democratic rival in the 1880 presidential election, in which over 9 million votes were cast. Chester A. Arthur, who became President in 1881 after Garfield's assassination, clearly had no mandate from anybody. In 1884 the Democrats succeeded in electing Grover Cleveland, the first successful candidate of their party since the Civil War, but the New Yorker received less than a majority of the total popular vote and won only 70,000 more votes than his Republican rival. Four years later, in 1888, that rival, Benjamin Harrison, defeated Cleveland by winning a majority in the electoral college, but the Democratic candidate had a plurality of the popular votes.

Even had these Presidents been elected by overwhelming majorities in order to carry out ambitious programs, they would have been frustrated by the fact that control of Congress was usually in the hands of their political enemies. To be sure, Grant started with safely Republican majorities in both Houses of Congress, but Carl Schurz, Charles Sumner, and other leading Republicans soon joined the Liberal Republican movement, voted with the Democrats, and blocked the administration's favorite measures. In the congressional elections of 1874, Democrats for the first time since the Civil War won a majority in the House of Representatives and, except for two years (1881–1883), they retained control of the House until 1889. It was not, therefore, until the inauguration of the Democratic President Grover Cleveland in 1885 that the executive and the legislative branches of the national government represented the same political party. Given these conditions, it is easy to understand why the politicians of the Gilded Age accomplished so little and why the few measures they succeeded in adopting had to be compromises.

Though untutored in politics, Grant seems to have sized up the political situation at once. The same strategic sense that dictated his offensive campaign against Vicksburg suggested his defensive, compromising role as President. "Let us have peace," the President urged in his inaugural address— but it was not clear whether he was addressing the white Ku Kluxers who were trying to overthrow the Reconstruction governments in the South or the Northern Radicals who wanted to impose further conditions on the Southern states. As it proved, Grant had both extremes in mind. On the one hand, the President warmly supported the immediate and unconditional readmission of Virginia to the Union, even though Radicals like Sumner warned that the Virginia legislature was "composed of recent Rebels still filled and seething with that old Rebel fire." On the other, Grant was outraged by the terrorism rampant in the South, and he insisted that Congress pass a series of Enforcement Acts (1870–1871) enabling him to crush the Ku Klux Klan. Under this legislation, the President proclaimed martial law in nine South Carolina counties where white terrorists were most active, and federal marshals arrested large numbers of suspected Klansmen in North Carolina, Mississippi, and other Southern states. In brief, then, Grant's policy was to warn Southern whites that the national government would not tolerate overt violence and organized military activity—but to let them understand that they would not be harassed if they regained control of their state governments through less revolutionary tactics.

Though a few old Radicals like Sumner attacked Grant's Southern policy and blamed him for shedding the blood of innocent white and black Unionists in the South, most Northerners accepted the President's program without difficulty. They were growing tired of the whole question of Reconstruction. Other issues claimed their attention, as debates over the resumption of specie payments and the annexation of Santo Domingo pushed stories about the South off the front pages of the newspapers.

Especially diverting were the revelations that newspapers began to make about corruption on all levels of government. During a war, as Lincoln said in 1863, "Every foul bird comes abroad, and every dirty reptile rises up." The Civil War inaugurated a period of low public morality in the United States, and wartime patterns of favoritism, fraud, and bribery continued into the Reconstruction era. Then, about 1870, reformers and crusading newspaper editors started to expose the corruption. The earliest revelations concerned New York City, which had fallen under the control of "Boss" William Marcy Tweed, who proceeded joyfully to loot the taxpayers. Tweed's ring began construction of a new county courthouse, which cost $3 million, but for which Tweed's board of audit charged taxpayers $11 million. Nearly $3 million went to a man named Garvey for plastering this and other municipal buildings; after the amount of his fees leaked out, he became known as the "Prince of Plasterers." Tweed approved the purchase of so many chairs, at $5 each, that if placed in line they would have extended seventeen miles. In 1871 when the New York *Times* began to expose the ring's padded bills, faked leases, false vouchers, and other frauds, the attention of the whole nation was attracted, and when *Harper's Weekly* started carrying Thomas Nast's devastating caricatures of the Boss, Tweed's face became more familiar to Americans than that of any other man except Grant. As readers followed the stories of Tweed's arrest, trial, escape from detention, flight to Spain, where he was identified by an official who had seen Nast's cartoons, and return to a New York prison, they had little time for or interest in the customary tales of terrorism in the South.

Soon revelations about the national government began to make equally fascinating reading. Shortly before the 1872 election, the New York *Sun,* a Democratic paper, began to expose the workings of the Credit Mobilier, the construction company that the Union Pacific Railroad Company paid to build its transcontinental route. Investigation proved that members of the Credit Mobilier were also members of the board of directors of the Union

"ROMISH POLITICS—ANYTHING TO BEAT GRANT"

Thomas Nast's cartoon ridicules Horace Greeley's attempt to make
his presidential candidacy acceptable to the Democratic Irish-
Americans, whom Nast portrayed as apelike creatures. Note the
Catholic priest, prepared to take control of the public schools
should Greeley win. (*Library of Congress.*)

Pacific, who were, thus, paying themselves huge profits. What was even
more damaging was the revelation that, in order to avert public inquiry,
the Credit Mobilier offered stock to Vice-President Schuyler Colfax, Representative (and future President) James A. Garfield, and other prominent
politicians. They were allowed to "purchase" the stock on credit, the down
payment being "earned" by the high dividends that the stock began to pay.

Though Republicans found it advisable to drop Colfax from their ticket
in 1872, scandal did not seriously touch the Grant administration until after the election. Then, in short order, stories of fraud began to appear about
almost every branch of the executive offices. In the treasury department,
unscrupulous customshouse officers, especially in New York, preyed on importers. Merchants who failed to pay off the brigands had their shipments

delayed, their imported goods subjected to minute, time-consuming inspection, and their crates and boxes that were not immediately removed from the docks stored at exorbitant rates. Corruption was rampant in the navy department, where political favoritism dictated everything from the employment of workers in the shipyards to the contracts for the construction of new vessels. Secretary of War William W. Belknap was proved to have accepted bribes from Indian traders, who had the exclusive and particularly remunerative franchise to sell goods to Indians and soldiers at frontier army posts.

Of all these scandals, the closest to the White House was the Whiskey Ring. In order to avoid heavy excise taxes, first levied during the war, whiskey distillers, especially those in St. Louis, had for years been conspiring with officials of the internal revenue service. During Grant's administration, they secured the cooperation of none other than Orville E. Babcock, the President's private secretary, who warned the swindlers whenever an inspection team was sent out from Washington. In return for his assistance, Babcock received such favors as a $2,400 diamond shirt-stud, which he found defective and asked to have replaced with another, more expensive one, and from time to time the ministrations of a "sylph." When Grant first learned of the frauds, he urged, "Let no guilty man escape." But as it became clear that his close friends and his personal staff were involved, he did everything possible to block further investigation. When Babcock went on trial, the President of the United States offered a deposition expressing "great confidence in his integrity and efficiency." Babcock was acquitted, and Grant retained him on the White House staff.

As news of these shabby scandals—and there were scores of others, on all levels of government—spread, large numbers of Northerners came to think it was more important to set their own house in order than to tell Southerners how to behave. As early as 1867, *The Nation* announced: "The diminution of political corruption is the great question of our time. It is greater than the [question of Negro] suffrage, greater than reconstruction. . . ."

The desire to reduce political corruption led to the emergence of the civil service reform movement during the Gilded Age. Though voices had been raised against the spoils system long before the Civil War, it was not until after Appomattox that an organized reform drive appeared. Knowledge of widespread wrongdoing among government officials, fear that President Johnson might convert the government bureaucracy into a tool to promote his renomination, and the example of the British system of appointing civil servants after competitive examinations gave strength to the movement. Early efforts of Representative Thomas A. Jenckes of Rhode Island to require federal appointees to pass competitive examinations failed in Congress, but the reformers, led by the politically ambitious George William Curtis, editor of *Harper's Weekly,* and by E. L. Godkin of *The Nation,* hoped for success under Grant's administration.

They were doomed to disappointment, for on this, as on all other controversial topics, Grant perfectly understood that compromise was the mood of the age, and he straddled. He made no mention of civil service reform in his first message to Congress, and Henry Adams—the son of Lincoln's minister to Great Britain and the grandson and great-grandson of American Presidents—remarked in his supercilious way that Grant was inaugurating

WILLIAM M. TWEED

Thomas Nast's devastating caricatures of the corrupt New York boss made Tweed's face familiar all over the world. When the "Boss" fled to Spain to escape prosecution, a Spanish immigration official identified him on the basis of Nast's drawings, and he was sent back to New York to serve his prison sentence. (*American Antiquarian Society.*)

"a reign of western mediocrity." But when disgruntled civil service reformers began to talk loudly about joining the Liberal Republican movement, Grant moved swiftly to head them off. In 1871 he pressured Congress into creating a Civil Service Reform Commission, and he neatly co-opted his chief critic by naming Curtis chairman. Though the commission had little power and achieved less success, the move kept Curtis and a sizable number of reformers as supporters of Grant's reelection. Once the election was over, Grant lost interest in the commission and so blatantly violated its rules that Curtis had to resign.

Strengthened by the news of the scandals that rocked Grant's second administration, civil service reformers claimed some of the credit for the nomination of Hayes in 1876, but they found him as difficult to manage as Grant. On the one hand, the new President did take on the powerful political machine of New York Senator Roscoe Conkling and he succeeded in ousting some of Conkling's supporters, including future President Chester A. Arthur, from the New York customshouse. On the other hand, at election time the President wanted his own appointees to contribute to Republican campaign funds and to help organize Republican state conventions, much as their predecessors had done. "I have little or no patience with Mr. Hayes," exclaimed the reforming editor of the New York *Times*. "He is a victim of . . . good intentions and his contributions to the pavement of the road to the infernal regions are vast and various."

Hayes's successor, Garfield, gave civil service reformers little more satisfaction. With cruel accuracy, one Massachusetts reformer characterized the new President as "a grand, noble fellow, but fickle, unstable, . . . timid and hesitating." Civil service reform advocates noted suspiciously that Garfield's Vice-President was Arthur, named by the Republican national convention in a vain attempt to placate Conkling. Consequently reformers felt no special sense of victory when Garfield chose James G. Blaine, leader of the "Half-breed" faction of the Republican party, as his secretary of state and began to oust more of Conkling's "Stalwarts" from the New York customshouse. Conceited and imperious, Conkling resigned in a huff from the Senate and rushed to Albany seeking vindication through reelection. To his surprise, Hayes's removal of Stalwarts from federal offices undercut the Stalwarts, and the New York legislature failed to send Conkling back to the Senate. Shortly afterward, a crazed office-seeker named Charles Guiteau assassinated Garfield, shouting that he was a Stalwart and rejoicing that Arthur was now President. Shocked by Garfield's assassination, Congress in 1883 passed the Pendleton Act, which required competitive examinations of applicants for some federal jobs. Though the measure covered only a fraction of all government employees, it was a genuine measure of

PRESIDENT CHESTER A. ARTHUR

President Arthur was typical of the chief executives of the Gilded Age, who had no popular mandate, and initiated no broad, controversial programs. (*Library of Congress.*)

civil service reform and permitted the emergence of a professional government bureaucracy.

⊱ II ⊰

While Northern opinion was focused on corruption and civil service reform, while it was further diverted by the depression, unemployment, and strikes, state after state in the former Confederacy was restored to what was euphemistically called "home rule"—which meant the rule of native white Democrats. The "Redeemers," as they called themselves, gained power first in Virginia, North Carolina, Tennessee, and Georgia. In 1875 they won control of Alabama, Mississippi, Arkansas, and Texas, and early in 1877 they ended Republican rule in Florida.

To the relatively few Northerners who were concerned about these developments, the new rulers of the South seemed much like the antebellum slavocracy. All stanch Democrats, the Redeemers sported the traditional Southern mustachios and goatees, they bragged about their records in the Confederate army, and they erupted in florid Southern oratory. In fact, however, they represented a substantially different interest from the plantation oligarchs of the prewar era; they allied themselves instead with the factory owners, railroad men, and city merchants of the New South. In public stance the Redeemers identified themselves with the romantic cult of the Confederacy and yearned over "the dignifying memories of the war," but they were really in favor, as a Vicksburg, Mississippi, editor admitted, "of the South, from the Potomac to the Rio Grande, being thoroughly and permanently Yankeeized."

But the process of creating a Yankee South, the Redeemers made abundantly clear, had to be directed by Southerners like themselves. Their experience during the Reconstruction years taught them to distrust Northerners, even Northerners of their own economic backgrounds and viewpoints. Consequently, in state after state, the Redeemers systematically went about overthrowing Republican rule. The tactics varied according to the locality, but the strategy was everywhere the same. White Republicans were subjected to social pressure, economic boycott, and outright violence; many fled the South. Though the Redeemers made some efforts to woo Negro voters, most realized the task was futile and instead devised ways of intimidating or coercing them. Sometimes they exercised economic pressure by threatening not to hire or extend credit to politically active blacks. In several states whites organized rifle clubs, which practiced marksmanship on the outskirts of Republican political rallies. When the blacks attempted to defend themselves, whites overpowered them and slaughtered their leaders. In state after state, Republican governors appealed to Washington for additional federal troops, but Grant, convinced that the public was tired of "these annual autumnal outbreaks" in the South, refused. As a result, by the end of Grant's second administration, South Carolina and Louisiana were the only Southern states with Republican governments.

The fate of these two remaining Republican regimes in the South became intricately connected with the outcome of the 1876 presidential election. The Democratic nominee, Samuel J. Tilden, undoubtedly received a majority of the popular votes—though, equally undoubtedly, thousands

A NOTICE FROM THE KU KLUX KLAN

The Ku Klux Klan and other Southern white terrorist organizations tried to intimidate both blacks and their white allies. This notice threatens death to a man who recommended a Negro's appointment as a United States mail agent.

of blacks who would have voted for his Republican rival, Hayes, were kept from the polls. But Tilden lacked one vote of having a majority in the electoral college unless he received some votes from South Carolina, Florida, and Louisiana, all of which submitted to Congress competing sets of Democratic and Republican ballots. (There was also a technical question of the eligibility of one Republican elector from Oregon.) Immediately after the election, "visiting statesmen" from both the Republican and Democratic national headquarters went to these states in an effort to influence the counting of the ballots. It soon became clear that Hayes really had received a majority in South Carolina. In Florida the outgoing Republican governor certified that Hayes electors had won, but his Democratic successor, installed early in 1877, gave certificates of election to the Tilden electors. Louisiana also sent in two sets of electoral votes, one representing the original count that showed Tilden the victor by some 9000 votes, the second arrived at by the notoriously corrupt state canvassing board, controlled by Republicans, that showed Hayes the victor by 3000 votes.

Consequently, when Congress assembled in December 1876, it confronted a crisis. If it decided to accept the disputed Democratic electoral votes, Republican control of the White House would be broken for the

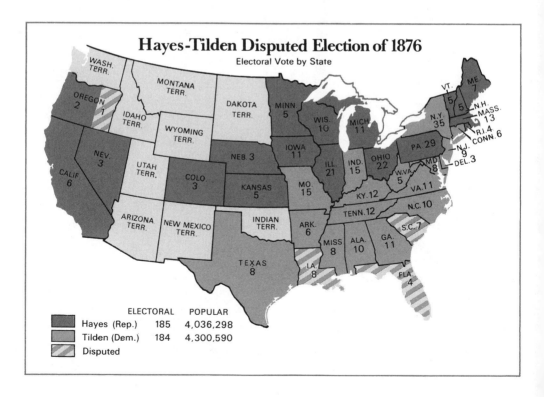

Hayes-Tilden Disputed Election of 1876

Electoral Vote by State

	ELECTORAL	POPULAR
Hayes (Rep.)	185	4,036,298
Tilden (Dem.)	184	4,300,590
Disputed		

first time in a quarter of a century and the reconstruction of the South would be ended. If Congress accepted the Republican electoral votes, that decision would run counter to the will of a majority of the voters in the country, and it would outrage Democrats, some of whom agreed with Henry Watterson's Louisville *Courier-Journal* that 100,000 Democratic "petitioners" should surround the Capitol while the votes were being tallied.

To resolve the impasse required a compromise—not a single compromise, but a complicated, interlocking set of bargains. After intricate and secret negotiations, several agreements were reached. First Congress decided that the disputed electoral votes should be referred to a special electoral commission, which consisted of five members of the House of Representatives, five members of the Senate, and five associate justices of the Supreme Court. This body was composed of eight Republicans and seven Democrats, and on every disputed ballot the commission ruled in favor of Hayes by that same vote. These decisions left Tilden's electoral vote at 184, while Hayes's slowly mounted to 185. In March 1877, for the fifth time in succession, a Republican President was inaugurated.

Democrats reluctantly accepted the election of Hayes because of some other bargaining that took place while the electoral votes were being counted. One set of compromises came to be known as the "Wormley agreement," because it was negotiated in the luxurious Washington hotel owned by the Negro restaurateur, James Wormley. Representing Hayes at these sessions were Senator Sherman, Representative Garfield, and other prominent Republicans; across the table sat Southern Democratic leaders, including Henry Watterson of Kentucky, Senator John B. Gordon, the former Confederate general who now represented Georgia in Congress, and L. Q. C. Lamar, once Confederate minister to Russia, who was senator from Mississippi. The Republicans promised the Southerners that, if allowed to be inaugurated, Hayes "would deal justly and generously with the south." Translated, that meant that Hayes's friends pledged he would withdraw the remaining federal troops from the South and would acquiesce in the overthrow of the Republican regimes in South Carolina and Louisiana. The Southerners found the terms acceptable, and they promptly leaked the news of their agreement, so as to protect themselves from charges that they had betrayed their section.

Behind the Wormley agreement lay other, less formal, compromises. Hayes's backers promised that the new President would not use federal patronage in the South to defeat the Democrats. They further pledged that he would support congressional appropriations for rebuilding levees along the flood-ridden Mississippi River and for constructing a transcontinental railroad along a Southern route. In return, Southerners agreed to allow the Republicans to elect Garfield speaker of the new House of Representatives, with the power to determine the membership of congressional committees. More important, they promised to protect the basic rights of blacks, as guaranteed in the Thirteenth, Fourteenth, and Fifteenth Amendments to the Constitution.

Once Hayes was inaugurated, nearly all of these informal agreements were flouted by both sides. Hayes, for his part, ordered the removal of federal troops from the South, and he did appoint a Southerner, former Confederate David M. Key, to his cabinet as postmaster-general. But two-thirds of the federal officeholders in the South remained Republicans, including sixteen officials connected with the notorious Louisiana canvassing board. Hayes also changed his mind about supporting a Southern transcontinental railroad. To "make possible any more Credit Mobilier operations," he said piously, "would be a serious mistake."

In turn, Southern Democrats reneged on their promises. They did not vote for Garfield as speaker but instead helped reelect to that powerful position a stalwart Democrat, Samuel J. Randall of Pennsylvania. Once the House was organized under Democratic control, the Southerners eagerly joined in an investigation of alleged fraud in Hayes's election. Only a few Southern Democratic politicians, like Governor Wade Hampton of South Carolina, remembered their promises to respect the rights of blacks. Instead, nearly all took the final withdrawal of federal troops from the South as a signal that the Negro, already relegated to a position of economic inferiority, could be excluded from Southern political life.

Southern whites had to act cautiously, so as not to offend public opinion in the North or to invite renewed federal intervention, but they moved steadily and successfully to reduce Negro voting. One of the simplest devices was the poll tax, adopted by Georgia in 1877 and quickly copied by other Southern states. To Northerners, the requirement that a voter had to pay $1 or $2 a year did not seem unreasonable, yet in fact, since three-fourths of the entire Southern population had an average income of only $55.16 in 1880, the poll tax was a considerable financial drain, especially for poverty-stricken blacks. More imaginative was the "eight box" law, adopted by South Carolina in 1882 and imitated by North Carolina and Florida. Under this system, ballots for each contested race had to be deposited in separate boxes. Thus a voter must cast in one box his ballot for governor, in another box his ballot for sheriff, and so forth. The system frustrated the illiterate Negro voter, who could no longer bring to the polls a single ballot, marked for him in advance by a Republican friend. To make the task of semiliterate voters more difficult, election officials periodically rearranged the order of the boxes. Still another device, which did

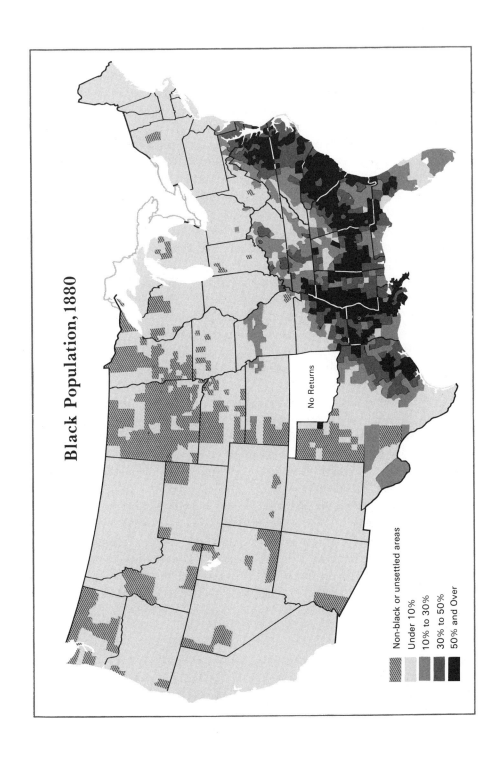

Black Population, 1880

No Returns

Non-black or unsettled areas
Under 10%
10% to 30%
30% to 50%
50% and Over

not become popular until the late 1880s, was the secret, or Australian, ballot. Ostensibly introduced in the South, as in the North, in order to prevent fraud, the secret ballot actually discriminated heavily against blacks, for as late as 1900 the number of illiterate adult Negro males ranged from 39 percent in Florida to 61 percent in Louisiana.

Despite all these devices, Southern blacks continued to vote in surprising numbers. In the 1880 presidential election, for example, more than 70 percent of the eligible Negroes voted in Arkansas, Florida, North Carolina, Tennessee, and Virginia, and between 50 percent and 70 percent voted in Alabama, Louisiana, South Carolina, and Texas. To the Redeemers, these black voters posed a double threat. They were numerous enough that ambitious Northern Republicans might be tempted again to try federal intervention in state elections, with the hope of breaking the now solidly Democratic South. Even more ominous was the possibility that poorer whites in the South, whose needs for public education and welfare the business-oriented Redeemers consistently neglected, might find common cause with their black peers. "The greatest danger that threatens democratic supremacy in the south," a Negro newspaper in Arkansas shrewdly noted in 1883, "is that the 'out faction' always gravitates toward the Negro and secures his aid to route [sic] the 'ins.'"

The Redeemers saw both these dangers materialize after 1890. Shortly after the Republicans gained control of the House of Representatives in 1889, Representative Henry Cabot Lodge of Massachusetts introduced a strong bill for federal control of elections, which was promptly christened the "Force Bill." Though Democrats in the Senate defeated Lodge's bill in January 1891, Redeemers saw in it a threat to renew "all the horrors of reconstruction days." Their fear was doubtless the greater because the almost simultaneous rise of the Populist movement promised, as never before, to split the white voters of the region. Appealing to farmers and small planters, the Populist party was the enemy of lawyers and bankers and of the rising commercial and industrial spokesmen of the "New South." Some of the Populist leaders, like Thomas Watson of Georgia, were openly critical of the Redeemers' policy of repressing the blacks and seemed to be flirting with the Negro voters.

Faced with this double threat, Southern states moved swiftly to exclude the Negro completely and permanently from politics. Mississippi led the way in 1890 with a requirement that voters be able to read and interpret the Constitution to the satisfaction of the registration officials, who were white. It is not hard to imagine how difficult even a graduate of Howard University law school would have found the task of satisfactory constitutional exegesis. In 1898 a Louisiana constitutional convention improved upon the Mississippi example by requiring a literacy test of all voters except for the sons and grandsons of persons who had voted in state elections before 1867. Since no Louisiana Negroes had been permitted to vote before that date, this provision allowed illiterate whites to vote, while the literacy test excluded most Negro voters.

State after state across the South followed, or elaborated on, these requirements. South Carolina held a disfranchising convention in 1895. North Carolina amended its constitution to limit suffrage in 1900. Alabama and Virginia acted in 1901–1902, and Georgia adopted a restrictive constitutional amendment in 1908. The remaining Southern states continued to rely on the poll tax and other varieties of legislative disfranchisement. When opponents of these measures accused their advocates of discriminating against the Negroes, Carter Glass of Virginia replied for his entire generation: "Discrimination! Why that is precisely what we propose; that exactly is what this convention was elected for."

It took time, then, for the complete working out of the political compromises of the Reconstruction era. Not until nearly the end of the century did white Southerners receive the full price they had exacted in permitting the election of Rutherford B. Hayes. But by 1900 that payment had been made in full. The Negro was no longer a political force in the South, and the Republican party was no longer the defender of Negro rights.

⋙ III ⋘

These political arrangements, which, in effect, ratified the American Compromise and excluded the Negro question from national politics for more than a generation, were probably less important in bringing the Civil War era to a close than the changes that were simultaneously occurring in the minds of Americans. If the American Compromise was to hold, it had to rest on a fundamental consensus, a desire to forget or ignore the differences that had hitherto divided sections, interests, and races. In short, the theme of reconciliation had to dominate the world of ideas as it did the world of economics and politics.

During the first few years after the Civil War, it was not at all clear that such an intellectual reconciliation could occur. Northern writers and intellectuals during the war had been intensely patriotic and highly nationalistic. Even the best of their productions were suffused with a tone of Northern superiority. Although Walt Whitman was compassionate toward the fallen soldiers of the South, he never concealed his belief in the righteousness of the Union cause, and his greatest war poems, "O Captain! My Captain!" and "When Lilacs Last in the Dooryard Bloom'd," were tributes to Lincoln,

**THE BLUE AND THE GRAY MEET AT SEVEN PINES
BATTLEFIELD AFTER THE WAR**

Union soldiers and Confederate veterans began to hold joint reunions on
the battlefields after the bitterness of the war faded. They increasingly
romanticized their reminiscences about the struggle and found enough
glory for both sides in the war. Note that each of the veterans here shown
has lost an arm. (*The Valentine Museum, Richmond, Virginia.*)

the fallen leader of the national cause. Similarly Herman Melville's *Battle-
Pieces* (1866), spare, gnomic verses whose greatness was not recognized
until a later generation, exulted in Union victory even while expressing
sympathy for individual Rebels. James Russell Lowell also turned literary
nationalist. At the time there was much enthusiasm for his long, rather
wooden *Ode Recited at the Harvard Commemoration, July 21, 1865,* which
combined exaltation of the Northern cause with a tribute to Lincoln, that
"kindly-earnest, brave, foreseeing man, sagacious, patient, dreading praise,
not blame." More enduring, however, was Lowell's second series of *Biglow
Papers,* which used Yankee characters and Yankee dialect to explain why
Southerners had to give up their sectional identity:

Make 'em Amerikin, an' they'll begin
To love their country ez they loved their sin;
Let 'em stay Southun, an' you've kep' a sore
Ready to fester ez it done afore.

In fiction as in verse, Northern writers during and immediately after the war insisted that Southerners must repent and accept Northern values. That was the central theme of *Miss Ravenel's Conversion from Secession to Loyalty,* John W. DeForest's 1867 novel, which remains perhaps the best novel ever written about the Civil War. A native of Connecticut, DeForest had spent some time in the South before the war, commanded a company of Union volunteers in Louisiana and in the Shenandoah Valley, and after Appomattox served with the Freedmen's Bureau in South Carolina. He was not, therefore, ignorant of the South, and some aspects of Southern life seem to have had a sensuous charm for this straitlaced New Englander. The most credible characters in his novel are the corrupt, whiskey-drinking Virginian, Captain Carter, whose animal magnetism is so strong that Lillie Ravenel marries him against her own better judgment, and the lurid Creole, Mrs. Larue, with whom Carter continues to carry on a torrid affair even after his marriage. But in the end it is not these Southern-born characters who have the strength to win victory. After Carter's fortunate death in battle, Lillie weds her patiently waiting Northern lover, Captain Colbourne—as stiff and as formal as DeForest himself. Sententiously, Colbourne and Miss Ravenel's father discuss the significance of the romances that have occurred, and of the war itself. "The right always conquers because it always becomes the strongest," Dr. Ravenel suggests. "In that sense 'the hand of God' is identical with 'the heaviest battalions.' " Agreeing, Colbourne summarizes in a sentence the theme of Northern superiority: "The Southern character will be sweetened by adversity as their persimmons are by frost."

Like DeForest, Whitman initially assumed that the national sentiment aroused by the Civil War would erase sectional feelings and ultimately would produce a national literature, which could provide for America's democratic society "that glowing, blood-throbbing, religious, social, emotional, artistic, indefinable, indescribably beautiful charm and hold which fused the separate parts of the old feudal societies together." But by the time Whitman got around to elaborating his theory in his strange, rambling essays, *Democratic Vistas,* published in 1871, his confidence had begun to wane. "Society, in these States, is cankered, crude, superstitious and rotten," he judged, and he feared that America might be suffering from "the lack of a common skeleton, knitting all close." The government was "saturated in corruption, bribery, falsehood, maladministration," and the cities reeked "with respectable as much as non-respectable robbery and scoundrelism." Despite obvious signs of material progress, he was tempted to conclude that the United States was "so far, an almost complete failure in its social aspects, and in really grand religious, moral, literary, and aesthetic results."

WALT WHITMAN

Shown here in his prime during the Civil War, Whitman in the Reconstruction years longed for the emergence of a "literatus," who could enunciate the new national spirit in literature. But Whitman himself was now too old and too tired to play the role. (*Library of Congress.*)

But that "so far" suggested that there was a possible remedy. It was the emergence of a powerful national literature, and Whitman longed for the appearance of "a single great literatus," who could issue a clarion call for American culture.

Whitman's hopes were not to be fulfilled. The giants of American literature belonged to a previous generation. Whitman himself was too exhausted, too old, to serve as "literatus" of the new age; in 1873 he suffered a stroke of paralysis and retired to Camden, New Jersey. Melville after the war sank into decades of silence, only to complete the manuscript of *Billy Budd* just before his death in 1891. Ralph Waldo Emerson, who during the pre–Civil War period had come nearest to fulfilling Whitman's specifications for an American "literatus," was now slowly slipping into senility.

The new generation of Northeastern writers offered little more hope for literary leadership. Once the intellectual capital of the country, New England was now stagnant. Its ablest poet, Emily Dickinson, lived a recluse in her house in Amherst, Massachusetts, her verse unseen by the public until after her death. Its ablest novelist, the transplanted New Yorker Henry James, found the American scene uncongenial and fled to Europe. Its supply of local talent was so bankrupt that in 1871 the editorship of the *Atlantic Monthly* went to a Middle Westerner, William Dean Howells. The New York publishing scene was, as always, bustling, but Whitman correctly dismissed the now deservedly forgotten poets and essayists of the era as "a parcel of dandies and ennuyees, dapper little gentlemen from abroad, who flood us with their thin sentiments of parlors, parasols, piano songs, [and] tinkling rhymes."

Instead of the national literature for which Whitman hoped, there emerged between 1865 and 1890 strong regional schools of literature— "local colorists," as they have somewhat condescendingly been called. It was in the Far West, where a motley group of Indians, Mexicans, Chinese, Yankees, and Southerners were engaged in the experiment of constructing an instant society, that the first of these regional writers appeared. The center of the group was the elegant former New Yorker Bret Harte, who had moved to California in the 1850s and, with the support of a lucrative but undemanding job in the United States mint at San Francisco during the 1860s, wrote prolific verse and fiction. Not until Harte became editor of the *Overland Monthly* in 1868, however, did he turn his imagination to the local scene, and the publication of "The Luck of Roaring Camp" and "The Outcasts of Poker Flat" proved that he had struck a literary pay lode in the garish, tawdry, but deeply romantic adventurers in the California mining country. Immediately lionized by both English and Eastern literary circles, Harte generously assisted his fellow Western local colorists. It was with Harte's encouragement that Mark Twain (Samuel L. Clemens) published *The Celebrated Jumping Frog of Calaveras County and Other Stories* (1867), a transposition of the traditional American tall tale to a Far Western setting, and became a world celebrity. Less enduring was the fame of another Harte protégé, Joaquin Miller, who compensated for his limited literary talents by self-dramatization; appearing at London dinner parties in his sealskin coat, his red plaid shirt, and his hip boots, Miller seemed so completely the personification of the Wild Westerner that the English forgot his limping rhymes.

A second regional school of writers emerged in the Middle West in the 1870s. Stimulated by reading Bret Harte, Constance Fenimore Woolson, the grand-niece of James Fenimore Cooper, sought in her stories of French voyageurs, of fur trappers and traders, and of rough lumbermen to recapture the traditions and the color of the Great Lakes region where she was brought up. In 1871 John Hay, who had served as Lincoln's private secretary, succumbed to the regional impulse and published his *Pike County Ballads,* which recaptured in frontier dialect both the crudeness and the humor of early Illinois. More prolific was Edward Eggleston, a Methodist minister who made a systematic study of life and language in his native southern Indiana before writing *The Hoosier Schoolmaster* (1871), *The Circuit Rider* (1874), and other novels that attempted to re-create life on a frontier that was beginning to slip from memory. Soon that frontier would be romanticized and subdued in the ever popular verse of the Hoosier poet, James Whitcomb Riley, who wrote his jingles about "just plain folks."

Regional writing emerged more slowly in the South than in other sections. Some older Southern writers could not break themselves of the habit of writing treatises in defense of slavery. Others were too embittered by the war to appeal to a national audience. Younger writers were for the most part less sore, but they were too exhausted to write the kind of regional romance that postwar readers sought. Paul Hamilton Hayne, the Charleston poet who saw his house and library burned in the bombardment of his city and had his silver stolen by Sherman's "bummers," lived out his days in north Georgia, in a rough "shanty of uncouth ugliness," so dilapidated that he tried to paper over the holes in the walls with pictures his wife cut from magazines. Henry Timrod, the South Carolina poet who died of tuberculosis at the age of thirty-nine, summarized his life after the war as "beggary, starvation, death, bitter grief, utter want of hope." The ablest of Southern poets, Sidney Lanier, whose health had been broken during service in the Confederate army and who was also destined for a premature death from tuberculosis, epitomized in a sentence the experience of Southern writers in the 1860s: "Pretty much the whole of life has been merely not dying."

Thanks largely to the enterprise of Northern magazine editors, Southern writers fared very differently during the 1870s and 1880s. The warm reception readers gave Western local color fiction and verse led the editors of *Scribner's Monthly Magazine* (after 1881, *The Century Magazine*) and *Lippincott's Magazine* actively to solicit contributions from Southern authors, and early Southern successes in these journals brought offers from *Harper's Monthly Magazine* and finally even from the formerly antislavery journal, *The Atlantic Monthly*. Publication of stories or serialization of novels in these prestigious monthlies usually led to book publication by a major Northern firm, so that for the first time writing became a remunerative occupation in the South.

The successful Southern writer had first to meet the terms and conditions of his Northern editors. *Scribner's,* which set the standard, sought to promote "a sane and earnest Americanism" and constantly "to increase the sentiment of union throughout our diverse sisterhood of States." Southern writers were "tacitly barred from any expression of the old hostility" between the sections. Northern editors wanted no polemics defending slavery or justifying secession, no jeremiads about what the North had done during the war, no objective reporting on the workings of Reconstruction. Instead, they sought stories set in the South, long on local color, heavy in Southern dialect, ingenious in plot, and romantic in tone.

These were terms that Southern writers of the new generation found it easy to accept. Most young Southerners were prepared to admit they were glad the Confederacy had failed; nearly all felt their section had a brighter future in the Union. Many consciously sought in their writing to bring about sectional reconciliation. The Virginia novelist Thomas Nelson Page declared that he had "never wittingly written a line which he did not hope might tend to bring about a better understanding between the North and the South, and finally lead to a more perfect Union." They agreed that regional literature must be part of a broad national literature. Joel Chandler Harris, author of the "Uncle Remus" stories, spoke for his generation in asserting "that whatever in our literature is distinctly Southern must ... be distinctly American." "My idea," Harris continued, "is that truth is more important than sectionalism, and that literature that can be labeled Northern, Southern, Western, or Eastern is not worth labeling at all."

In return for accepting American nationality, Southern writers were allowed great freedom in their choice of subjects. George Washington Cable's fiction explored the mysteries of that least American of cities, New Orleans, where Creoles and Yankees, 'Cajuns, quadroons, and slaves mixed together in a cosmopolitan and fascinatingly decadent society. Mary Noailles Murfree wrote of Southern Appalachian folk, so isolated from the American mainstream that their dialect, which she laboriously attempted to replicate, was full of Elizabethan idioms. Harris wrote scores of conventional novels and stories about Southern life, but his readers identified him as author of the Uncle Remus tales, stories that he had heard as a boy in Georgia and now re-created to give American literature the never-to-be-forgotten Br'er Rabbit, that defenseless yet preternaturally clever animal, who was able— perhaps like the slaves who had originally told Harris the tales—to outwit his more powerful enemies like Br'er Fox and Br'er Bear. Page's stories had a courtly Virginia setting, and the lush bluegrass country of Kentucky was the scene of James Lane Allen's impressionistic tales.

In all this postwar Southern writing, the Negro played a surprisingly small part. As in the Uncle Remus stories, a black was often allowed to be the narrator, a gentle, aged former slave, full of folk wisdom and glowing with happy memories about "dose times befoah de wah." "Dem wuz good ole times, marster," said Sam, the former slave who narrated Page's most popular story, *Marse Chan* (1884), "de bes' Sam uver see! Niggers didn' hed nothin' 'tall to do.... Dyar warn 'no trouble no' nuthin'." Though the point was never made explicitly, the implication was that race relations in the South had been exemplary until disrupted by Northern invaders. Though the recommendation was never given overtly, the promise was that if white Southerners were left alone there would be a return to the good old days.

If slaves and slavery were peripheral in this Southern literature, the theme of reconciliation was central. Again and again the stories dealt with the Civil War as the result of misunderstanding, of a failure of Northerners and Southerners to recognize how much they had in common. In one of Harris's stories, a wounded Union officer, "captured" by a black "mammy" and nursed back to health by her white mistress, proved to have such a noble character as to shatter the Southerners' stereotypes about Yankees. "He gave ... a practical illustration of the fact that one may be a Yankee and a Southerner too, simply by being a large-hearted, whole-souled American." Typically in these romances, understanding leads to marriage. Time and again the Union officer, befriended by a Southern planter's family during the conflict, returns South after Appomattox to claim the hand of the planter's daughter and to save the plantation from foreclosure for debts.

The product of changing sectional sentiment after the Civil War, Southern fiction also helped to produce that change. Both sides in the recent conflict had been right. Both sides shared equally in the glory and the gallantry.

UNCLE REMUS

AND HIS

LEGENDS OF THE OLD PLANTATION

BY JOEL CHANDLER HARRIS

WITH ILLUSTRATIONS BY F. CHURCH AND J. MOSER

𝔏𝔬𝔫𝔡𝔬𝔫

W. SWAN SONNENSCHEIN & Co.

PATERNOSTER SQUARE

—

1884

UNCLE REMUS

In the Southern literature of reconciliation, the Negro played a surprisingly small part. Sometimes he appeared as the narrator of tales, like Joel Chandler Harris's Uncle Remus. More frequently, he reminisced happily about "dose times befoah de wah." (*General Research and Humanities Division, The New York Public Library, Astor, Lenox and Tilden Foundations.*)

To Northern readers, as well as to Southern, these were ideas immensely appealing, immensely consoling. They permitted the Civil War generation to gloss over the brutal past, and they allowed the postwar generation of Northerners to shed any guilt it felt over abandoning the Negro. Indicative of the power of Southern romance was the response of Thomas Wentworth Higginson to Page's *Marse Chan,* a tale about a political quarrel that kept two Southerners from marrying before the young man rode away to the war. By the time the girl's father relented, the hero had bravely died on the battlefield, and shortly afterward the girl too expired of grief. Sitting in his study in Cambridge, Massachusetts, Higginson—who had once organized the attempt to free the fugitive slave Anthony Burns; who had been a co-conspirator with John Brown; who had heroically commanded a regiment of brave Negro soldiers during the Civil War—let the tears trickle down his cheeks as he grieved over the death of a fictional Southern slaveholder.

Thus Americans of the Reconstruction generation became emotionally reconciled to a series of compromises that ended decades of conflict between majority power and minority interests. In foreign policy and in economic organization, in race relations and in politics, informal agreements were hammered out that served to guarantee the primacy of the nation but also to protect local and regional rights. These compromises made no provision for the protection of Native Americans, who were being ruthlessly pushed into barren reservations. They systematically relegated Afro-Americans to the category of second-class citizens. They took little account of the needs of labor. They gave no recognition to the special problems of women. But, when veiled by literary sentimentality, the compromises seemed to most white middle-class Americans to provide a tolerable way of life that preserved both the national Union and their own individual freedom.

Bibliographical Essay

The literature on the era of sectional conflict in nineteenth-century American history is enormous, highly specialized, and richly rewarding. I cannot list here all of even the most basic books and articles on the period. What follows is a personal, highly selective list of some titles that have helped to shape my own thinking. For a fuller enumeration, see the extensive bibliography in *The Civil War and Reconstruction* (1969), by J. G. Randall and David Herbert Donald.

Though the literature on the period is extensive, there have been, as I mentioned in the preface, surprisingly few attempts to view the years from 1845 to 1890 as a whole. The one notable exception is James Ford Rhodes, *History of the United States from the Compromise of 1850* [*to the Final Restoration of Home Rule at the South*] (7 vols., 1893–1906), a work that is outdated in many sections, that is marred throughout by racism, and that is anti-Southern, anti-Negro, antilabor, and anti-inflationist. It remains, nevertheless, a basic work, grand in conception, scope, and execution. Of several briefer works that cover the whole period, Roy F. Nichols, *The Stakes of Power* (1961), is outstanding.

The history of American nationalism, which is the main subject of the present book, has been surprisingly neglected by historians. The best general treatment is Hans Kohn, *American Nationalism* (1957), and there is much valuable material in Herbert W. Schneider, *A History of American Philosophy* (1946). Two able studies of American national consciousness, both written by Paul C. Nagel, are *One Nation Indivisible* (1964) and *This Sacred Trust* (1971). A difficult but important book is Major L. Wilson, *Space, Time, and Freedom* (1974).

Majority Rule and Minority Rights (1943), by Henry Steele Commager, is a brilliant introduction to this unsolvable problem. Since Commager's sympathies are so clearly majoritarian, it would be well to consult also the leading spokesman of minority interests, John C. Calhoun, who formulated his ideas in *A Disquisition on Government* (1853). For a fuller exposition, see August O. Spain, *The Political Theory of John C. Calhoun* (1951). Alexis de Tocqueville voiced his fears of the tyranny of the majority in *Democracy in America*; the edition by Phillips Bradley (2 vols., 1948) is invaluable for its introduction and commentary, but George Lawrence's translation (1966) is more fluent and accurate. David M. Potter, *The South and the Concurrent Majority* (1972), explains how Southerners during the century after Calhoun's death were often able to block legislation desired by the national majority.

GENERAL WORKS ON THE ANTEBELLUM ERA

Even though left incomplete at its author's death, *The United States, 1830–1850* (1935), by Frederick Jackson Turner, is a work of astonishing insight and erudition, which anticipated the findings of many subsequent studies. Avery Craven, *The Coming of the Civil War* (1957), is a provocative work, with pro-Southern sympathies. Arthur C. Cole, *The Irrepressible Conflict* (1934), is valuable on social and economic changes. The most comprehensive work on the period, however—one that covers political, social, economic, diplomatic, and intellectual history—is Allan Nevins, *Ordeal of the Union*, Vols. I–IV (1947–1950) (the third and fourth volumes bear the subtitle, *The Emergence of Lincoln*).

The Age of Enterprise (1940), by Thomas C. Cochran and William Miller, deals perceptively with economic change during the antebellum era. Stuart Bruchey, *The Roots of American Economic Growth* (1965), is an admirable synthesis of recent scholarship. More technical is Douglass C. North, *The Economic Growth of the United States* (1961). George R. Taylor, *The Transportation Revolution* (1951), is a work of broad scope.

History of Transportation in the United States before 1860 (1917), by Caroline E. MacGill et al., remains a standard work. For conflicting views on the impact of the railroads on the American economy, see Albert Fishlow, *American Railroads and the Transformation of the Ante-Bellum Economy* (1965); and Robert W. Fogel, *Railroads and American Economic Growth* (1964).

Victor S. Clark, *History of Manufactures in the United States* (3 vols., 1929), is an invaluable compendium. Arthur H. Cole, *The American Wool Manufacture* (2 vols., 1926), is a model history. On cotton manufacturing, see Caroline F. Ware, *The Early New England Cotton Manufacture* (1931); and Hannah Josephson, *The Golden Threads* (1949). For the social ideas of New England manufacturers, Robert F. Dalzell, Jr., "The Rise of the Waltham-Lowell System and Some Thought on the Political Economy of Modernization in Ante-Bellum Massachusetts," *Perspectives in American History,* 9 (1975), 229–270, is important. The authoritative study of the management of American business corporations is Alfred D. Chandler, Jr., *The Visible Hand* (1977).

On banking during the antebellum period, there are two indispensable works: Bray Hammond, *Banks and Politics in America from the Revolution to the Civil War* (1957); and Fritz Redlich, *The Molding of American Banking* (2 vols., 1947–1951).

John R. Commons et al., *History of Labor in the United States* (4 vols., 1918–1935), is full and scholarly. Norman Ware, *The Industrial Worker, 1840–1860* (1924), is an admirable monograph. Herbert G. Gutman, "Work, Culture, and Society in Industrializing America," *American Historical Review,* 78 (1973), 531–588, breaks new ground in labor history.

Paul W. Gates, *The Farmer's Age* (1960), is a comprehensive history of agriculture during the pre–Civil War era. See also two authoritative studies: P. W. Bidwell and J. I. Falconer, *History of Agriculture in the Northern United States* (1925); and Lewis C. Gray, *History of Agriculture in the Southern United States* (2 vols., 1933).

Standard histories of immigration include Maldwyn A. Jones, *American Immigration* (1960); Marcus L. Hansen, *The Atlantic Migration* (1940); and Carl Wittke, *We Who Built America* (1939).

The complex story of the relation of government to the economy has to be pieced together from a variety of sources. Four exemplary studies show how the government intervened in, and regulated, economic affairs in key states: Oscar and Mary F. Handlin, *Commonwealth* [Massachusetts] (1947); Louis Hartz, *Economic Policy and Democratic Thought* [Pennsylvania] (1948); Milton S. Heath, *Constructive Liberalism* [Georgia] (1954); and James N. Primm, *Economic Policy in the Development of a Western State* [Missouri] (1954). Morton J. Horwitz's brilliant *The Transformation of American Law* (1977) shows how the courts shaped economic policy.

On the national level, after the destruction of the Bank of the United States by the Jacksonians, the federal government intervened in the economy most directly through the tariff, and consequently the tariff was the subject of endless sectional controversy. For general treatments, see

F. W. Taussig, *The Tariff History of the United States* (1910); and Edward Stanwood, *American Tariff Controversies in the Nineteenth Century* (2 vols., 1904). For a superb account of the controversy aroused by the Tariff of Abominations in South Carolina, see William W. Freehling, *Prelude to Civil War* (1966). See, however, Paul H. Bergeron, "The Nullification Controversy Revisited," *Tennessee Historical Quarterly,* 35 (1976), 263–275, for the view that Freehling has overemphasized the slavery issue in the Nullification crisis. Charles M. Wiltse, *John C. Calhoun* (3 vols., 1944–1951), is a masterful full-length portrait of the chief South Carolina leader in that crisis. Theodore D. Jervey, *Robert Y. Hayne and his Times* (1909), does not do justice to his chief lieutenant. Daniel Webster, the chief congressional spokesman against nullification, still has no really satisfactory biography. Claude M. Fuess, *Daniel Webster* (2 vols., 1930), is thin and uncritical; Richard N. Current, *Daniel Webster and the Rise of National Conservatism* (1955), is incisive but brief. One has, therefore, to prepare a kind of composite biography of Webster from four excellent monographs: Maurice G. Baxter, *Daniel Webster and the Supreme Court* (1966); Norman D. Brown, *Daniel Webster and the Politics of Availability* (1969); Robert F. Dalzell, Jr., *Daniel Webster and the Trial of American Nationalism* (1972); and Sydney Nathans, *Daniel Webster and Jacksonian Democracy* (1973).

On American thought during the pre–Civil War decades, Ralph H. Gabriel, *The Course of American Democratic Thought* (1940), remains the invaluable exposition of basic, widely held values. Three excellent surveys are Russel B. Nye, *Society and Culture in America* (1974); Vernon L. Parrington, *Main Currents in American Thought* (3 vols., 1927–1930); and Rush Welter, *The Mind of America* (1975). Though left incomplete at its author's death, Perry Miller, *The Life of the Mind in America* (1965), is a profound analysis of American attitudes toward religion, law, and science.

For a cynical view of the American sense of mission, see Albert K. Weinberg, *Manifest Destiny* (1935). Frederick Merk, *Manifest Destiny and Mission in American History* (1963), is a valuable corrective. Two recent studies, which recognize the ambiguities inherent in the idea of mission, are Fred Somkin, *Unquiet Eagle* (1967); and Lawrence J. Friedman, *Inventors of the Promised Land* (1975).

THE OLD SOUTH AND SLAVERY

The three best studies are books by Clement Eaton: *A History of the Old South* (1966); *The Growth of Southern Civilization* (1961); and *The*

Mind of the Old South (1967). William E. Dodd, *The Cotton Kingdom* (1919), is a brief, brilliant interpretation. Charles S. Sydnor, *The Development of Southern Sectionalism* (1948), and Avery O. Craven, *The Growth of Southern Nationalism* (1953), trace the history of the section from 1818 to 1861.

Some of the best studies of the Old South emphasize its distinctiveness. The most influential contemporary account was Frederick Law Olmsted, *The Cotton Kingdom,* which emphasized Southern backwardness, inefficiency, and provincialism; the best edition is that edited by Arthur M. Schlesinger (1953). Ulrich B. Phillips, *Life and Labor in the Old South* (1929), which presented a happier picture, also portrayed the South as a separate culture. In *The Political Economy of Slavery* (1965) and *The World the Slaveholders Made* (1969), Eugene D. Genovese also argues that the South had "a social system and a civilization with a distinct class structure, political community, economy, ideology, and set of psychological patterns."

On the other hand, a number of studies, like the present book, find fundamental similarities between the South and the rest of the nation. These include Carl N. Degler, *Place Over Time* (1977); Fletcher M. Green, *Democracy in the Old South and Other Essays,* edited by J. Isaac Copeland (1969); Grady McWhiney, *Southerners and Other Americans* (1973); Frank L. Owsley, *Plain Folk of the Old South* (1949); Owsley, *The South: Old and New Frontiers,* edited by Harriet C. Owsley (1969); and Charles G. Sellers, ed., *The Southerner as American* (1960).

In a special category are the deeply thoughtful essays in David M. Potter, *The South and the Sectional Conflict* (1968).

The literature on slavery is so extensive that only a few of the major titles can be mentioned here. Like the books on the Old South, some of the best studies emphasize the fact that slavery was indeed a peculiar institution—one that gave to both blacks and whites in the South a peculiar social structure and a peculiar set of values. Ulrich B. Phillips, *American Negro Slavery* (1918), long the standard history, with a pronounced racial bias, stressed the economic irrationality of the system. This theme was even more explicitly developed in Phillips's essays, *The Slave Economy of the Old South,* edited by Eugene D. Genovese (1968). Comparing the slave system to the Nazi concentration camps, Stanley M. Elkins, *Slavery* (1959), depicted both the horrors and the uniqueness of the peculiar institution. For evaluations of the Elkins thesis, see *The Debate over Slavery,* edited by Ann J. Lane (1971). In his superb, broad-ranging history of slavery, *Roll, Jordan, Roll* (1974), Eugene D. Genovese analyzes the symbiotic relationships between slaves and masters that created a distinctive culture. For critical appraisals of this major work from two very different perspectives, see the reviews by David Herbert Donald in *Commentary,* 59 (1975), 86–90; and by James D. Anderson in *Journal of Negro History,* 41 (1976), 99–114. Finally, both John W. Blassingame, *The Slave Community* (1972), and Herbert G. Gutman, *The Black Family in Slavery and Freedom* (1976), a pioneering work of great scope and methodological interest, depict a distinctive Afro-American culture in the South.

Other studies, with which the present book is in general agreement, describe slavery as a special, if extreme, form of labor that was perpetuated because planter-capitalists found it profitable to do so. Both Avery Craven, in *The Coming of the Civil War,* and Lewis C. Gray, in *The History of Agriculture in the Southern United States,* previously cited, advanced this view. Not slighting any of the atrocities incident to the slave system, Kenneth M. Stampp portrayed slavery, in *The Peculiar Institution* (1956), as a highly profitable capitalistic enterprise. Three seminal articles generally sharing this point of view are Thomas P. Govan, "Was Plantation Slavery Profitable?" *Journal of Southern History,* 8 (1942), 513–535; Robert R. Russel, "The General Effects of Slavery upon Southern Economic Progress," *Journal of Southern History,* 4 (1938), 34–54; and Alfred H. Conrad and John R. Meyer, "The Economics of Slavery in the Ante Bellum South," *Journal of Political Economy,* 66 (1958), 95–130. *Time on the Cross* (2 vols., 1974), by Robert W. Fogel and Stanley L. Engerman, is a major study of the economics of American Negro slavery; it stresses not merely the essentially capitalistic nature of the slave system and its profits for the masters but also the extent to which the slaves shared the traditional American values of individualism, family stability, and economic mobility. *Time on the Cross* has been subjected to exceptionally severe substantive and methodological criticism; see, for example, Herbert G. Gutman, *Slavery and the Numbers Game* (1975); and Paul A. David et al., *Reckoning with Slavery* (1976). But it is not clear that these critics have undermined the essential conclusions of Fogel and Engerman. Finally, Nathan I. Huggins, *Black Odyssey* (1977), suggests the similarities between the experience of Africans brought to America and the Europeans who emigrated to this country.

ABOLITION AND ANTISLAVERY

The best general history of abolitionism is James Brewer Stewart, *Holy Warriors* (1976). Also valuable are Merton L. Dillon, *The Abolitionists* (1974); Dwight L. Dumond, *Antislavery* (1961); and Louis Filler, *The Crusade against Slavery* (1960). Benjamin Quarles, *Black Abolitionists*

(1969), deals with a topic frequently neglected, as does Larry Gara, *The Liberty Line* (1967).

On the intellectual background of abolitionism, there are three broad-ranging and indispensable works: Aileen Kraditor, *Means and Ends in American Abolitionism* (1969); Lewis Perry, *Radical Abolitionism* (1973); and Ronald G. Walters, *The Antislavery Appeal* (1977).

Some of the best biographies of abolitionist leaders are: Benjamin Quarles, *Frederick Douglass* (1948); Walter M. Merrill, *Against Wind and Tide* [Garrison] (1963); John L. Thomas, *The Liberator* [Garrison] (1963); Merton Dillon, *Elijah P. Lovejoy* (1961); Dillon, *Benjamin Lundy and the Struggle for Negro Freedom* (1966); Irving H. Bartlett, *Wendell Phillips* (1961); and Benjamin P. Thomas, *Theodore Weld* (1950).

Russel B. Nye, *Fettered Freedom* (1949), shows how abolitionists broadened their appeal by connecting their cause with that of civil liberty. David B. Davis, *The Slave Power Conspiracy and the Paranoid Style* (1969), traces the spread of Northern belief in a proslavery conspiracy. On early moves to make abolitionism a political movement, see Gilbert H. Barnes, *The Antislavery Impulse* (1933); Betty Fladeland, *James Gillespie Birney* (1955); and James B. Stewart, *Joshua R. Giddings and the Tactics of Radical Politics* (1970).

The best book on antislavery politics is Richard H. Sewell, *Ballots for Freedom* (1976), which traces the continuities from the Liberty to the Free-Soil to the Republican parties. On the Free-Soil party itself, see Joseph G. Rayback, *Free Soil* (1970); and Frederick J. Blue, *The Free Soilers* (1973).

EXPANSIONISM AND THE MEXICAN WAR

In addition to Albert K. Weinberg, *Manifest Destiny,* and Frederick Merk, *Manifest Destiny and Mission in American History,* both previously cited, see Merk, *The Monroe Doctrine and American Expansionism* (1966); and Norman Graebner's important *Empire on the Pacific* (1955).

The origins of the Mexican War can be traced in George L. Rives, *The United States and Mexico* (2 vols., 1913); Glenn W. Price, *Origins of the War with Mexico* (1967); and Charles G. Sellers, *James K. Polk: Continentalist* (1966). David M. Pletcher, *The Diplomacy of Annexation: Texas, Oregon, and the Mexican War* (1973), is a landmark of historical scholarship and understanding.

On the Mexican War itself, the old but still standard account is Justin H. Smith, *The War with Mexico* (2 vols., 1919). For shorter modern studies, consult Otis Singletary, *The Mexican War* (1960); Seymour V. Connor and Odie B. Faulk, *North America Divided* (1971); K. Jack Bauer, *The Mexican War* (1974); and John E. Weems, *To Conquer a Peace* (1974).

A useful account of Northern hostility toward the war is John H. Schroeder, *Mr. Polk's War: Opposition and Dissent, 1846–1848* (1973). James C. N. Paul, *Rift in the Democracy* (1951), shows how the Texas issue divided the Democrats. Kinley J. Brauer, *Cotton Versus Conscience* (1967), and Thomas H. O'Connor, *Lords of the Loom* (1968), tell how annexation and the ensuing war split the Whigs, especially in Massachusetts. Chaplain W. Morrison, *Democratic Politics and Sectionalism* (1967), is the authoritative account of the Wilmot Proviso, but see also Eric Foner, "The Wilmot Proviso Revisited," *Journal of American History,* 56 (1969), 262–279.

THE POLITICS OF SECTIONALISM

The political history of the period from 1848 to 1861 is admirably treated in David M. Potter, *The Impending Crisis* (completed and edited by Don E. Fehrenbacher, 1976). A fuller account appears in Allan Nevins, *Ordeal of the Union* and *The Emergence of Lincoln,* previously cited. Because both these works are so comprehensive, only a very few additional titles need to be mentioned here.

On the Compromise of 1850, the indispensable monograph is Holman Hamilton, *Prologue to Conflict* (1964). See also Hamilton's biography of Zachary Taylor (2 vols., 1941–1951) and the studies of Calhoun and Webster previously mentioned. Clay lacks a good biography; the best study is George R. Poage, *Henry Clay and the Whig Party* (1936). For an overstated, but nevertheless interesting, account of the role played by Texas bonds in the settlement, see Elgin Williams, *The Animating Pursuits of Speculation* (1949). Robert W. Johannsen, *Stephen A. Douglas* (1973), is essential for an understanding of the part the "Little Giant" played in the settlement. The connection between the compromise and the Illinois Central Railroad is largely inferential, but see Paul W. Gates, *The Illinois Central Railroad and Its Colonization Work* (1934); and John F. Stover, *History of the Illinois Central Railroad* (1975).

The history of the Democratic party in the 1850s is elaborately traced in three basic works by Roy F. Nichols: *The Democratic Machine, 1850–1854* (1923); *Franklin Pierce* (1931); and *The Disruption of American Democracy* (1948).

George H. Mayer, *The Republican Party* (1964), is the best general history. A much more valuable account, rewarding especially for its exploration of Republican ideology, is Eric Foner, *Free Soil, Free Labor, Free Men* (1970). Michael F. Holt, *Forging a Majority* (1969), stresses the ethnocultural bases of the Republican party. James L. Sundquist, *Dynamics of the Party System* (1973), argues that the Republican party was not just an extension of the Whig party but the product of a general realignment of voters. Ronald P. Formisano, *The Birth of Mass Political Parties* (1971), seems to confirm this view, at least for Michigan.

For an understanding of the American (Know-Nothing) party, Ray A. Billington, *The Protestant Crusade* (1938), is indispensable. W. Darrell Overdyke, *The Know-Nothing Party in the South* (1950), is useful. Jean H. Baker, *Ambivalent Americans* (1977), is a model study, combining literary excellence and methodological sophistication, of nativism in Maryland. Three important essays are David B. Davis, "Some Ideological Functions of Prejudice in Ante-Bellum America," *American Quarterly,* 15 (1963), 115–125; Michael F. Holt, "The Politics of Impatience: The Origins of Know Nothingism," *Journal of American History,* 60 (1973), 309–331; and Dale Baum, "Know-Nothingism and the Republican Majority in Massachusetts; The Political Realignment of the 1850s," *ibid.,* 64 (1978), 959–986.

On the Kansas-Nebraska Act, which precipitated the party struggles of the 1850s, there is a complex and controversial literature. The best introduction to it is Roy F. Nichols, "The Kansas-Nebraska Act: A Century of Historiography," *Mississippi Valley Historical Review,* 48 (1956), 187–212.

Alice Nichols, *Bleeding Kansas* (1954), is a brief popular treatment of the incredibly complex history of Kansas during this period, but serious students will learn more from Paul W. Gates, *Fifty Million Acres* (1954), a study of land policy in the territory, and from James C. Malin's difficult *John Brown and the Legend of Fifty-Six* (1942). The national repercussions of the territorial struggle are traced in James A. Rawley, *Race and Politics: Bleeding Kansas and the Coming of the Civil War* (1969).

The fullest account of the Sumner-Brooks affair is in David Donald, *Charles Sumner and the Coming of the Civil War* (1960).

The background required for an understanding of the issues in the Dred Scott case is supplied in Arthur Bestor, "State Sovereignty and Slavery: A Reinterpretation of Proslavery Constitutional Doctrine, 1846–1860," *Journal of the Illinois State Historical Society,* 54 (1961), 117–180; Mark DeWolfe Howe, "Federalism and Civil Rights," *Proceedings of the Massachusetts Historical Society,* 77 (1966), 15–27; Allan Nevins, "The Constitution, Slavery and the Territories," in *The Caspar G. Bacon Lectures on the Constitution of the United States, 1940–1950* (1953), 95–141; and Robert R. Russel, "Constitutional Doctrines with Regard to Slavery in Ter-

ritories," *Journal of Southern History,* 32 (1966), 466–486. On the celebrated suit itself, the standard monograph is Vincent C. Hopkins, *Dred
Scott's Case* (1951). Appendix I of Allan Nevins, *The Emergence of Lincoln,* II, 473–477, is particularly important on the motivation of the justices.
On the chief justice, see Don E. Fehrenbacher's perceptive essay, "Roger
B. Taney and the Sectional Crisis," *Journal of Southern History,* 43 (1977),
555–566.

Edwin E. Sparks, ed., *The Lincoln-Douglas Debates of 1858* (1909),
contains the full texts of the speeches by both candidates. On Lincoln, the
best one-volume biography is Stephen B. Oates, *With Malice Toward
None* (1977), though there is also merit in Benjamin P. Thomas, *Abraham
Lincoln* (1952). Robert W. Johannsen, *Stephen A. Douglas,* previously
cited, is definitive. Two important commentaries and interpretations of the
debates are Don E. Fehrenbacher, *Prelude to Greatness* (1962); and Harry
V. Jaffa, *Crisis of the House Divided* (1959).

Graphic accounts of John Brown's raid at Harpers Ferry are presented in
two full-length biographies: Stephen B. Oates, *To Purge This Land With
Blood* (1970); and Oswald G. Villard, *John Brown* (1910). The best un-
derstanding of Brown himself can be gained from Richard O. Boyer, *The
Legend of John Brown* (1973), which, however, carries the story only to
1855, when Brown went to Kansas. For Southern reactions to the raid, see
"John Brown's Private War," in C. Vann Woodward, *The Burden of
Southern History* (1968), 41–68.

No single work adequately re-creates the growing Southern mood of
disaffection toward the Union during the 1850s. Part of the story can be
captured in the biographies of two Southern fire-eaters: Laura A. White,
Robert Barnwell Rhett (1931); and Avery O. Craven, *Edmund Ruffin,
Southerner* (1932). Volume I of *The Diary of Edmund Ruffin,* edited by
William K. Scarborough (1972), traces the thought of one of these ex-
tremists from 1856 to 1861. How economic discontent spurred on Southern
sectionalism is the theme of five excellent studies: Weymouth T. Jordan,
Rebels in the Making (1958); Robert R. Russel, *Economic Aspects of
Southern Sectionalism* (1924); John G. Van Deusen, *The Ante-Bellum
Southern Commercial Conventions* (1926); Van Deusen, *Economic Basis
of Disunion in South Carolina* (1928); and Herbert Wender, *Southern
Commercial Conventions* (1930). The Southern sense of political distinctiveness is sketched in Jesse T. Carpenter, *The South as a Conscious Minority* (1930). Two important books by William Barney stress the feeling
of Southerners that the slave system had to expand or perish: *The Road to
Secession* (1972); and *The Secessionist Impulse* (1974). The frustration
of Southern hopes to annex new slave territories is ably traced in Robert E.
May, *The Southern Dream of a Caribbean Empire* (1973).

Three monographs cover the election of 1860: Ollinger Crenshaw, *The Slave States in the Presidential Election of 1860* (1945); Emerson D. Fite, *The Presidential Campaign of 1860* (1911); and Reinhard H. Luthin, *The First Lincoln Campaign* (1944).

Dwight L. Dumond, *The Secession Movement* (1931), remains a standard work, but it should be supplemented by William Barney's two books, just cited. Ralph A. Wooster, *The Secession Conventions of the South* (1962), is a careful statistical analysis of the membership in those bodies. Two valuable recent state studies of secession are Steven A. Channing, *Crisis of Fear* [South Carolina] (1970); and Michael Johnson, *Toward a Patriarchal Republic* [Georgia] (1977). "Class and Party in the Secession Crisis: Voting Behavior in the Deep South, 1856–1861" by Peyton McCrary, Clark Miller, and Dale Baum, *Journal of Interdisciplinary History,* 8 (1978), 429–457, is a sophisticated statistical examination of the popular support for secession.

Two persuasive, but somewhat conflicting, explanations of why Northerners refused to compromise with the secessionists are found in David M. Potter, *Lincoln and His Party in the Secession Crisis* (1962); and Kenneth M. Stampp, *And the War Came* (1950). Albert Kirwan, *John J. Crittenden* (1962), is a fine biography of the principal advocate of compromise. For the belated and ill-fated peace convention, see Robert G. Gunderson, *Old Gentlemen's Convention* (1961); and Jesse L. Keene, *The Peace Convention of 1861* (1961).

CAUSES OF THE CIVIL WAR

Nearly every historian mentioned in this bibliographical essay has offered at least an implicit judgment on the causes of the Civil War, and many have written at length on this subject. It is obviously impracticable to enumerate all these books and essays here. Fortunately, however, there are two excellent guides to the vast literature: Howard K. Beale, "What Historians Have Said About the Causes of the Civil War," in *Theory and Practice in Historical Study* (Social Science Research Council *Bulletin,* No. 54 [1946]), 55–102; and Thomas J. Pressly, *Americans Interpret Their Civil War* (1954). Three important approaches not discussed in these guides are: Lee Benson and Cushing Strout, "Causation and the American Civil War: Two Appraisals," *History and Theory,* 1 (1961), 163–185; Gerald Gunderson, "The Origins of the American Civil War," *Journal of Economic History,* 34 (1974), 915–950; and John S. Rosenberg, "Toward a New Civil War Revisionism," *American Scholar,* 38 (1969), 250–272.

Extensive extracts from writings by contemporaries and by subsequent historians are offered in Edwin C. Rozwenc, ed., *The Causes of the American Civil War* (1972); and Kenneth M. Stampp, ed., *The Causes of the Civil War* (1974).

GENERAL HISTORIES OF THE CIVIL WAR

The best one-volume history is Peter J. Parish, *The American Civil War* (1975). William Barney, *Flawed Victory* (1975), is an original and provocative work. The fullest modern account of the Civil War is in the four final volumes of Allan Nevins, *Ordeal of the Union*, which bear the subtitle *The War for the Union* (1959–1971). *The Centennial History of the Civil War* (3 vols., 1961–1965), by Bruce Catton, is eloquent and moving.

Civil War Books, edited by Allan Nevins, James I. Robertson, Jr., and Bell I. Wiley (2 vols., 1967–1969), is a huge annotated bibliography.

Mark M. Boatner III, *The Civil War Dictionary* (1959), is a valuable reference work. For maps, see Vincent J. Esposito, ed., *The West Point Atlas of American Wars* (2 vols., 1959).

The best Civil War anthologies are Henry S. Commager, ed., *The Blue and the Gray* (2 vols., 1950); and William B. Hesseltine, ed., *The Tragic Conflict* (1962). Francis T. Miller, *The Photographic History of the Civil War* (10 vols., 1911), offers the most complete pictorial coverage, but the photographs are poorly reproduced. Better pictorial histories, using modern photographic techniques, are David Donald, ed., *Divided We Fought* (1952); and Richard M. Ketchum, ed., *The American Heritage Picture History of the Civil War* (1960).

THE CONFEDERACY

There are several good general histories of the Confederate States of America: E. Merton Coulter, *The Confederate States of America* (1950); Clement Eaton, *A History of the Southern Confederacy* (1954); Nathaniel W. Stephenson, *The Day of the Confederacy* (1919); and Charles P. Roland, *The Confederacy* (1960). Albert D. Kirwan, ed., *The Confederacy* (1959), is a valuable anthology.

There is no fully satisfactory life of the Confederate President. The fullest biography is Hudson Strode, *Jefferson Davis* (3 vols., 1955–1964); the most perceptive is Clement Eaton, *Jefferson Davis* (1977). Students will learn much about the Confederate government from Rembert W. Patrick, *Jefferson Davis and His Cabinet* (1944). Jon L. Wakelyn, *Biographical Dictionary of the Confederacy* (1976), is an invaluable reference work. On the Southern Congress, see Ezra J. Warner and W. Buck

Yearns, *Biographical Register of the Confederate Congress* (1975); Yearns, *The Confederate Congress* (1960); and Thomas B. Alexander and Richard E. Beringer, *The Anatomy of the Confederate Congress* (1972). Biographies of cabinet members tell much about the operations of the Confederate government: Robert D. Meade, *Judah P. Benjamin* (1943); Joseph T. Durkin, *Stephen R. Mallory* (1954); Ben H. Proctor, *Not Without Honor* [John H. Reagan, the postmaster-general] (1962); and William C. Davis, *Breckinridge* (1974). Three Confederate diaries are invaluable: Mary B. Chesnut, *A Diary from Dixie* (1949); John B. Jones, *A Rebel War Clerk's Diary* (2 vols., 1866); and Robert G. H. Kean, *Inside the Confederate Government,* edited by Edward Younger (1955).

The best treatment of social and economic conditions in the wartime South is John C. Schwab's authoritative *The Confederate States of America* (1901). Richard C. Todd, *Confederate Finance* (1954), untangles a very complex subject. Charles W. Ramsdell, *Behind the Lines in the Southern Confederacy* (1944), is a thoughtful treatment of affairs on the home front. The impact of the war on ordinary citizens is graphically described in Bell I. Wiley, *The Plain People of the Confederacy* (1943). Mary Elizabeth Massey, *Bonnet Brigades* (1966), deals with the life of women in both the North and the South. Bell I. Wiley, *Confederate Women* (1975), concentrates on the South. Mary Elizabeth Massey, *Ersatz in the Confederacy* (1952), and *Refugee Life in the Confederacy* (1964), recount the hardships caused by the war. The student who has time to read only one book on life in the Confederacy should choose *The Children of Pride,* edited by Robert M. Myers (1972), an incomparably rich collection of the correspondence of the Jones family of Georgia.

On disaffection and disloyalty in the Confederacy, see Frank L. Owsley, *State Rights in the Confederacy* (1925); Albert B. Moore, *Conscription and Conflict in the Confederacy* (1924); Ella Lonn, *Desertion during the Civil War* (1928); and Georgia L. Tatum, *Disloyalty in the Confederacy* (1934). Frank W. Klingberg, *The Southern Claims Commission* (1955), shows the extraordinary amount of Unionism that persisted in the South. For accounts of two of President Davis's bitterest critics, see James Z. Rabun, "Alexander H. Stephens and Jefferson Davis," *American Historical Review,* 58 (1953), 290–321; and Joseph H. Parks, *Joseph E. Brown of Georgia* (1977).

THE UNION

Abraham Lincoln has been the subject of many distinguished biographies. The best one-volume biographies are those by Stephen B. Oates and Benjamin P. Thomas, already mentioned. The fullest and most flavorful life is

Carl Sandburg, *Abraham Lincoln: The War Years* (4 vols., 1939). The most scholarly and critical is *Lincoln the President* (4 vols., 1945–1955), by J. G. Randall and Richard N. Current. Several volumes of essays deal with important and controversial aspects of Lincoln's career: Richard N. Current, *The Lincoln Nobody Knows* (1958); David Donald, *Lincoln Reconsidered* (1956); Norman A. Graebner, ed., *The Enduring Lincoln* (1959); and J. G. Randall, *Lincoln the Liberal Statesman* (1947). See also Edmund Wilson's thoughtful essay on Lincoln in his *Patriotic Gore* (1962).

Indispensable for the understanding of wartime politics in the North are several diaries: Howard K. Beale, ed., *The Diary of Edward Bates* (1933); Theodore C. Pease and J. G. Randall, eds., *The Diary of Orville Hickman Browning* (2 vols., 1927–1933); David Donald, ed., *Inside Lincoln's Cabinet* [Salmon P. Chase] (1954); Allan Nevins and Milton H. Thomas, eds., *The Diary of George Templeton Strong* (4 vols., 1952); and Howard K. Beale and Alan W. Brownsword, eds., *Diary of Gideon Welles* (3 vols., 1960).

On the Union Congress, Leonard P. Curry, *Blueprint for Modern America* (1968), is an important, pioneering study. The best general account of politics in the North is James A. Rawley, *The Politics of Union* (1974). There has been disagreement among historians over the nature and significance of factionalism within the dominant Republican party. For a sampling of this literature, see T. Harry Williams, *Lincoln and the Radicals* (1941); David Donald, *The Politics of Reconstruction* (1965); Grady McWhiney, ed., *Grant, Lee, Lincoln and the Radicals* (1964); Allan G. Bogue, "Bloc and Party in the United States Senate, 1861–1863," *Civil War History*, 13 (1967), 221–241; and Bogue, "The Radical Voting Dimension in the U.S. Senate during the Civil War," *Journal of Interdisciplinary History*, 3 (1973), 449–474. Also important is Allan G. Bogue, "Some Dimensions of Power in the Thirty-Seventh Senate," in *The Dimensions of Quantitative Research in History*, edited by William O. Aydelotte et al. (1972), 285–318.

On constitutional issues, the authoritative work is J. G. Randall, *Constitutional Problems under Lincoln* (1951).

Emerson D. Fite, *Social and Industrial Conditions in the North during the Civil War* (1910), remains the best survey. A valuable anthology of firsthand accounts is George W. Smith and Charles Judah, eds., *Life in the North during the Civil War* (1966). Paul W. Gates, *Agriculture and the Civil War* (1965), gives attention to developments in the South as well as in the North. Thomas C. Cochran's article, "Did the Civil War Retard Industrialization?" in *Mississippi Valley Historical Review*, 48 (1961),

197–210, opened the ongoing debate among historians on that subject. For reactions and responses to Cochran's thesis, see Ralph Andreano, ed., *The Economic Impact of the American Civil War* (1962); and David T. Gilchrist and W. David Lewis, eds., *Economic Change in the Civil War Era* (1965).

For intellectual life in the North during the Civil War, see George M. Fredrickson, *The Inner Civil War* (1965); and Edmund Wilson, *Patriotic Gore* (1962). *Union Pamphlets of the Civil War,* edited by Frank Freidel (2 vols., 1967), is an invaluable collection of source material.

The fullest account of disaffection and disloyalty in the North is Wood Gray, *The Hidden Civil War* (1942). In *The Copperheads in the Middle West* (1960) and *The Limits of Dissent* (1970), Frank L. Klement argues that much of this "disloyalty" was simply Democratic opposition to the Republican party and Western objection to economic legislation that aided Eastern interests. For Northern draft riots, see Adrian Cook's fascinating *Armies of the Streets* (1974).

WARTIME DIPLOMACY

For the impact of the Civil War abroad, see the essays in Harold M. Hyman, ed., *Heard Round the World* (1969).

The standard work on Anglo-American relations remains Ephraim D. Adams, *Great Britain and the American Civil War* (2 vols., 1925). Frank L. Owsley, *King Cotton Diplomacy* (1959), stresses economic factors. David P. Crook, *The North, the South, and the Powers* (1974), and Brian Jenkins, *Britain & the War for the Union* (1974), are recent accounts.

Franco-American relations are admirably covered in Lynn M. Case and Warren F. Spencer, *The United States and France: Civil War Diplomacy* (1970); and Daniel B. Carroll, *Henri Mercier and the American Civil War* (1971).

Lincoln's role in foreign policy is overdramatized in Jay Monaghan, *Diplomat in Carpet Slippers* (1945). For valuable correctives, see Glyndon G. Van Deusen, *William Henry Seward* (1967); Norman B. Ferris, *Desperate Diplomacy: William H. Seward's Foreign Policy, 1861* (1976); and Ferris, *The Trent Affair* (1977). Two biographies that deal extensively with Northern diplomacy are Martin B. Duberman, *Charles Francis Adams* (1961); and David Donald, *Charles Sumner and the Rights of Man* (1970).

Robin Winks, *Canada and the United States: The Civil War Years* (1960), treats an important, but usually neglected, topic.

MILITARY ACCOUNTS

Marcus Cunliffe, *Soldiers and Civilians: The Martial Spirit in America, 1775–1865* (1968), is brilliant intellectual history, indispensable as background for a proper understanding of the military operations of the war.

On the Northern armies, the most comprehensive works are Fred A. Shannon, *The Organization and Administration of the Union Army* (2 vols., 1928); and Kenneth P. Williams, *Lincoln Finds a General* (5 vols., 1949–1959). Bruce Catton has written an absorbing trilogy on the Army of the Potomac: *Mr. Lincoln's Army* (1951); *Glory Road* (1952); and *A Stillness at Appomattox* (1953). For biographical sketches of all Union commanders, see Ezra J. Warner, *Generals in Blue* (1964). Among the best biographies of Union generals are: Warren W. Hassler, Jr., *General George B. McClellan* (1957); Bruce Catton, *Grant Moves South* (1960) and *Grant Takes Command* (1969); Lloyd Lewis, *Sherman* (1932); William M. Lamers, *The Edge of Glory* [Rosecrans] (1961); and Francis F. McKinney, *Education in Violence* [Thomas] (1961). For Lincoln's relationship to the army and its commanders, see T. Harry Williams, *Lincoln and His Generals* (1952); and Robert V. Bruce, *Lincoln and the Tools of War* (1956). *Stanton* (1962), by Benjamin P. Thomas and Harold M. Hyman, is an outstanding work.

The most elaborate account of military operations from a Southern point of view is Shelby Foote, *The Civil War* (3 vols., 1958–1974). Douglas S. Freeman, *Lee's Lieutenants* (3 vols., 1942–1944), is an important examination of Confederate commanders in the Eastern theater. Western operations receive excellent treatment in Thomas Connelly, *Army of the Heartland* (1967) and *Autumn of Glory* (1971). For biographical sketches of all Confederate commanders, see Ezra J. Warner, *Generals in Gray* (1959). The most imposing and appealing biography of any Southern general is Douglas S. Freeman, *R. E. Lee* (4 vols., 1934–1935). But for a critique of the Lee legend, see Thomas L. Connelly, *The Marble Man* (1977). Other excellent lives of Confederate commanders are Frank E. Vandiver, *Mighty Stonewall* (1957); T. Harry Williams, *P. G. T. Beauregard* (1955); Grady McWhiney, *Braxton Bragg and Confederate Defeat* (1969); Charles P. Roland, *Albert Sidney Johnston* (1964); Gilbert E. Govan and James W. Livingood, *A Different Valor* [Joseph E. Johnston] (1956); and Herman Hattaway, *General Stephen D. Lee* (1976).

For astute discussions of Confederate strategy, see Frank E. Vandiver, *Rebel Brass* (1956); Archer Jones, *Confederate Strategy from Shiloh to Vicksburg* (1961); and Thomas L. Connelly and Archer Jones, *The Politics of Command* (1973).

Two books by Bell I. Wiley provide a fascinating social history of the common soldier of the Civil War: *The Life of Johnny Reb* (1943) and *The Life of Billy Yank* (1952).

NAVAL OPERATIONS

The best general account is Virgil C. Jones, *The Civil War at Sea* (3 vols., 1960–1962). More analytical is Bern Anderson, *By Sea and By River* (1962). Two comprehensive accounts of the Union navy are James M. Merrill, *The Rebel Shore* (1957); and Richard S. West, Jr., *Mr. Lincoln's Navy* (1957). There is much of value in John Niven's fine biography, *Gideon Welles* (1973). Charles L. Lewis, *David Glasgow Farragut* (2 vols., 1941–1943), is a workmanlike job, and there is an enormous amount of revealing source material in John D. Hayes, ed., *Samuel Francis Du Pont: A Selection from his Civil War Letters* (3 vols., 1969).

For the often neglected story of Union naval operations on the rivers, see H. Allan Gosnell, *Guns on the Western Waters* (1949); and John D. Milligan, *Gunboats Down the Mississippi* (1965).

A great deal has been published about the duel between the *Merrimack* and the *Monitor*. The most recent study is William C. Davis, *Duel Between the First Ironclads* (1975).

On the Southern side, J. T. Scharf, *History of the Confederate States Navy* (1887), is old but still invaluable. Some of the best modern accounts include: Frank J. Merli, *Great Britain and the Confederate Navy* (1970); Milton F. Perry, *Infernal Machines: The Story of Confederate Submarine and Mine Warfare* (1965); William N. Still, Jr., *Confederate Ship-Building* (1969); Still, *Iron Afloat: The Story of the Confederate Armorclads* (1971); and Tom H. Wells, *The Confederate Navy* (1971). Joseph T. Durkin's biography of the Confederate Secretary of the Navy, *Stephen R. Mallory* (1954), is extremely useful.

THE NEGRO IN THE CIVIL WAR

Benjamin Quarles, *The Negro in the Civil War* (1953), is a comprehensive study. James M. McPherson, ed., *The Negro's Civil War* (1965), consists of documents skillfully woven into what amounts to a history of how Negroes felt and acted.

Two books that stress Northern racist attitudes are V. Jacque Voegeli, *Free But Not Equal: The Midwest and the Negro during the Civil War* (1967); and Forrest G. Wood, *Black Scare: The Racist Response to Emancipation and Reconstruction* (1968). It is well to remember, as James M. McPherson shows in *The Struggle for Equality* (1964), that many Northerners, and particularly abolitionists, had a sincere interest in the rights of blacks.

As a background for understanding the Emancipation Proclamation, Benjamin Quarles, *Lincoln and the Negro* (1962), is valuable. John Hope Franklin, *The Emancipation Proclamation* (1963), is the standard study. For an account of how emancipation affected one key border state, see Charles L. Wagandt, *The Mighty Revolution: Negro Emancipation in Maryland, 1862–1864* (1964).

For the service of Negroes in the Union army, the old but indispensable work is George W. Williams, *A History of the Negro Troops in the War of the Rebellion* (1888). *Army Life in a Black Regiment* (1870), by Thomas W. Higginson, is a classic account by a white officer who commanded black troops. A standard modern study is Dudley T. Cornish, *The Sable Arm: Negro Troops in the Union Army* (1956).

Bell I. Wiley, *Southern Negroes, 1861–1865* (1938), has long been a recognized authority. It can be supplemented by studies of the black experience in individual states—for example, C. Peter Ripley, *Slaves and Freedmen in Civil War Louisiana* (1976); and John W. Blassingame, *Black New Orleans, 1860–1880* (1973). James H. Brewer, *The Confederate Negro: Virginia's Craftsmen and Military Laborers* (1969), is an important study of a neglected topic.

The Gray and the Black (1972), by Robert F. Durden, is the definitive account of the Confederate debate over enrolling Negroes in the Southern armies.

RECONSTRUCTION

The most comprehensive study of the postwar period is Ellis P. Oberholtzer, *A History of the United States Since the Civil War* (5 vols., 1917–1937). Though containing much good political history and interesting material on social and economic conditions, Oberholtzer's work is prejudiced against both the Southern Negro and the Western farmer.

Of the several one-volume histories of the period, William A. Dunning, *Reconstruction, Political and Economic* (1907), and Claude G. Bowers, *The Tragic Era* (1929), share Oberholtzer's biases. Two Marxist accounts are W. E. B. DuBois, *Black Reconstruction* (1935); and James S. Allen, *Reconstruction: The Battle for Democracy* (1937). Three balanced modern treatments of the era are John Hope Franklin, *Reconstruction After the Civil War* (1941); Kenneth M. Stampp, *The Era of Reconstruction* (1965); and Rembert W. Patrick, *The Reconstruction of the Nation* (1967). Morton Keller, *Affairs of State* (1977), is in a class of its own; this objective and insightful analysis of politics, law, and government in late nineteenth-century America is the best single book on the period.

Some of the most important work on Reconstruction has appeared in the form of articles and monographs. For a useful selection from this literature, see Kenneth M. Stampp and Leon Litwack, eds., *A Reconstruction Reader* (1969). The following articles serve as guides to the changing interpretations of the period: Howard K. Beale, "On Rewriting Reconstruction History," *American Historical Review,* 45 (1940), 807–827; John Hope Franklin, "Whither Reconstruction Historiography?" *Journal of Negro Education,* 17 (1948), 446–461; Bernard A. Weisberger, "The Dark and Bloody Ground of Reconstruction Historiography," *Journal of Southern History,* 25 (1959), 427–447; and T. Harry Williams, "An Analysis of Some Reconstruction Attitudes," *Journal of Southern History,* 12 (1946), 469–486. There are also important essays in Harold M. Hyman, ed., *New Frontiers of American Reconstruction* (1966).

PRESIDENTIAL RECONSTRUCTION

The fullest account of steps taken during the Civil War to reorganize the Southern states is Herman Belz, *Reconstructing the Union* (1969). Charles H. McCarthy, *Lincoln's Plan of Reconstruction* (1901), is a detailed, sympathetic treatment. William B. Hesseltine's book of the same title (1960) argues that Lincoln had not one but many approaches to Reconstruction, all of them unsuccessful.

There are several rather unsatisfactory biographies of President Andrew Johnson: Lloyd P. Stryker, *Andrew Johnson: A Study in Courage* (1929); Lately Thomas, *The First President Johnson* (1968); and Robert W. Winston, *Andrew Johnson: Plebeian and Patriot* (1928). For a sampling of the conflicting interpretations of the postwar President, see Eric L. McKitrick, ed., *Andrew Johnson: A Profile* (1960).

Two early studies of the struggle between Johnson and the Republicans in Congress strongly favor the President: George F. Milton, *The Age of Hate* (1930); and Howard K. Beale, *The Critical Year* (1930). Recent scholarship has been mostly critical of Johnson—for example, Eric L. McKitrick, *Andrew Johnson and Reconstruction* (1960); LaWanda Cox and John H. Cox, *Politics, Principle, and Prejudice* (1963); and W. R. Brock, *An American Crisis* (1963).

THE SOUTH AFTER THE WAR

E. Merton Coulter, *The South during Reconstruction* (1947), though biased on political questions, contains much useful information about social and economic changes. Fred A. Shannon, *The Farmer's Last Frontier* (1945), includes a full discussion of the problems of postwar Southern agriculture. Recently the conventional account of those problems has been challenged by historians and economists using sophisticated quantitative methods: Stephen J. DeCanio, *Agriculture in the Postbellum South* (1974); Robert Higgs, *Competition and Coercion: Blacks in the American Economy* (1977); and Roger Ransom and Richard L. Sutch, *One Kind of Freedom: The Economic Consequences of Emancipation* (1977). For a thoughtful appraisal of this new literature, see Harold D. Woodman, "Sequel to Slavery: The New History Views the Postbellum South," *Journal of Southern History*, 43 (1977), 525–554.

On the alleged breakup of the plantation system, see Roger W. Shugg, *Origins of Class Struggle in Louisiana* (1939); but note Joseph G. Tregle's critique, "Another Look at Shugg's Louisiana," *Louisiana History*, 17 (1976), 245–281. For the continuing dominance of the planter class, see Jonathan M. Wiener, "Planter Persistence and Social Change: Alabama, 1850–1870," *Journal of Interdisciplinary History*, 12 (1976), 235–260.

The standard work on the transition from slavery to freedom is George R. Bentley, *A History of the Freedmen's Bureau* (1955), but it should be supplemented with William S. McFeely, *Yankee Stepfather: General O. O. Howard and the Freedmen* (1968); and Louis S. Gerteis, *From Contraband to Freedman* (1973). James L. Roark, *Masters Without Slaves* (1977), is particularly good on the former slaveowners' perception of this transition.

Henderson H. Donald, *The Negro Freedman: . . . The American Negro in the Early Years after Emancipation* (1952), is the only comprehensive work on its subject, but it is marred by a readiness to accept any discreditable tale about Negroes. Far more sensitive and revealing are several state studies: Peter Kolchin, *First Freedom* [Alabama] (1972); Willie Lee Rose, *Rehearsal for Reconstruction* [South Carolina] (1964); Joe M. Richardson, *The Negro in the Reconstruction of Florida* (1965); Alrutheus A. Taylor, *The Negro in Tennessee, 1865–1880* (1941); Taylor, *The Negro in the Reconstruction of Virginia* (1926); Vernon L. Wharton, *The Negro in Mississippi, 1865–1890* (1947); and, especially, Joel Williamson, *After Slavery: The Negro in South Carolina during Reconstruction* (1965).

On the education of blacks after the war, the best studies are Henry A. Bullock, *A History of Negro Education in the South* (1967); William P. Vaughn, *Schools for All* (1974); and Roger A. Fischer, *The Segregation Struggle in Louisiana* (1974).

For white attempts to repress the Negroes during Reconstruction, see the harrowing account in Allen W. Trelease, *White Terror* (1971). Michael Perman, *Reunion Without Compromise* (1973), also stresses the intransigence of Southern whites.

There is a considerable literature on the history—and particularly the political history—of nearly every Southern state in the postwar period. On Alabama, the most comprehensive work is Walter L. Fleming, *Civil War and Reconstruction in Alabama* (1905), but it needs to be supplemented and corrected by Thomas B. Alexander, "Persistent Whiggery in Alabama and the Lower South, 1860–1867," *Alabama Review,* 12 (1959), 35–52; Horace Mann Bond, "Social and Economic Forces in Alabama Reconstruction," *Journal of Negro History,* 23 (1938), 290–348; and Sarah Woolfolk Wiggins, *The Scalawag in Alabama Politics* (1977).

On Arkansas, the standard studies are Thomas S. Staples, *Reconstruction in Arkansas* (1923), and David Y. Thomas, *Arkansas in War and Reconstruction* (1926), but there is much fresh material in George H. Thompson, *Arkansas and Reconstruction* (1976).

On Florida, the older work of William W. Davis, *The Civil War and Reconstruction in Florida* (1913), is now largely superseded by *Nor Is It Over Yet* (1974), by Jerrell H. Shofner.

The standard account of Georgia, C. Mildred Thompson, *Reconstruction in Georgia* (1915), is admirably supplemented by Alan Conway, *The Reconstruction of Georgia* (1966); Elizabeth S. Nathans, *Losing the Peace* (1968); and Olive H. Shadgett, *The Republican Party in Georgia* (1964).

Joe G. Taylor, *Louisiana Reconstructed* (1974), largely replaces two older accounts: John F. Ficklen, *History of Reconstruction in Louisiana (through 1868)* (1910); and Ella Lonn, *Reconstruction in Louisiana after 1868* (1918). Three other studies that continue to be useful are Willie M. Caskey, *Secession and Restoration of Louisiana* (1938); Charles Vincent, *Black Legislators in Louisiana during Reconstruction* (1976); and T. Harry Williams, "The Louisiana Unification Movement of 1873," *Journal of Southern History,* 11 (1946), 349–369.

For Maryland and the other border states, the essays in *Radicalism, Racism, and Party Realignment,* edited by Richard O. Curry (1969), are valuable. On Maryland politics, there is also Jean H. Baker's brilliant monograph, *The Politics of Continuity* (1973).

Reconstruction in Mississippi (1901), by James W. Garner, continues to be a basic book, but William C. Harris, *Presidential Reconstruction in Mississippi* (1967), is also useful.

For Missouri, see William E. Parrish, *Missouri under Radical Rule* (1965); and Norma L. Peterson, *Freedom and Franchise: The Political Career of B. Gratz Brown* (1965).

The standard work on North Carolina, J. G. de Roulhac Hamilton, *Reconstruction in North Carolina* (1914), is badly out of date. W. McKee Evans, *Ballots and Fence Rails* (1966), is a fine account of Reconstruction on the lower Cape Fear. Allan W. Trelease, "Republican Reconstruction in North Carolina," *Journal of Southern History,* 42 (1976), 319–344, offers a quantitative analysis of the work of a Republican legislature.

A basic work is Francis B. Simkins and Robert H. Woody, *South Caro-*

lina during Reconstruction (1932). *Black Over White* (1977), by Thomas Holt, is a careful, methodologically sophisticated study of Negro political leadership in that state.

On Tennessee, two older monographs remain useful: James W. Fertig, *The Secession and Reconstruction of Tennessee* (1898); and James W. Patton, *Unionism and Reconstruction in Tennessee* (1934). See also two valuable later studies: Thomas B. Alexander, *Political Reconstruction in Tennessee* (1950); and Robert L. Hart, *Redeemers, Bourbons & Populists* (1975).

Reconstruction in Texas (1910), by Charles W. Ramsdell, should be supplemented by Paul C. Casdorph, *A History of the Republican Party in Texas* (1965); and W. C. Nunn, *Texas under the Carpetbaggers* (1962).

H. J. Eckenrode's inadequate *Political History of Virginia during the Reconstruction* (1904), needs to be read in conjunction with Jack P. Maddex, *The Virginia Conservatives* (1970); and Allen W. Moger, *Virginia: Bourbonism to Byrd* (1968).

RADICAL RECONSTRUCTION

To understand the Radical Republicans, one must first understand the rise of American nationalism during the war and the postwar years. George M. Fredrickson, *The Inner Civil War* (1965), is indispensable for this purpose. Frank Freidel, *Francis Lieber* (1947), is the authoritative biography of one of the principal nationalists, but see also the valuable discussion of Lieber in Philip S. Paludan, *A Covenant With Death* (1975).

An old, but still useful, study of constitutional changes during the postwar years is William A. Dunning, *Essays on the Civil War and Reconstruction* (1897). Harold M. Hyman, *A More Perfect Union* (1973), is a careful modern analysis. The definitive history of the Supreme Court in this period is Charles Fairman, *Reconstruction and Reunion* (1971), which, however, takes the story only to 1874. Stanley I. Kutler, *The Judicial Power and Reconstruction Politics* (1968), is an incisive revisionist study.

Joseph B. James, *The Framing of the Fourteenth Amendment* (1959), is a standard work. A basic source on the drafting of that amendment is *The Journal of the Joint Committee on Reconstruction* (1914), edited with an important, but frequently overlooked, explanatory essay by Benjamin B. Kendrick. The "conspiracy theory" of the Fourteenth Amendment (the view that its framers designed to protect corporations from state regulation) is now discredited; see Louis B. Boudin, "Truth and Fiction about the Fourteenth Amendment," *New York University Law Review,* 16 (1938), 19–82; Howard J. Graham, *Everyman's Constitution* (1968); and Andrew C. McLaughlin, "The Court, the Corporation, and Conkling," *Amer-*

ican Historical Review, 46 (1940), 45–63. Whether the framers intended to outlaw racial segregation and whether the amendment, regardless of their intent, does forbid segregation have been topics of heated controversy. Jacobus ten Broek, *The Antislavery Origins of the Fourteenth Amendment* (1951); Alexander M. Bickel, "The Original Understanding and the Segregation Decision," *Harvard Law Review,* 69 (1955), 1–65; and Alfred H. Kelly, "The Fourteenth Amendment Reconsidered: The Segregation Question," *Michigan Law Review,* 54 (1956), 1049–1086, believe that the amendment left the way open to subsequent sweeping decisions by the Supreme Court outlawing segregation. Raoul Berger, *Government by Judiciary* (1977), trenchantly argues that the Court has read into the Fourteenth Amendment meanings that its framers and supporters never intended.

On the Fifteenth Amendment, William Gillette, *The Right to Vote* (1965), is a model study, which has, however, been attacked in LaWanda Cox and John H. Cox, "Negro Suffrage and Republican Politics," *Journal of Southern History,* 23 (1967), 303–330; and Phyllis F. Field, "Republicans and Black Suffrage in New York State," *Civil War History,* 21 (1975), 136–147. Everette Swinney, "Enforcing the Fifteenth Amendment," *Journal of Southern History,* 28 (1962), 202–218, is a valuable essay.

On Reconstruction politics, the literature has grown so complex that one needs a guide. Two excellent introductions to the controversial writing are Larry G. Kincaid, "Victims of Circumstances: An Interpretation of Changing Attitudes toward Republican Policy Makers and Reconstruction," *Journal of American History,* 57 (1970), 48–66; and Michael L. Benedict, "Preserving the Constitution: The Conservative Basis of Radical Reconstruction," *ibid.,* 61 (1974), 65–90.

The Radical Republicans and Reconstruction, edited by Harold M. Hyman (1967), presents an extensive sampling from the Radicals' own writings. For general treatments, see Hans L. Trefousse, *The Radical Republicans* (1969); David Donald, *The Politics of Reconstruction* (1965); and Michael L. Benedict, *A Compromise of Principle* (1974). Biographies of some principal Radical leaders include Fawn Brodie, *Thaddeus Stevens* (1959); David Donald, *Charles Sumner and the Rights of Man* (1970); Hans L. Trefousse, *Ben Butler* (1957); and Trefousse, *Benjamin Franklin Wade* (1963).

C. Vann Woodward, "Seeds of Failure in Radical Race Policy," *American Philosophical Society Proceedings,* 210 (1966), 1–9, stresses the racist strain in the thinking of most Radicals. On the other hand, James M. McPherson, *The Struggle for Equality* (1964), shows that many abolitionists maintained an interest in the Negro during the postwar years. David Montgomery, *Beyond Equality* (1967), is an important study of the attitudes of Radical Republicans toward the labor movement. The essays in *Radical Republicans in the North,* edited by James C. Mohr (1976), are valuable.

Much less has been written about the Democratic party during Reconstruction. The best studies are Joel H. Silbey, *A Respectable Minority* (1977); and Lawrence Grossman, *The Democratic Party and the Negro* (1976).

David M. DeWitt, *Impeachment and Trial of Andrew Johnson* (1903), strongly pro-Johnson in tone, is the recognized authority on its subject. Michael L. Benedict's book of the same title (1973) is a useful, anti-Johnson corrective. Martin E. Mantell, *Johnson, Grant, and the Politics of Reconstruction* (1973), contains valuable insights on the events leading up to impeachment. The best explanation of why impeachment occurred when it did is found in Hans L. Trefousse, *Impeachment of a President* (1975).

POSTWAR DIPLOMACY

The easiest way to follow American foreign policy in the postwar era is through the biographies of the secretaries of state who helped frame it. The best life of Seward, who served under both Lincoln and Johnson, is that by Glyndon G. Van Deusen (1967). Allan Nevins, *Hamilton Fish* (1936), fully covers the career of Grant's secretary. On Hayes's secretary of state, see Chester L. Barrow, *William M. Evarts* (1941); and Brainerd Dyer, *The Public Career of William M. Evarts* (1933). The best life of James G. Blaine, who served under Garfield and, briefly, under Arthur, is that by David S. Muzzey (1934). There is no adequate biography of Frederick T. Frelinghuysen, who was secretary of state during most of Arthur's administration. For a massively detailed treatment of Cleveland's secretary of state, see Charles C. Tansill, *The Foreign Policy of Thomas F. Bayard* (1940).

The general expansionist temper of the postwar era is well treated in Joe P. Smith, *The Republican Expansionists of the Early Reconstruction Era* (1933); and in Donald F. Warner, *The Idea of Continental Union* (1960). Donald M. Dozer, "Anti-expansionism during the Johnson Administration," *Pacific Historical Review,* 12 (1943), 253–276, and William M. Armstrong, *E. L. Godkin and American Foreign Policy* (1957), treat the opposition to expansion.

On the collapse of Maximilian's regime after the withdrawal of French troops from Mexico, see Henry Blumenthal, *A Reappraisal of Franco-American Relations* (1959); and Dexter Perkins, *The Monroe Doctrine, 1867–1907* (1937).

The best accounts of the purchase of Alaska are Victor Farrar, *The An-*

nexation of Russian America to the United States (1937); and Ronald J. Jensen, *The Alaska Purchase and Russian-American Relations* (1975).

For Grant's ill-advised attempt to annex Santo Domingo, read Charles C. Tansill, *The United States and Santo Domingo* (1973). David Donald, *Charles Sumner and the Rights of Man* (1970), explains the course of a principal opponent of annexation.

Anglo-American relations during the postwar years involved talk of annexation of Canada, United States support of the Fenian movement to liberate Ireland, and the settlement of the Alabama claims. The Canadian aspect of this story is well treated in Hugh L. Keenleyside and Gerald S. Brown, *Canada and the United States* (1952); and in Lester B. Shippee, *Canadian-American Relations, 1849–1874* (1939). On the Fenian movement, see Charles C. Tansill, *America and the Fight for Irish Freedom* (1957); Thomas N. Brown, *Irish-American Nationalism* (1966); and W. S. Niedhardt, *Fenianism in North America* (1975). The Alabama claims, which receive attention in Allan Nevins, *Hamilton Fish*, and David Donald, *Charles Sumner and the Rights of Man*, are fully discussed in Adrian Cook, *The Alabama Claims* (1975).

For American foreign policy in the 1880s, see Walter LaFeber, *The New Empire: American Expansionism, 1860–1898* (1963); Milton Plesur, *America's Outward Thrust* (1971); David M. Pletcher, *The Awkward Years: American Foreign Relations under Garfield and Arthur* (1962); and Alice F. Tyler, *The Foreign Policy of James G. Blaine* (1927).

POSTWAR SOCIAL AND ECONOMIC CHANGES

The best general treatment of social and economic changes during the post–Civil War period is Allan Nevins, *The Emergence of Modern America, 1865–1878* (1927). Edward C. Kirkland, *Industry Comes of Age* (1961), is authoritative.

The Visible Hand (1977), by Alfred D. Chandler, is the definitive account of the managerial revolution that took place in American business during these years. There is not room here to list the literature on the growth of individual American industries, but every reader will enjoy Allan Nevins, *Study in Power: John D. Rockefeller* (2 vols., 1953); and Joseph F. Wall, *Andrew Carnegie* (1970).

A path-breaking book on labor during these years is Herbert Gutman, *Work, Culture, and Society in Industrializing America* (1976). Norman J. Ware, *The Labor Movement in the United States, 1860–1890* (1929), is a classic in its field, and Gerald N. Grob, *Workers and Utopia: A Study in Ideological Conflict in the American Labor Movement, 1865–1900* (1961), is a basic work.

On westward expansion, Oscar O. Winther, *The Transportation Frontier: Trans-Mississippi West, 1865–1890* (1964), is a good introduction. Walter P. Webb, *The Great Plains* (1931), is a brilliant account, which traces the rise of the range cattle industry. On the same subject, see Robert R. Dykstra, *The Cattle Towns* (1968). For some of the economic difficulties faced by settlers in the West, consult Allan G. Bogue, *Money at Interest* (1955); and Robert O. Swierenga, *Pioneers and Profits: Land Speculation on the Iowa Frontier* (1968).

The American Heritage History of the Indian Wars (1977), by Robert M. Utley and Wilcomb E. Washburn, is a spirited, illustrated account, chronicling the final defeat of the Native Americans. Accounts that attempt to present this story from the point of view of the Indians include Dee Brown, *Bury My Heart at Wounded Knee* (1970); T. H. Fehrenbach, *Comanches* (1974); William Brandon, *The Last Americans* (1974); and, best of all, Angie Debo, *Geronimo* (1976). More conventional accounts are Francis P. Prucha, *American Indian Policy in Crisis* (1975); and Loring B. Priest, *Uncle Sam's Stepchildren* (1975).

There are no good studies of postwar tariff controversies, but there are three excellent, sophisticated accounts of the complex currency question: Robert P. Sharkey, *Money, Class, and Party* (1959); Irwin Unger, *The Greenback Era* (1964); and Walter T. K. Nugent, *The Money Question during Reconstruction* (1967). A little more specialized, but highly valuable, is Allen Weinstein, *Prelude to Populism: Origins of the Silver Issue, 1867–1878* (1970).

The standard works on farmers' unrest have long been two books by Solon J. Buck: *The Granger Movement* (1913) and *The Agrarian Crusade* (1920). George H. Miller, *Railroads and the Granger Laws* (1971), shows the influence of Western businessmen on the so-called Granger legislation.

POLITICS DURING THE AGE OF RECONCILIATION

The best account of Grant's presidency remains William B. Hesseltine, *Ulysses S. Grant, Politician* (1935). On the disastrous campaign to prevent Grant's reelection in 1872, see Earl D. Ross, *The Liberal Republican Movement* (1919); John G. Sproat, *"The Best Men"* (1968); and Richard A. Gerber, "The Liberal Republicans of 1872 in Historiographical Perspective," *Journal of American History*, 62 (1975), 40–73. Ari A. Hoogenboom, *Outlawing the Spoils* (1961), is a model history of the civil service reform movement.

Paul L. Haworth, *The Hayes-Tilden Presidential Election of 1876* (1906), has long been the standard account, but it needs to be supplemented by C. Vann Woodward, *Reunion and Reaction* (1951), which explores the economic forces behind the political façade. Keith I. Polakoff, *The Politics of Inertia* (1973), gives full attention to the Democratic party during the election and the compromise.

On post-1877 politics, H. Wayne Morgan, *From Hayes to McKinley* (1969), is the most comprehensive work. *The New Commonwealth* (1968), by John A. Garraty, is, however, more insightful and interpretive. Matthew Josephson, *The Politicos, 1865–1896* (1938), is a spirited, irreverent account. Harry Barnard, *Rutherford B. Hayes and His America* (1954), is the best biography of that President. Allan Peskin, *Garfield: A Biography* (1978), promises to be definitive. Thomas C. Reeves, *Gentleman Boss* (1975), is an excellent biography of Arthur. Allan Nevins, *Grover Cleveland: A Study in Courage* (1932), is both monumental and readable. Harry J. Sievers, *Benjamin Harrison* (3 vols., 1960–1966), tells rather more than one needs to know about that President.

David J. Rothman, *Politics and Power* (1966), is an original account of the organizational changes in the Senate from 1869 to 1901. Robert D. Marcus, *Grand Old Party* (1971), analyzes the Republicans during the 1880s and 1890s. Horace S. Merrill, *Bourbon Democracy in the Middle West* (1953), and J. Rogers Hollingsworth, *The Whirligig of Politics* (1963), do the same for the Democrats. There is a fascinating comparison of the Democracy of Tilden and Cleveland with the Liberalism of Gladstone in Robert Kelley, *The Transatlantic Persuasion* (1969).

Recent studies have emphasized the ethnocultural bases of politics during the Gilded Age—for example, Paul Kleppner, *The Cross of Culture* (1970); and Richard J. Jensen, *The Winning of the Midwest* (1971). But, using even more sophisticated statistical methods, Melvyn Hammarberg, in *The Indiana Voter* (1977), has seriously challenged this view.

Two excellent treatments of Republican attitudes toward the South during this period are Vincent P. DeSantis, *Republicans Face the Southern Question* (1959); and Stanley P. Hirshson, *Farewell to the Bloody Shirt* (1962).

THE SOUTH AFTER 1877

C. Vann Woodward, *Origins of the New South, 1877–1913* (1951), is a masterful work, unequalled in its comprehensiveness and its originality. A recent revisionist work of great importance is J. Morgan Kousser, *The Shaping of Southern Politics: Suffrage Restriction and the Establishment of the One-Party South* (1974). Also valuable is Dewey Grantham, Jr., *The Democratic South* (1963).

One of the few studies that attempts to understand, rather than to censure, the Southern Redeemers is William J. Cooper, Jr., *The Conservative Regime: South Carolina, 1877–1890* (1968).

There are several valuable books that trace the disaffection with the Redeemers and the rise of Populism in the Southern states: Francis B. Simkins, *"Pitchfork" Benjamin Tillman* (1944); C. Vann Woodward, *Tom Watson: Agrarian Rebel* (1955); Alfred D. Kirwan, *Revolt of the Rednecks: Mississippi Politics, 1876–1925* (1951); William I. Hair, *Bourbonism and Agrarian Protest: Louisiana Politics, 1877–1900* (1969); and William W. Rogers, *The One-Gallused Rebellion: Agrarianism in Alabama, 1865–1896* (1970). Two important recent studies of the Southern origins of Populism are Robert C. McMath, Jr., *Populist Vanguard: A History of the Southern Farmers' Alliance* (1976); and Lawrence Goodwyn, *Democratic Promise: The Populist Movement in America* (1976).

LITERARY RECONCILIATION

Robert E. Spiller et al., *Literary History of the United States*, Vol. II (1948), contains some good chapters on postwar literature. One of America's great literary critics tackles the writing on the Civil War in *Patriotic Gore* (1962), by Edmund Wilson. Robert A. Lively, *Fiction Fights the Civil War* (1957), is a readable survey. The best general account of the literary reconciliation between North and South is Paul H. Buck, *The Road to Reunion* (1937). My account of Higginson's weeping over Page's novel is derived from Buck, and I see no reason to doubt the story though Higginson's most thorough biography, Tilden G. Edelstein, *Strange Enthusiasm* (1968), calls it "very unlikely."

On the local colorists, there is much in Van Wyck Brooks, *New England: Indian Summer* (1940), and *The Times of Melville and Whitman* (1947). Thomas Nelson Page deserves a fuller biography than the short sketch by Theodore L. Gross (1968). Joel Chandler Harris also needs a good modern biography; but see two fine articles by Michael Flusche: "Joel Chandler Harris and the Folklore of Slavery," *American Studies*, 9 (1975), 347–363, and "Underlying Despair in the Fiction of Joel Chandler Harris," *Mississippi Quarterly*, 29 (1975), 91–103. There are two excellent biographies of George W. Cable, by Arlin Turner (1956) and Louis D. Rubin (1969). *Walter Hines Page: The Southerner as American* (1977), by John M. Cooper, Jr., is a thoughtful study of one of the most influential Southern intellectual leaders. For an engaging, sympathetic account of Northern as well as Southern writers in the postwar era, see Daniel Aaron, *The Unwritten War: American Writers and the Civil War* (1973).

Acknowledgments

My principal debt in writing this book is to my students, whether at Columbia University, Princeton University, the Johns Hopkins University, the University of Oxford, or Harvard University. For nearly a generation they have let me try out on them my ideas about the meaning of the Civil War years in American history. Their reactions to my courses, their searching questions, and their thoughtful criticisms have helped me clarify my thinking.

A somewhat different version of portions of the last five chapters of this book appeared in *The Great Republic: A History of the American People*. To my co-authors in that work I am indebted for incisive criticism, both stylistic and substantive. The manuscript has been improved because of the acute and sympathetic suggestions given by Mr. Roger Donald, senior editor at Little, Brown and Company. I am also deeply grateful to members of the superb professional staff at D. C. Heath and Company. To Mr. Alexander Bloom of Wheaton College and Mr. Richard Immerman of Boston College I owe much for their careful checking of my manuscript, a tedious labor that saved me from making dozens of errors. My thanks also go to Mr. Daniel L. Cloyd and Mr. Robert C. Kenzer, both of Harvard University, who caught dozens of factual and typographical errors while reading proofs. So did Dr. Aïda DiPace Donald, of the Harvard University Press, to whom I am indebted for numerous stylistic suggestions as well.

My dear friend and former colleague, Professor Eric F. Goldman of Princeton University, encouraged me to undertake this book, and in a thousand ways I am indebted to him for his unflagging support.

Part of this book was written while I had a leave of absence from my teaching duties, thanks to the generous support given by the Charles Warren Center for the Study of American History at Harvard. To the Warren Center and its director, Professor Donald Fleming, I am deeply grateful for this assistance.

Through the kindness of the Rockefeller Foundation I completed this book in what must be the most nearly ideal surroundings for a scholar: the Bellagio Study and Conference Center on Lake Como in Italy. For the many kindnesses extended to me during my stay at the Villa Serbelloni, I want to thank Dr. William O. Olson and Mrs. Elizabeth Olson.

Finally, for superb typing of a difficult manuscript I must express my gratitude to my secretary, Miss Jackie Zeltzer.

Index

Radical Republicans
  and the Fourteenth amendment,
    193–96
  and the impeachment of Andrew
    Johnson, 199–201
  and Johnson's plan of Reconstruc-
    tion, 191–92
  and Lincoln's plan of Reconstruc-
    tion, 158, 166
  and the Military Reconstruction Act,
    197–98
  and the Supreme Court, 198–99
  literature on, 295–96
Radical Review, 242
Raiders, Confederate, 133
Railroads, 101, 136, 164, 225, 227–28,
  244–45
Rains, George W., 102
Randall, Samuel J., 260
Randolph, George W., 100
Range-cattle industry, 231–32
Reconstruction; *see also* Congressional
  Reconstruction, Presidential Reconstruction
  alternative scenarios for, 171–75
  basic questions concerning, 169–71
  limited by constitutionalism, 175–83
  limited by economic theory, 183–90
  limited by political expediency, 190–
    201
  limited by racism, 201–11
  literature on, 290–96
Red Cloud, Chief, 225
Red River campaign, 129
Redeemers, 256, 262
Reid, Whitelaw, 190
Republican party
  before the Civil War, 62–63, 69, 76
  during the Civil War, 158–60, 167
  during the postwar era, 190–201,
    234–35, 248–49
  literature on, 280–81
Resumption Act of 1875, 237–38

Resumption of specie payments; *see*
  Currency controversies
Revels, Hiram R., 208
Rhett, Edmund, 185
Rhett, Robert Barnwell, 14, 20, 46, 59
Rhode Island, 7, 9, 203
Richmond, Va., 96, 140, 161–62, 176–
  77
Richmond *Examiner,* 149
Riley, James Whitcomb, 268
Roanoke Island, N.C., 131
Robber barons, 228–29
Rockefeller, John D., 135, 229
Rockefeller, William, 229
Roman Catholics; *see* Catholics
Rosecrans, W. S., 126, 128
Ross, John, 92
Ruffin, Edmund, 91
Russell, Lord John, 83, 106, 108, 150,
  152
Russia, 105, 107, 108, 222–23
Russian North America; *see* Alaska

"Sambo's Right to Be Kilt," 147
San Francisco, Calif., 40, 201–202
Santa Fe, N.M., 39, 113
Santo Domingo, 105, 219–20, 221, 223
Savannah, Ga., 162
Scalawags, 208–209
Scandals; *see* Corruption
Schurz, Carl, 34, 78, 105–106, 150,
  249
Schuyler, Robert, 47
Scott, Dred, 63–69
Scott, Thomas A., 229
Scott, Walter, 23
Scribner's Monthly Magazine, 269
Sea Islands, 130–31, 180–82
Secession, 283
  of states of lower South, 76–77
  of states of upper South, 89–97
Secret ballot, 262
Sedalia, Mo., 232

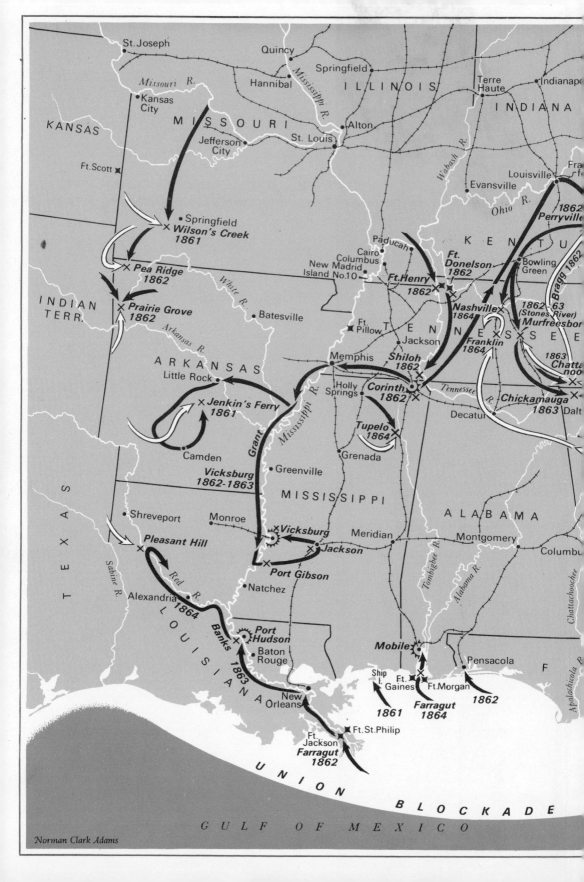

St. Joseph • Quincy • Springfield • Terre Haute • Indianapo

Missouri R. ILLINOIS INDIANA

Kansas City • Hannibal • Alton • St. Louis • Louisville • Fra fe

KANSAS MISSOURI Evansville

Ft. Scott ✕ Jefferson City • *Ohio R.* Louisville •

KEN TU

Springfield ✕ **Wilson's Creek 1861** Paducah • Columbus • New Madrid • Island No.10 **Ft. Donelson 1862** Bowling Green

Bragg 1862

✕ **Pea Ridge 1862** *White R.* **Ft. Henry 1862** **Nashville 1864**

INDIAN TERR. ✕ **Prairie Grove 1862** Batesville • Ft. Pillow ★ T E N N E S S E E **1862-'63 (Stones River) Murfreesbor**

Arkansas R. Jackson • **Franklin 1864** **1863 Chatta noo**

ARKANSAS Memphis • **Shiloh 1862** *Tennessee R.* ✕ **Chickamauga 1863** Dalt

Little Rock • Holly Springs • **Corinth 1862** ✕

✕ **Jenkin's Ferry 1861** *Mississippi R.* Decatur •

Tupelo 1864 ✕

Camden • **Grant** Grenada •

Vicksburg 1862-1863 Greenville • MISSISSIPPI ALABAMA

Shreveport • Monroe • Meridian • Montgomery • Columbu

T E X A S **Pleasant Hill** ✕ **Vicksburg** ✕ **Jackson** *Tombigbee R.* *Alabama R.* *Chattahoochee*

Sabine R. *Red R.* ✕ **Port Gibson** Natchez •

Alexandria • **1864** LOUISIANA **Banks 1863** **Port Hudson** Baton Rouge • **Mobile** ✕ Pensacola •

F

New Orleans • Ship I. Ft. Gaines Ft. Morgan **1862** *Apalachicola R*

Ft. Jackson ★ ★ Ft. St. Philip **1861** **Farragut 1864**

Farragut 1862 U N I O N B L O C K A D E

G U L F O F M E X I C O

Norman Clark Adams